the Father of HOLLYWOOD

2-25-2011

Eva,

Enjoy the journey.
Its a wonderful life!

gaelyn Whitley Keith

the Father of HOLLYWOOD

Gaelyn Whitley Keith

TATE PUBLISHING & Enterprises

Published by Tate Publishing & Enterprises, LLC
127 E. Trade Center Terrace | Mustang, Oklahoma 73064 USA
1.888.361.9473 | www.tatepublishing.com

Tate Publishing is committed to excellence in the publishing industry. The company reflects the philosophy established by the founders, based on Psalm 68:11,
"The Lord gave the word and great was the company of those who published it."

Published in the United States of America

ISBN: 978-1-61663-475-9
1. Biography & Autobiography / Historical
2. Biography & Autobiography / Cultural Heritage
10.05.28

Dedicated to HJ and Gigi.

Foreword

From the earliest silent films made by pioneering American filmmakers to the multimillion-dollar blockbusters of today, the movie industry of America has always had a home: Hollywood. But how did Hollywood itself get started? Who were the driving forces behind its creation and development, the visionaries and kingmakers who built the infrastructure of a worldwide industry but only received a fraction of the credit that was heaped upon the stars of the silver screen?

Movie buffs nowadays have no idea that so much of what we take for granted about Hollywood was largely planned, designed, and built by Hobart Johnstone Whitley, an extraordinary individual who is not nearly as well known as he should be. HJ was the primary developer of Hollywood, a central figure in attracting and keeping the talent needed to make such an ambitious project successful and, in turn, transform a formerly sleepy part of California into a hugely profitable and exciting industry.

Gaelyn Whitley Keith's remarkable book, *The Father of Hollywood*, goes a long way toward erasing the misconceptions concerning HJ's life and career and paints a truly charming portrait of the man who lived a life that itself is worthy of a fine movie.

—Ellen Tanner Marsh
New York Times best-selling author

Note from the Author

One of my earliest childhood memories was listening to stories of my father's family. The tales were like little uniquely shaped pieces that belonged to a five-thousand-piece jigsaw puzzle. How could I resist putting such an interesting enigma together?

So what was the appeal of this historical mystery? One simple word: Hollywood. Most people only have a few pieces of this puzzle. Putting them together is especially difficult because few know what the finished picture should look like. HJ Whitley plays a central role in this mystery. He is buried in the Hollywood Forever Cemetery, and his historic gravesite plaque reads, "The Father of Hollywood."

I started to ask my family to tell me all the stories they could remember about HJ and Gigi's lives. With their help, I built the story from the ground up, using witty sayings, fantastic stories, and hundreds of yellowed, brittle, black-and-white photographs that, under my family's watch, I handled like treasure found on an archeological dig.

As HJ Whitley's great-granddaughter, I acquired an extensive base of information from over fifty boxes of business records and personal correspondences that were kept by the family. Much of the actual events in the book were recorded in my great-grandmother's private journals, letters, and diaries. I am sure that the more personal parts of her diaries were never intended to be made public. This book is her story of the founding of Hollywood. Some of the experiences are recorded as they occurred, yet others are retrospective. My father lived with his grandmother, Gigi, for the last twenty years of her life and, therefore, heard many of the stories firsthand.

The number of pieces of information I dealt with was astonishing. They were little flashes of his life that were bright, quick, and inspiring, a sliver of truth echoing from the past. As I dug through the historical facts, I realized that even if a piece of information did not connect to anything I had previously found, it would fit in later. I just placed the information in what I thought was the appropriate section and continued to research.

For me, most of the facts rarely showed up in perfect order. Trying to make sense out of the information that randomly appeared was challenging, like solving a murder mystery. Nearly everyone loves a mystery. Putting this puzzle together resembles the work of detectives in many aspects. Like detectives, the reader will sift through the evidence in order to build the true picture of the founding of Hollywood.

Facts first seemed unconnected and awkward, but once they were sifted through and linked, they began to make sense. Events seemed to overlap in random order, linked by one underlying element: HJ Whitley. While working in Hollywood he was also involved in ten major projects. These projects spanned many decades and seemed to overlap one another. I felt that the reader would understand the picture being created better if the book was more topical than chronological. Understanding the Whitleys' influence on Hollywood provides one with a greater appreciation of the rich tapestry of its founding. Wouldn't you love to find the one piece of the puzzle that explains the true story of how Hollywood was named?

It is important to know what this book is and is not. This book is a book of stories about the family that influenced the founding of Hollywood. It is not a formal discourse of early Hollywood life. It is an examination of writings by Gigi Whitley, business journals, business correspondence, and newspaper articles. I did not conduct any primary research using the Internet, as some of its information is unreliable. I believe that the best way to obtain information is to have physical contact with the sources. Every trip to my father's house (where I asked every conceivable question about the stories his grandmother and family told him about the founding of Hollywood), the UCLA library, Hollywood, and family archives was like a small detective adventure. There were many moments on these trips when history came to life, like a motion picture on the big screen. The more I have learned about Hollywood, the more entranced I have become. HJ Whitley built something so big and novel that it has changed world history forever.

The historical characters, achievements, and state of affairs in this book are the truth uncovered by my exhaustive research of more than ten years. I acquired facts from reliable sources and verified their authenticity. I am now sharing them with the reader. The conversations and dialogues were not transcribed verbatim but were reconstructed.

The reader may hear many voices in the story, each one painting a part of the puzzle that unfolds. I tried not to modernize the writings too much so that the picture produced gave the reader a snapshot of life just as it was, little over one hundred years ago. Life at that time was not yet centered around movies, television, radios, or computers. It was a unique time to live, when women were declaring their independence and social mores were changing. By the 1900s, the number of inventions introduced was astronomical.

I hope the reader will be amazed as HJ's awe-inspiring saga unfolds. Thousands of details are offered to help the reader fully understand the dynamics of Hollywood's founding. Understanding the creation of Hollywood is like putting together a puzzle of a spring scene. I know that you have seen them, the ones with all the tree pieces looking the same. It seemed impossible that the pieces were different enough to fit together and make anything; yet with even one piece missing, the picture would be incomplete.

The picture created in this saga will reveal HJ Whitley as one of the iconic characters of United States history. As the reader learns more I hope it will explain much of the feelings they carry in their hearts and minds about Hollywood. Many of the hot social topics of today can be found in Hollywood's past. Headlines were dominated by scandals, drugs, big business, terrorism, women's rights, war, politics, fashion, and the environment.

One of the delights of weaving history into an enchanting picture was the trivia I found in my great-grandmother's writings. They were used to bring color to the characters and explain their motives and feelings. My great-grandparents, HJ and Gigi Whitley, are the patriarchs who presided over the creation of Hollywood. Their city has forever changed the course of history, portraying visions of glamour and romance to a degree unmatched anywhere else. Nestled in hills covered with towering eucalyptus and citrus groves, Hollywood was built as part of the grand scheme by visionary developer HJ Whitley, "The Father of Hollywood." Why did the *Los Angeles Times, Hollywood Citizen,* and others in the community consider him the founding father? Whitley Heights was the Beverly Hills of yesteryear, and some of the most impressive homes in Hollywood are located there. Stars like Jean Harlow, Ethel Barrymore, Charlie Chaplin, Marion Davies, W.C. Fields, Harold Lloyd, Carole Lombard, Rudolph Valentino, and many others lived and held legendary parties in the Heights. How did he get them to settle there? What was the magical draw this amazing man possessed?

For most of my life, he was like a superhero up on the cinema screen. I learned piece by piece that he was friends with Teddy Roosevelt, ran the Oklahoma run, and named Hollywood and was responsible for it becoming world renowned. As years and even decades passed, I began to wonder if I could uncover more about this amazing man or if he would just remain a man of secrets I would never know. I began to think that a man like that deserves a book. Thanks to the help of so many kind people I am happy to present the reader with the Whitley Family Saga.

And, of course, one last huge thanks to family and friends. Without their support, this book would never have reached completion. I would like to thank: my great-grandmother, Gigi Whitley; my grandmother, Irene Whitley; my father, Johnstone Whitley; my mother, Mary Ellen Whitley; my daughters, Michelle Thurber and Tiffeny Damico; my sons-in-law, Jason Thurber and Michael Damico; my sister, Bonnie Merrick; my nephew, Gregory Merrick; my niece, Christi Merrick; my grandsons, Ryan Michael Keith Damico and Christopher Gunnar Keith Thurber; and my granddaughters, Grace Elizabeth Damico and Annelies Elena Thurber. Additionally, I would like to thank my PEO family: Tristine and Heath Lorains, Malia La Vallee, Naomi Burney, and Loni Montgomery who were kind enough to help in the editing process.

My deepest appreciation goes to my husband, Randy Keith. He encouraged me every day to fulfill my dream of being published and to write my great-grandfather's story so that people could enjoy the legendary saga of the making of Hollywood.

Looking back on it, I do not think I have ever had so much fun as I have had in learning and sharing the stories of a man who shaped Hollywood. I wrote this story for a lot of reasons; but most of all, it was to give one more glimpse into a vanishing culture. I am proud of HJ Whitley. I want my great-grandfather to walk out of the past with Gigi at his side.

Preface

Lord, keep my memory green. I am writing this book in memory of all the beautiful things it has been my privilege to have enjoyed while traveling as well as at home in Hollywood. My lingering thoughts are of the bird's greetings with their sweet carols, flowers with their wonderful colors, fragrances that waft here and there, and the mountains and valleys with their divine power to impart peace and give inspiration to my faith. These lasting memories inspire me with courage to carry on, even as death has cast its shadow across my path. The influence of these lovely memories whisper to me and cheer me on my way.

—Margaret Virginia Ross Whitley
1867–1951

Chapter One

The beginning of the story goes way back, before the great developer arrived, to the green foothills that are in the heart of California. Summers came, and summers went. The passage of time gave false assurance that everything would remain the same. This all changed as a little village was born. Sun-kissed and serene, it was amongst the foothills of the Cahuenga Valley. Calling across the virgin landscape, a warbler sang its melodic, caroling song. Flowers bloomed in gorgeous array, painting the meadows in various shades of purples and yellows. The bouquets made by the flowers along the trail were too beautiful to describe. Oranges and lemons hung abundantly on the trees in a fashion that seldom grew elsewhere.

In the spring of 1886, nearing yet another summer, HJ came along with his golden inspiration. That was not the first time he had been there and stood on the highest of those splendid hills as he gazed at the valley below. He stood there with Gigi, his bride of only a few short weeks; and they were both overwhelmed with the impressive scene. As they scanned the horizon, the land stretched on forever—a land of sensuous delights. The soft breeze carried the breath of sweet alyssum. HJ turned to Gigi with a familiar gleam in his eyes and said, "This is what I have been yearning for all my life."

He breathed the fragrant, fresh air as he surveyed the land in every direction. Suddenly, he took out his pencil and notebook and began to write. HJ envisioned the hilltop overlooking the valley covered with cream-colored homes with red tile roofs set amongst narrow, winding streets, becoming one of the most romantic and beautiful cities in the world. He hoped that it would be renowned for its elegant, brick-style office buildings and tree-lined boulevards. He planned to pattern it after the *Champs-Elysées,* the most beautiful avenue in Paris. Yet he desired it to have its own unique American flavor. The city would be comprised of a variety of retail stores, restaurants, banks, and luxury hotels. HJ's experience, money, and time would be spent altering the West forever. He visualized sections changing rapidly from open fields, orchards, and vegetable gardens to fine residential and commercial districts. All that was left was to purchase the first five hundred acres. A quick sketch and a few words for future memory helped him record his majestic vision.

With a twinkle in his eye and a snap of his fingers, HJ excitedly murmured, "This town will be my crowning jewel. The Boulevard will be like a magical oasis. It will be like an acquaintance that makes a great first impression. With the lure of the hills, the sea, and the sunshine, it will be a little piece of heaven."

HJ was sharp-witted, honest, moral, and sincere, just as his father and grandfather had been. They came from an unusually sturdy, far-seeing stock. Each had a reputation of immeasurable wisdom. This wisdom made it possible for them to live more productive lives than most. HJ found it easy to accomplish in one year what it took most men a lifetime to complete. He radiated confidence and was endlessly interesting, jaunty, creative, highly intelligent, and occasionally reticent.

HJ was a handsome man, with thick, dark hair and blue eyes, someone who looked like someone you would read about in a best-selling novel. He had a Roman nose and a groomed mustache and was known to carry a little pistol in his coat pocket. His face was thin, and he had a high-toned presence, reflecting his social standing.

As a young boy, HJ loved to hear his father tell stories about his grandfather, the Honorable Nicholas Whitley of Liverpool, England, who won fame as a naval commander and was a member of Parliament. At bedtime, his father's robust voice brought amazing stories to life. Grandfather was assigned to a British ship in the Indian Ocean. His orders were to monitor the coasts for pirate activity. Disguised as a commercial sailing vessel, the ship prowled the shores acting as bait.

The pirates were in good spirits, having discovered what they thought was a defenseless ship with a large bounty. Their side cannons were aimed at Grandfather's ship. After the first shot was fired, a heated battle ensued. A section of the pirate ship's mast was lost to the sea. The ships tossed and turned in the ocean waves. Grappling hooks were employed to pull the ships together.

With sword in hand, Grandfather yelled orders into the salty wind. "Board the ship!" An intense sword fight ensued. The air smelled of blood and smoke. As the pirate ship began to burn, the powder kegs in the helm of the ship exploded in a burst of bright orange. The ship lurched and then began to sink. He cried, "Surrender, or drown in the open sea!" Quickly, the motley crew abandoned ship. Under Grandfather's competent command, the pirates were easily subdued and taken prisoner. Upon his return to England, he was awarded a Naval General

Medal for his bravery. As dreamy thoughts of the battle danced in his mind, HJ finally dozed off to sleep.

Grandfather had many achievements to his credit and was anxious for HJ's father, Joseph, to carry on in the family enterprise. In 1793, Lieutenant Governor John Graves Simcoe selected a site for the capital of Upper Canada. It was to serve as the judicial and administrative center of Ontario. A courthouse and homes for government officials were built. To Grandfather, this town appeared to be a lucrative opportunity for his son to make a name for himself. He insisted that Joseph's appointment to an administrative post in Canada would be a good thing, a positive one. So it happened that Father was persuaded to accept a government post. Taking with him fourteen servants, even a bootblack, he arrived in his new hometown four months later. As a "gentleman farmer," his home was located in Katesville, a settlement a few miles northwest of Strathroy on the Syndenham River, a pioneer hamlet in Upper Canada.

Joseph was a highly educated man, with careers as a government administrator, a college professor, and a distinguished writer. He had dark, wavy hair; penetrating eyes; and a warm smile. With a strong character and sunny disposition, he spent his life and means facilitating others to accomplish their dreams. Many of his creative ideas were criticized and joked about, considered foolish. He wrote papers on such diverse topics as the need to manufacture and mass-market soap in bar form and the introduction of time zones as a solution to the problems in scheduling activities across the railroad lines. Many years after Joseph's death, HJ realized that his father's ideas became viable knowledge. Anything that was intellectually challenging served as a stimulus to generate Joseph's novel business ideas. He reminded HJ that, "Traditionally, people scoff at ideas they do not understand. How long did it take man to discover and accept that the world was round? I hope you will be a leader, directing others into uncharted territories."

His father's words were like little seeds carried by a gusty breeze. They flew straight out of his mouth and into HJ's heart, where they germinated in the fertile, receptive soil of his spirit. His father's chief objective in life was to help others and benefit mankind. He taught HJ never to forget a favor or forsake a friend. Fortunately, the wisdom his father passed on to him generated astonishing traits that would be the basis of HJ's business affairs.

Joseph was married to Eleanor Johnstone, the daughter of Colonel William Johnstone, an officer in the British Army. William was a direct descendant of a noted Scottish family, the Johnstones of Annandale. Eleanor was highly educated. She had a rare charm and inner beauty that radiated when she smiled. Her golden brown eyes were often half-hidden under amber curls. Her nose was thin and delicate, cheeks rosy and fair. With perfect posture, bearing, poise, and grace, she immediately took command of any room she entered.

Regrettably, the vast wilderness of those pioneer days frightened her. Danger and death lurked at every turn. She wondered if it could ever be tamed. The backwoods were so large that no effort to cultivate it seemed worthwhile. It might as well have been the ocean for all the use it was. The frontier simply forbade the presence of man. After HJ's birth, she finally convinced Joseph to move to Flint, Michigan.

Joseph was in the process of taking off his gloves and snow-laden boots when he heard the faint cry of his newborn son. On October 7, 1847, in Toronto, Canada, Hobart Johnstone Whitley was born, the seventh and youngest child of Joseph and Eleanor

Whitley. That same year, General Kearney secured Los Angeles and ended hostilities in California. It was almost as if a magical force paved the way for HJ's future in Hollywood.

HJ was a beautiful and healthy baby with the most enormous, bright, blue eyes. His brownish red fuzz for hair quickly turned pale blonde in the summer sun. He was a precious child. HJ did everything early: sitting up, crawling, talking, and after only nine months, walking.

Early in life, HJ had a structured and formal education. He knew basic Latin and Greek and spoke English and French fluently. From the start of his education, he was a model student, possessing a photographic memory. Sensing, perhaps, that he was destined for great leadership in his manhood, HJ found reading books delightful. He became a voracious reader of philosophy, history, and psychology and quickly acquired a fine vocabulary. HJ wrote with clarity. This educational regiment came pleasantly and with ease.

Like most great men, HJ was always careful about his dress. He possessed a silent pride and would not tolerate anything that might tarnish his dignity. No one was more disciplined than him. He meticulously kept his accounts. Even as a young man, he wrote the events of his day in a journal. At the early age of sixteen, he was a portrait of a perfect Victorian gentleman. HJ refused to move, read, or speak unless he considered the impact it would have on others. In the true spirit of the era, he learned to respect men of superior social standing. He felt that thoughtless laughter and stories that relayed idle gossip were unacceptable.

Tragedy plagued HJ's early life. As a young boy, he lost four of his six siblings to cholera. It appears that a hog and her babies accidentally fell into the family's water supply and drowned. Foul water then ignited the outbreak. HJ would have died had he not been away with his parents. For HJ, who was old enough to understand the struggle between life and death, the year was profoundly engraved in his mind. They were buried next to one another not long before sundown. HJ stood on the hill and watched tears run down his mother's cheeks. A cold and empty feeling crept through his veins. He became reluctant to commit unguarded affection to others, who, to him, seemed like impermanent objects of love.

With a pang of sorrow, HJ learned that his parents had been killed in a buggy accident. HJ was barely eighteen. His parents drove to town to purchase supplies. They proceeded south on Main Street, turning east between the buildings, attempting to cross the railroad tracks just past the depot. A large lumber warehouse concealed the approaching freight train from their view. The train was not scheduled to stop at the depot. As the train rumbled forward, the tower operator showed a green sign from the tall, wooden tower, which meant that all was clear. As he stopped to record the train's passing, his hand froze at the sight of a train snaking around the curve, blind to what was ahead. How had he missed seeing the buggy the first time he looked?

It seemed likely that his parents were talking about their purchases. The various noises along the crowded street blocked the roar of the locomotive on the tracks, which bore down on them at a terrific speed. As the eighty-ton engines met the buggy, a crushing sound shot through the town. The buggy was smashed to splinters. After the accident, people rushed to the scene and started searching for the bodies. His mother was found first, her body lying next to the railroad tracks, twenty-five feet east of where the buggy was struck. Across her head was a large, bloody gash. Death was instant. On the opposite side of the tracks, down the embankment, was HJ's father, who was found alive but unconscious. His right side was mangled, and he had difficulty breathing. He was taken home in a neighbor's wagon. The pain that marred his face warned his children that something was not quite right. It was something they feared that not even a doctor or medicine could help. Sadly, he was found dead in bed the next morning.

The funeral was held at the old stone church on the hill overlooking the river on the western edge of town. At half past nine on Tuesday morning, the service began. The church was crowded with friends of the unfortunate family. There were many floral offerings, both at the church and at the cemetery, and a long procession of friends who followed them to their resting place. HJ was glad that his sister, Grace, was with him at the funeral. She sat quietly while tender tears crawled down her cheeks. Grace clasped his hand, giving it a warm squeeze; but HJ appeared unemotional, never shedding a tear and speaking in a monotone voice.

He then attended the short graveside service, looking on with grief. All around him, the fragrant flowers smelled sweet. The quiet psalm read by the reverend resonated with the whispering trees. Although the flowers were a symbol of purity and peace, they offered him none. A few large men gradually lowered the large, dark boxes into the ground. He stared at the ample, gray stone leaning close to his parent's gravesite, names chiseled into its face. Every stroke cut hard and deep and cold. He watched them toss the first shovelful of dirt into the grave, the sounds painfully echoing in his ears, the scent of grief and uncertainty in the air. Turning away in a daze, he began to walk home, not really recognizing all of the others in attendance. His spirit was paralyzed.

In April of 1865, only a few weeks after his parents' death, Abraham Lincoln was assassinated. HJ thought that this act seemed so un-American, vicious, and desperate. Sorrow engulfed him like a black smoke. A penetrating loneliness covered him; his world stood forever changed. He abandoned any hope of a bright future. For a time, his withdrawal from the world seemed complete. His thoughts centered without conscious realization on things of the past. He would talk about his parents and his childhood. Sometimes he thought that if he could go back in time he could be happy again.

Fortunately, his father's encouraging words called, urging him to progress onward. A glimmer of sunlight shined upon his spirit. His parents' tragic death forced him to seek employment at a young age. His education from Toronto Business College enabled him to abruptly throw himself into the commercial world. His close associates marveled at his business ability. Like a hermit crab seeking a larger shell, HJ left his childhood to seek his adult identity.

It was no surprise to Grace that he headed for Chicago, a place where he could hide among the crowd and establish a grocery and mercantile enterprise. With the money he inherited from his parents' estate, he was able to keep a full stock of dry goods, furnishings, shoes, hats, and clothing. Eager to please his customers, he hired a first-class tailor to make alterations. With the arrival of the railroads, the city of Chicago really started to boom. The true secret to Chicago's growth was the willingness of its capitalists to guarantee the quality of the products they sold. HJ's business was one of the first to offer customers a money-back guarantee.

HJ was a progressive man, one of the first to accept new ideas. Even at a young age, he was a leader. Additionally, HJ had a strong constitution, artistic talent, business sense, and sheer gumption. He did not smoke, drink, or curse. He worked relentlessly, procured large profits, had a good eye for detail, and stood his ground against trying clients. His success as a businessman was aided in good measure by people who wanted what he had to offer.

Discontented with his cramped business quarters, his heart yearned for the freedom of open space. The stuffy conditions made him restless until one day he was attracted to the picture hanging in his room. He had possessed it for some time but never studied it very seriously. In his boyhood, he had admired the drawing: a pen sketch by Uncle T.W. Whitley, drawn in 1842. The scenic drawing showed waving fields of grain. It called to him, "Go to the West, young man." His uncle had been a partner of Horace Greeley, a political reformer and newspaper editor who used his paper to sound his support for labor, homesteads, and the frontier. After reading several articles about the frontier, HJ took Horace's advice and headed to the West. Before he could begin his new life, he needed to apply for naturalization papers so he could purchase land in the new territories. Once completed, HJ, a man of considerable means, embarked wholeheartedly on his commercial adventure.

In search of additional fortune, opportunity, and a new life, HJ began his journey at age twenty-three. Even though many years had passed since the California Gold Rush of 1849, its land still held a glittering allure. HJ yearned for the potential riches the area offered. He wanted to play his part in defining and shaping America's values and history. He would leave a permanent mark using two aspects of his personality: inventiveness and courage. America promised him free reign in his thirst for self-determination and land ownership. Its vast territory and untapped potential offered him a tantalizing freedom. America was everything, truly a land of opportunity. The history, skills, and experience of his family ideally equipped him for this challenge.

In the course of business at the mercantile, HJ became associated with some of the leading railroad officials from the Northern Pacific Railroad and Chicago Rock Island and Texas Railway who were laying tracks through to the Pacific Coast. The railway company's primary aim was to carry finished goods from the East to the developing areas of the West and then return with raw materials for the East. They had plans to complete a line west of the Missouri. This new line would include Kansas, Nebraska, Colorado, Texas, the Dakotas, and the Indian Territory.

Through exploratory conversations with railroad executives, HJ decided to pursue a job with the Rock Island Railroad. He was pleased when they asked him to manage the expansion of towns along the rail lines. Development provoked too many disagreements. Slapdash planning triggered controversy. The railroad company became entwined with political hagglers and investment speculators, all vying to influence the railroad on where it should establish its towns. In order to prevent outside intervention, HJ assured them that he would maintain utmost secrecy about towns' locations. To the revenue-conscious railroads, careful consideration in selecting town sites hinged on investment returns.

HJ had a vision of building towns, and the frontier meant open opportunity. Described as the frontrunner of the Bismarck and Missouri territories, HJ built settlements along the Chicago Rock Island and Pacific Railway and the Chicago Rock Island and Texas Railroad. Between 1870 and 1894, HJ launched more than one hundred towns. He hammered together cities, got railway tracks laid, built stations, and cut roads; and the designs they carved in the landscape are still here today. The frontier was like a safety valve for him. When people became too emotionally connected to him, he simply sold his land, packed up, and left, moving farther west to build another town.

The building of the Rock Island Railway through Texas opened a large section of rich country. HJ put together numerous towns in Indian Territory that surpassed those built along other railroad lines. He carefully selected the sites to control the trade of the rich farming sections. HJ watched the little cities spring up as if by magic as the shrill whistle of the great civilization echoed through the rich valleys. Fortunes were made by enterprising men who built and sold buildings in the new towns. They were men who loved the excitement that the new frontier offered.

For a number of years, his headquarters were in Kansas City and Minneapolis, where he became interested in banking and large land developments. As a self-taught civil engineer, he easily stepped into the position as the railroad's pitchman (a.k.a. developer). His business required him to do extensive travel.

Providence seemed to bring HJ and Gigi together. As Gigi had written in her journal:

> It seems not long ago, in one of the most perfect places on Earth, at the western edge of California, that HJ and I met. I will remember that hour forever; I still see it before me. I recall how peaceful I felt when I saw HJ looking so intently at me for the first time. Little did I know that I was just beginning a journey that would become a legend.

Chapter Two

It was from a beautiful Southern mother and a very religious Northern father, William Ross, from which she was born, Margaret Virginia Ross, on February 10, 1867, in Mobile, Alabama. She was familiarly known as Gigi and was the seventh child in a happy Southern home. There was one curious thing at the time of her birth. Gigi was born with a caul over her face. Her mother told her that she would be gifted in some way or another, with a highly developed ability of second sight. As a small child, her dreams started to become very vivid and full of particular detail. Gigi noticed that things she had dreamed about were happening in reality, usually only weeks or days later. At first, this frightened her. She began to talk to her mother about them. Based on her knowledge, which was limited, her mother explained to her that her dreams were messages from God. Gigi's mother was the first person to make her aware of this gift. She helped Gigi accept, embrace, and become comfortable with her newfound ability.

The year Gigi was born earmarked a change in Victorian society. For the first time, a woman in the United States, Lucy Hobbs, became a certified dentist. Women's position in society was changing. Women would slowly shift from being home-bound housewives to wage-earning consumers. Years later, Gigi thought that this event foreshadowed Hollywood's beginning.

Gigi's mother, Margaret Hart Ross, was a woman of beauty and unusual courage. Her mother taught her to think no evil of another. All beautiful things appealed to Gigi's mother, especially flowers and poetry. When her mother left a room, the scent of rose or some magical fragrance lingered. The silk of her dress rustled softly as she climbed the stairs.

Her mother was a member of the Methodist Episcopal Church, and all her children were brought up to revere God. They attended services; and while the sermons were very long to a small child, her mother's gentle love had a way of helping Gigi enjoy the services, forming a habit that would remain her entire life.

Women in the South were liberated from taking part in the common, more ordinary requirements of life. Therefore, Gigi developed great skill in the fine arts of the era. She was an eager reader as a child. As a teenager, she lost her thoughts in Jane Austen's *Emma* and *Pride and Prejudice,* Charlotte Bronte's *Jane Eyre,* and her sister Emily's *Wuthering Heights.* Gigi's head was filled with images of Heathcliff, Mr. Darcy, and Frank Churchill. She spent many hours devouring these classics, both poetry and prose. As Gigi grew, she gradually fell under the spell of poets who wrote of love. Robert Burns, her favorite poet, wrote delightfully romantic visions. "The Red Red Rose" described the lover's feelings the way she pictured them: fresh and springlike. Their love would endure forever.

Besides reading, she spent many hours singing, playing the piano, dancing, and doing needlework. Gigi developed a sweet, loving disposition. She had the kindest heart. Her spirit was pure. Gigi was acknowledged as a rising beauty. By her fifteenth birthday, in 1882, men's heads turned as she walked down the street. Several boys had asked to call on Gigi, but Uncle Samuel felt that she was too young and naive. Gigi's sweet, loving nature would be the cornerstone of her married life.

Tragedy haunted Gigi's early childhood. Her father died when she was barely two years old. She really had no memories of him except the ones created from pictures. While the family was at her sister Alabama's funeral, they were robbed of an assortment of valuable treasures. Yet the most tragic event was the death of Gigi's mother when she was fourteen. Fortunately, the memory of her mother remained vivid.

Gigi was very fortunate that Samuel Ross was chosen to be her guardian. He was a kind and inspiring man with fire in his eyes and passion in his words. His nose was perfectly straight, accentuating his broad brow and hazel eyes. Uncle Samuel was a widower who had buried a wife and two children.

It was early summer of 1885. Uncle Samuel had given Gigi a special treat: a trip to California. Summer vacation was like a breath of fresh air. Leaving her studies was like having a weight lifted from her shoulders, one that she was not even aware of carrying. Now that she was reaching womanhood, Uncle Samuel decided to travel with her, as he wanted to create one more precious memory of their time together.

At the time of their trip, Los Angeles was inhabited by fewer than sixty thousand people. Not much more than the remains of an adobe Spanish settlement, it was still very quaint and interesting. Trains were not their only mode of travel. Carriages and steamers were employed to augment their train travel once they reached California. The roads were primitive and incredibly bumpy. Clouds of dust were stirred up by the horses because of the rainless weather. Wanting to see everything, they traveled north along the Los Angeles River. It etched its way through the alluring nooks and valleys of the territory. As they traveled farther, they entered a spacious valley, densely populated with cottonwoods, among which snaked the beautiful river. The plain where the river ran was very extensive. As Gigi and Uncle Samuel made their way farther north, the land became dotted with shallow ponds and marshes. Droopy willows towered over a ragged blanket of alder and hackberry while thorny masses of California roses sprinkled tints of crimson and smooth pink across the landscape.

Farther upriver, in the San Fernando Valley, soft greenery grew on small plateaus shaded by massive oaks, whose thick roots clung into the earth. The air was perfectly delicious; every breath gave a clear and distinctive piece of pleasure. Deer grazed in the plains, passing by to drink from the river once in a while. Gigi was told that coyotes, raccoons, gray foxes, and bobcats also foraged along the river. Oriole calls flittered in the air like endless flute songs while trees whispered in the wind. Ducks and geese floated down the river as though they were on a magic carpet ride. A graceful, broad wing hawk soared in the sky, coming in for a leisurely pass directly over them. This river flowed steadily and consistently year round. California's scenery was so magnificent that Gigi told Uncle Samuel, "One day, I hope to live here. I feel happier in the West than any place I have ever been. Something about the music of the ocean, the towering ranges of snowcapped mountains, the myriads of precious flowers of every hue, and the scenery delights and stirs my soul."

After a short stay, they decided to continue their journey back East. Uncle Samuel and Gigi were to travel on the Great Northern Pacific Railroad until they reached Minnesota. Gigi planned to visit her sister and attend music classes. As fate would have it, HJ had received a letter from his business associates requesting his presence in the East. He would be traveling on the train with them. HJ later told Gigi, "I noticed you the moment I entered the car. There was just something about you that caught my eye."

He requested the porter change his seat so that he could get a closer view. He liked what he saw. HJ was close enough to capture the sparkle in Gigi's wide eyes, which "seemed to be sapphire," he told her, "a marvelous shade of the blue sky." HJ thought they were unusual eyes, with an intriguing angelic quality. He noticed too how her head rose proudly, just as his mother's had. Her complexion was very fair and her cheeks delicately rosy. Gigi's thick, golden hair was pulled together at the back of her neck with a baby-blue satin ribbon. She wore a blue dress with a lace collar. HJ decided that he would have to find some way to meet her.

How fortunate for Gigi that Uncle Samuel was introduced to one of the greatest pioneer developers while they were eating lunch that afternoon. The dining room was full, so HJ asked permission to dine at Uncle Samuel's table, knowing that it was a perfect opportunity to meet Gigi. A lively conversation ensued. Uncle Samuel and HJ were instant friends, like two entwined threads of gold on black fabric. Laughter and camaraderie instantly flowed between them. On one of the stops, HJ invited Uncle Samuel to accompany him on business. Upon returning to the train, Uncle Samuel told Gigi with much enthusiasm, "HJ is an amazing man."

Uncle Samuel encouraged HJ to take Gigi out to see the cowboys and the great herds of cattle. They saw many miles of splendid country filled with rolling hills, valleys, and the picturesque Missouri River. The atmosphere was truly romantic as the sun's light stretched across the rolling fields, creating a golden hue. Suddenly—too late—Gigi realized that her heart had opened up. She was falling into a deep, sweet trance called love.

Uncle Samuel instantly recognized that her eyes shined with the desire that her heart held. Encouragingly, he stated, "HJ is a man of high principles, someone who will make some young girl a wonderful husband."

Gigi charmed HJ. No one was surprised when he asked permission to call on her. Gigi looked forward to his visits, and he often brought her small gifts: books, a bouquet of flowers, and fruit, but never chocolate candy. She wondered why. If there was anything she loved, it was candy.

Their romance had hardly begun when, once again, HJ had the feverish call to return to work. He was afraid that things were getting too serious. He needed to end the relationship before his heart got the best of him. The loss of his first wife and infant daughter still haunted him, and he was not willing to take a chance at losing another. The fear of death had made him a prisoner, and he preferred to live his life in loneliness.

Having returned from California, Gigi went to live with her sister, Mary. It was a more convenient spot to complete her studies. The home had been lovely when she arrived, with all its flowers gloriously blooming. Mary's home was frequently visited by young intellectuals who spent several hours a day discussing philosophical works of Thoreau, Emerson, and Fuller. Gigi hated that women's self-reliant impulses were held against them. These young men seemed to appreciate that women really wanted the freedom to unfold their powers as needed for self-development. Women hoped to shape the new society that was emerging. Gigi spent the evenings on the porch with the young gentlemen strumming banjoes or went for long, slow buggy rides in the country. That year, Mary's home became a treasure trove of fond memories, yet Gigi still longed to see HJ.

Thankfully, after their first formal encounter, she had written in her diary:

> It is Sunday morning. I went to my first formal party with HJ last night, and now I am frightened. He was wonderful, intelligent, tender, humorous, handsome, and fascinating—a complete gentleman. And this has all caught me completely by surprise; I realized—like a bolt of lightning striking me—that he is the man I am going to marry. I had dreamed of him nearly a month before I was introduced to him. I am afraid that all his wonderful accomplishments will eclipse my identity. I do not want to live in someone's shadow. I am still young and quite impulsive. I have a great deal to learn. Do I have the wisdom he desires in a wife? But there is just something about him, a strange feeling telling me that he will be my husband. There is something about "us." The "us" that could be, the "us" that will be. My only prayer is that our love will be the awe-inspiring union of two souls, each with their own identity, akin to a singer and songwriter.

Being wise even at the young age of eighteen, Gigi decided that she needed to fill the void left by HJ's hasty departure. She devoted herself to music. Their time apart gave her the opportunity to attend Carleton College, complete her education, and study at one of the best conservatories of music. While HJ was gone, music cascaded from her heart, tiny melodies without words.

The adventures she had with HJ during her summer vacation were gradually becoming like a long-lost dream. Yet, during their time apart, she realized that he would return to her. Gigi could sense things as though they had already happened, something she had learned in childhood. One night, she had a very ordinary, almost dull dream. It was about normal, everyday things, except that it included a visit from HJ. Gigi knew that HJ would appear just as he had in the dream.

Life was strenuous in the Wild West. Before long, HJ realized that he had overlooked his need for love. In his long evenings alone, he began to think of the sweetheart he had left behind in Minnesota. He could visualize Gigi standing by a carved banister with fair, curly hair and shining, bright blue eyes. Although this industrious man, now thirty-eight, had attempted to drive all sentiment out of his life, he began to think of the young woman who had been waiting quite long enough for him. HJ had known Gigi for a little over six months. Suddenly, his heart required him to write to her.

When Gigi heard that her sister had received a letter from the post office addressed to her, she knew that HJ had finally written. Her heart raced as she opened the letter. Gigi was excited yet nervous to hear what he had to say.

> My dear Gigi,
>
> It astonishes me how much the state of my mind influences the powers of my body. I have been thinking of you night and day and find it difficult to sleep. I had no choice but to write you a letter this evening to let you know that I will soon be there to visit. I want to say a thousand loving and heartfelt things to you, but lack the mastery of words in the arena of love. I will wait until I see you to tell you in person. I wake filled with thoughts

of you and the intoxicating evenings which we spent together. My senses are in turmoil; longing to hold you near to me. Sweet, amazing Gigi, what a strange effect you have on my heart! You draw from my heart a love which consumes me with fire. It was late last night that I fully realized how much I wanted you to be part of my life. I am planning to arrive next Thursday on the five o'clock train and I am looking forward to meeting you at the depot.

Forever yours,

HJ

As Gigi walked down the path toward the train station, the little heels of her shoes clicking on the pavement kept beat with the rush of her heart. A lucent haze generally encircled the city, giving indescribable softness and exquisite dreamy charm to the day. She was so anxious that she had trouble keeping herself from running to see HJ. Gigi looked up and down the tracks and through the crowds, hoping to see him. Finally, she heard the footsteps behind her, almost lyrical as they followed closely behind. Gigi glanced back, seeing HJ in the lingering vapor of the train. He was more handsome than she had remembered. The smile on his face was angular and peaceful. His forehead was lofty and fair; his nose flawless; and his eyes large, dramatic, and expressive. As he set down his suitcase and briefcase, he slowly removed his hat and sweetly inquired, "Hello. Did you miss me?"

The look in her eyes and her diminutive grin told more than the words she spoke. They quickly embraced as though they had never parted. As he picked her up and set her down, she could tell that HJ was in love with her. That evening, he took her to the finest restaurant in town. He sweetly whispered, "Your eyes are sparkling like jewels." The dinner was enhanced by a table dressed with a white silk tablecloth and a sparkling crystal vase with a loose arrangement of pretty garden peonies. The crystal gaslight chandeliers' lighting was subtle and intimate.

HJ's cheeks were flushed. His good-natured smile and clammy hands were outward indications to her that something important was on his mind. He found it difficult to talk. Smiling radiantly, he told her that he had fallen in love with her from the first time they had met. He said that he was attracted to her vibrant spirit and beauty. Gigi knew immediately that he was going to propose. After dessert was served, he took her hand, and then, on bended knee, HJ proposed. Gigi gasped, sitting there without breathing for a few moments. He waited. Gigi still had not given him the answer. Teary-eyed and tenderly smiling, she leaned forward and gently kissed him on the cheek, whispering, "Yes. With all my heart!"

Gigi felt intoxicated. Her vision was blurry, her stomach fluttering with butterflies. Her wobbly legs did not let her stand. Her symptoms could only mean one thing: love. HJ pulled out a box that held the most exquisite engagement ring. He gently slid the ring on her finger, an intricate design of rubies surrounded by a series of small diamonds, set in a gold band. Gigi just stared at it. It was perfect. Applause could be heard coming from the surrounding tables.

Before they selected a wedding date, it was important for Gigi to make sure that HJ understood that she was different from the other women he had courted.

Gigi declared, "I want to continue my music lessons and writing."

HJ replied, "I would not have it any other way."

He was unclear what her statement was implying. At that time, Gigi had a piano, a riding horse, and about twenty thousand dollars (equivalent to more than one half million dollars in twenty-first-century valuation) that her father and uncle had given her. She was strong-willed, and her passion for living enticed HJ. Gigi was a tiny woman who barely broke five feet. However, when she made up her mind about something, getting her to change it took an act of Congress. She was a hard person to ignore. When HJ proposed, he thought that, in addition to being able to sing, play an instrument, and speak a little French, Gigi should also be innocent, virtuous, dutiful, and ignorant of intellectual opinion. Her place was to be in the background, being submissive and supportive. HJ thought that women were weak and helpless, fragile, delicate flowers incapable of making decisions beyond ensuring that their children were taught moral values. He had no idea that Gigi wanted to control her own destiny. Gigi would never be content living in a man's shadow. She did not think that HJ realized this the night he proposed.

Even at this happiest of times, uneasiness had set in. HJ refused to have a church wedding. He wanted to be married in a place that was more comfortable for him. He thought that churchgoers were legalistic and hypocritical. After telling her sister, Mary, of her dilemma, her sister advised, "You must remember that marrying simply for love and love alone does create some realistic obstacles. One problem is that you have to live *and* love. HJ cannot do everything just the way you want, but he is a man of means that will let you live as you are accustomed. In other words, would you marry a respectable poor man just because he let you have your way? How could you afford to live comfortably and support your children? *You* would be miserable!

Think twice before you say too much, Gigi. HJ is a wonderful man."

Gigi's personality was strong, and her anger burned hot. Her sense of justice would not allow her to compromise her beliefs. Yet, because of her kind heart, her happiness flashed brighter than was true for most people. When Gigi was happy, she drew everyone around her into a circle of warmth; but just as easily, she conceded that she had often given others what she felt were needed rebukes and insults. Gigi realized that a word spoken to HJ in a moment of anger could leave painful wounds. As spoiled as she was, Gigi could not always have her own way. She recognized that sometimes HJ did have a point and that in insisting on getting her own way all the time, without regard for his feelings or needs, she was in some way undermining herself. After discarding all sense of caution, she finally decided to move forward with the marriage.

HJ was anxious to return to his business affairs but knew he would have to tell Gigi some of his bitter past. He felt it only fair that she know that he was a widower and had loved his first wife. He did not want to cheat Gigi out of having a husband who loved her with all his heart and was 100 percent there in mind, body, and soul. The more time he spent thinking of his first wife, the less time he spent thinking of Gigi. He promised himself that he would change and let go of the past.

The wedding was planned for spring, giving Gigi only three short months to prepare. Grace, HJ's sister, helped her buy her trousseau and linens. Gigi considered what she felt was the only alternative: a garden wedding in the atrium because she felt the weather would still be cold outside. She envisioned them exchanging their vows surrounded by flowers. The wedding would then have the feeling of country charm and informality, a setting that HJ was agreeable to.

On a beautiful springlike day in 1886, Uncle Samuel met Gigi at the foot of the stairs and escorted her down the aisle. Her wedding gown was a lovely, full-length, satin skirt covered with Venetian lace studded with pearls. Tiny pearl buttons adorned the back. The sleeves were lace with tiny rosebuds at the wrist. The skirt was long, with an artistically draped overskirt. HJ was clad in a formal suit. There, in the presence of family and friends, the Episcopalian rector performed the wedding ceremony.

This day was the beginning, not the end. They both had vowed not to work on the marriage but to work on themselves. Gigi hoped that HJ knew that it was impossible for him to change her; they could only change themselves. Whatever the years of their lives had in store would be the result of what they both put into it in the form of their individual lives.

Chapter Three

Only a few short hours en route to their honeymoon destination, HJ told Gigi that he needed to stop at the next town and tend to important business. Gigi held her tongue but secretly felt that she should have been his most important business.

As they descended from the train, HJ took Gigi's arm and led her to the steps of the streetcar.

"I am a bride!" she cried. "Do you think I am going to arrive at the most extravagant hotel in the city riding in a streetcar? No! I would rather go to a less expensive hotel than be humiliated this way. If we go to the best, we will go in a carriage."

"No!" HJ said firmly. "We are going to the hotel on the streetcar."

"No, I will not!" Gigi stomped her foot in anger.

HJ stared at her, anger flashing in his eyes. He turned away, picked up the suitcases, and handed them to the porter. HJ took Gigi by the arm and tried to lead her onto the streetcar, but she began to kick and scream. The passengers who were also waiting for the streetcar turned to look, staring in confusion. HJ, so irritated by Gigi's tantrum, picked her up, put her traveling cape over her face, and carried her onto the streetcar. Gigi's anger quickly turned to shame. She wished she could walk off the streetcar and never see any of those people again. Gigi wanted to crawl under a seat and die.

Freeing herself from HJ's arms, she rushed to the end of the streetcar, trying to regain her composure before they reached the hotel. In ten minutes, HJ sent the porter to get her. She walked back to HJ without a trace of resentment on her face.

As they descended the steps of the streetcar, walking toward the hotel's magnificent entrance, HJ exclaimed, "My heavens. That is my best friend, Mr. Steele, from Dakota." He looked at Gigi. "Now, dear, he is a very wealthy man, and I want you to be charming. We are working on a very important business transaction."

"Yes, dear," she whispered.

Mr. Steele, a handsome man in his forties, had high cheekbones, piercing eyes, and a long and delicate nose like an archangel.

"Well, well, HJ," Mr. Steele exclaimed, eyeing Gigi. "What is this? A surprise you've sprung upon us?"

As HJ introduced Gigi to Mr. Steele, he smiled and gently kissed her hand.

"Mr. Steele, do you think a lot of HJ?"

Looking slightly puzzled, "Indeed, my dear lady."

"Well then, will you do something for me please?"

He bowed. "Anything in the world, with pleasure, for HJ and his charming bride."

"Well." Gigi glanced at HJ and leaned closer to Mr. Steele. "I want you to instruct HJ that it is improper for a lady to be brought to such an elegant hotel in anything *but* a carriage." Gigi impishly smiled.

"Well, you just leave him to me." Mr. Steele smirked.

As Gigi hastened to the hotel, she turned to see that HJ and Mr. Steele stood there laughing. They thought it was the greatest joke they had ever heard. Disgusted, Gigi rushed to the hotel lobby. She was welcomed by polished marble floors and shiny chandeliers suspended from an arching ceiling; but, too angry to care, she asked for a room with twin beds and signed in as Mr. and Mrs. HJ Whitley. The hotel clerk recognized the name and looked up at her, realizing that she was one of the newlyweds that the bridal chamber had been reserved for over a month ago.

The hotel room was elegantly carpeted and lit with gaslights. This was the first time Gigi had stayed in a hotel that had a magnetized enunciator that enabled guests to request room service by merely pushing a button. She sat on the pillow top bed, admiring the fireplace and looking at the lovely garden she could see though the open window. The dry, sweet-scented air was reminiscent of a rose garden in full bloom. The fragrance reminded her of her mother.

As she shut her eyes, she could almost hear the rustling of her mother's silk dresses as she climbed the stairs and smell the magical scent she left behind, smelling of roses. As Gigi lay down onto the hotel bed, she could hear her mother's sweet voice reciting Henry David Thoreau's *Friendship*, a verse she had learned from her youth.

> I think awhile of Love, and while I think,
> Love is to me a world,
> Sole meat and sweetest drink,
> And close connecting link,
> Tween heaven and earth…

Her mother made sure that she had a refined upbringing and Southern charm. It was something that Gigi was struggling with at the moment. As HJ entered the suite, he walked up to the porter, who was placing their trunks in the room, and requested that they be moved to the bridal suite—the room he had telegraphed for.

"I am perfectly satisfied," Gigi informed the porter smugly. "But if *he* wishes to occupy the bridal suite, it's fine with me."

HJ informed Gigi he had an important appointment. "When I return, we will have dinner in the bridal suite."

He and the porter left with the trunks. Gigi could hear the porter laughing. "Well, Colonel, tats one on youse," he said.

HJ failed to return by tea time. Gigi regretted that she had been so demanding, more difficult than most men would tolerate. Secretly ashamed of her blind rage, a cloud of misery and disgust lingered in her mind. She questioned if she would ever understand how to handle a man that had a will that matched her own.

To appease herself, she decided to have tea at a quaint spot down the street from the hotel. As she entered the establishment, she was particularly attracted to a landscape painting of the countryside, much like she imagined the property of Wuthering Heights—cold, damp, and foggy, traces of snow lingering about. Gigi sat at a small, linen-lined table set with fragrant roses. The waiter, a cheery man, was so happy in his work that he instantly put her at ease. The smell of yeast and sugary baked goods filled the air. The finger sandwiches arrived, along with delectable scones. She spent nearly an hour enjoying the many delicacies served; but she felt uneasy about a remark she heard from the ladies at another table. "How strange to see such a sweet girl dining alone." Gigi finished with haste and walked back to the hotel.

As she entered the lobby, all eyes turned toward her. She could hear the porter whisper to the hotel clerk, "There is the bride."

Gigi hurried to the bridal suite and was greeted with a bouquet of yellow and white lilies in full bloom, mingled with irises and wildflowers. Sitting next to the bouquet was a basket of ruby red apples, little yellow apricots, and golden peaches. But still no candy! Why didn't he ever get her candy? A nice box of chocolates would beat out those apples any day. She was uncertain if she should suggest it to him but decided that it might be better to mention it another day.

Young as Gigi was, she realized even then that the principle game was business for her energetic husband. HJ was a wonderful businessman, but she was afraid that he would never confide his business affairs with her. She hoped to learn more about the business so that she could understand why he had to give all his time to it. Why did men think they had the right to neglect their home and family for business? Perhaps, with her help, he could learn a little moderation in the things he did. Gigi would use her feminine influence to cause him to regard his home life above any other obligation. She cheered up and decided that she would try to be the wife HJ needed. With a quick prayer, Gigi knew that God would help her find that path.

Gigi had been in the bridal suite for two hours when HJ returned. He was pleased to see her sitting on the settee, reading Defoe's *Moll Flanders*. Being a little wiser, she held her tongue. Rather than complaining, she thanked him for the fruit and flowers. Gigi asked him if he had been in time to meet his friends for the important business appointment. HJ seemed delighted that she had asked. Feeling assured that the way was clear to begin explaining, he told her the events of the day.

"Of course, you understand, dear. I had to finish my business with them. When they urged me to take dinner with them, I felt obliged to accept. You do understand, dear?" he cautiously said.

No answer.

"When I asked the hotel clerk, he told me you had just gone out to take a walk." He hesitated. "Where did you go?"

"Oh, I just went to a nice tea room down the street. I knew you were with important friends. When do we start our journey again?"

"Tomorrow, but maybe it is still early enough to go somewhere tonight. Where would you like to go?" His eyes swept her face and settled on her parted lips.

As he kissed her, she murmured that she preferred to stay home alone with him. "I love you. You make me feel things, things I have always dreamed about."

He held her tightly around the waist and kept them intimately joined. Nothing was stopping him from the thoughts that raced through his mind. With that, he carried her to their bed.

Early the next morning, Gigi lay watching him sleep. She had been watching him for a while, never wanting to forget the wonderful evening, especially his soft, caressing touches. Gigi just liked to look at him, especially when he smiled. His strong physique and face appeared boyish to her, despite his age. She followed a path with her eyes over his face when she suddenly realized that it must be time to get up. HJ was awakened from his deep slumber by her whispering in his ear, "You must hurry. It is nearly eight, and we have to catch the ten o'clock train." A sly grin grew slowly across HJ's face as he threw the covers back to get out of bed.

Though Gigi had rebelliously wanted her own way the day before, somehow last night had brought them together in a way she could barely comprehend. Gigi sensed that the rest of the honeymoon would be magnificent.

HJ and Gigi were both fascinated with California, so it had been decided that Los Angeles was where they would spend the majority of their honeymoon. Even at that early date, it had become quite a famous tourist attraction. Los Angeles had changed very little since their last visit. It was still not more than a small Spanish settlement, yet it was the countryside surrounding it that attracted HJ's attention. It was a lovely California day when they arrived. There were very few good hotel accommodations at that time, the Westminster being the best. There, they became acquainted with General Harrison Gray Otis, the cofounder of the *Los Angeles Times*. General Otis was a true military hero, having courageously fought in the Civil War. He proudly told them about his military career and the ghastly battle wounds he had received. He desired to talk with HJ because he had heard of the progressive work he had done in the great Northwest. He tried to persuade HJ to join him in developing southern California.

Otis declared, "There is plenty of room to spread out, and such a man as you is needed to build the new empire. Drive out in the country and see our beautiful surroundings. There are no streetcars to speak of. The Santa Monica car line to the beach is our only direct road toward the West. You can hire some fine driving horses that will afford you a better view of the surrounding country. There are plenty of narrow paths leading up to the hills, delightful wildflowers, some orchards, but mostly garden sections farmed by Chinese men."

Treasuring horseback riding, HJ and Gigi made plans to explore the hills the next morning at daylight. With a knapsack lunch in hand, they headed to the stables to get the horses. In those days, it was not customary for ladies to ride astride, so HJ insisted that Gigi start her ride wearing a skirt. HJ wore his tan suit and cap while she had on a black skirt, red jacket, and cap with her hair tucked up inside. When they were out of the city limits, she stopped and took off the skirt. Flaunting her riding britches, she hastily stuck the skirt in her pack. Soon, they left the city far behind.

The horseback ride was breathtaking. The horses seemed to dance and prance gracefully, as though the rhyme of the ride was timed to a lively ballet of classical music. Gigi adored the cadence of water flowing over rocks in the creek mixed with the highs and lows of chirping birds. The pungent scent of wild-flowers flavored the air as they rode along the meandering trail. After traveling north for several hours, they began to pass small ranches and country places where fruits and vegetables were grown. They even enjoyed picking a variety of luscious produce and savoring its sweetness. Gigi appreciated that oranges were once considered the fruit of the gods.

HJ asked one of the farmers along the trail, "Where would you go if you wanted to purchase some land?"

"Go through the Cahuenga Pass to the San Fernando Valley. It is very productive," he replied.

"Well, someday we will go out there, but today I think I will show my bride Lookout Mountain."

They rested for an hour after enjoying the lovely picnic lunch provided by the hotel.

Gigi remarked, "Can we journey up higher and get a better view of the valley?"

As they neared the top, they stopped and dismounted their horses to admire the view below. As HJ was making a few sketches in his notebook for future memory, he spied off to the left an old rickety wagon full of wood pulled by one horse with a Chinese man driving pell-mell down the narrow road. The Chinese man was singing at the top of his voice. HJ and Gigi stood to one side of the road as the man appeared around the cluster of trees. He had also caught a glimpse of them, so he drew up his reins to stop the wagon full of firewood. Getting out of the wagon, he put his palms together in front of his chest and bowed his head a little, closing his eyes as an expression of respect. HJ and Gigi were delighted with his greeting. Gigi still remembered those two tall men talking to each other. Much to her surprise, the Chinese man spoke an intelligible but broken English with a thick Chinese accent.

"What are you doing?" HJ asked.

"I up sunrise. Old trees fall down. Pick up wood. All time haully wood."

"Holly wood … Hollywood!" HJ declared as he gazed off to the valley below.

After a long silence, the Chinese man climbed back in the wagon. He continued on his way down the trail. HJ was lost in thought and had not meant to ignore the man. All of a sudden, HJ turned to Gigi and said, "Hollywood! That is a perfect name! I will name this new town Hollywood. Holly will represent my British ancestors and Wood for our Scottish. Yes, *Hollywood!*"

Dusk arrived as they returned to the hotel. They were welcomed with Spanish music flowing into the courtyard. A delightful, passionate, and romantic melody was playing while a male dancer dominated the beat of the music with short bursts of powerful footwork. HJ's eyes were drawn to the female dancer's graceful movements as she seductively glided past him. Her movements were accented by the expressive twists and turns of her hands. Gigi was intrigued that the dancer could express sensual femininity without being vulgar. As the provocative dancer proceeded across the courtyard, her tempting appearance and movements, obviously reliant upon the power of feminine allure, threw HJ, who was a very sophisticated man, off balance. "This Spanish dancer is magnificent!" he observed as he moved to take care of the horses.

After they hurried inside and freshened up, they watched the rest of the performance from the piazza. With the mood for romance set, HJ and Gigi decided to dine in their room on the fresh vegetables and fruit they had handpicked on their afternoon trip.

Anticipation of what the evening would hold was half the pleasure for them. The scent of him after his bath enveloped Gigi in the heady fragrance of rosemary. They gazed through the window at the starlit sky. Gigi rested her head on HJ's chest and heard his steady heartbeat. Then he lifted his head and looked at her. There was a soft twinkle in his eyes as their glances met.

The next morning, Gigi pulled back the curtains as she spoke, letting light flood into the room where HJ was just waking. After a sleepless night, she felt it imperative to plead with him to leave her in California. Gigi understood that he had work to finish in the Dakotas, but she reasoned that he would complete it faster if he went alone.

He declared, "I cannot stand to leave you. I have never loved anyone the way I love you. I promise if you come with me, we will return to California as soon as possible. We will stay for another week to rest up, and then we will leave for the Dakotas."

The weather was lovely, so they traveled to the ocean. The beach was deserted. It was the perfect place to be. Gigi loved being with her handsome, blue-eyed man. They were an odd couple. HJ was over six feet tall while Gigi barely surpassed five feet. His sturdy shoulders offered her never-ending support and comfort. Gigi cherished the thought that his strong arms would hold her like no other. When she was wrapped in his arms—arms that would be open just for her—she felt completely loved, safe, and secure.

They watched the waves from the shore as they crested and then crashed on the sandy beach. Tiny sandpipers played tag with the gentle waves. Gigi could taste the salt in the air, watching little rainbows glisten through the prisms of the ocean's spray. She loved the way her skin felt in the damp air with the ocean breeze all around her. It was a perfect day, with the water appearing warm and inviting, calling as it crashed upon the shore. On a whim, she tossed her dress in the sand. The water felt cool and refreshing as she dove through a breaking wave. It was daring, but love leads one to many uncharted places. As she swam freely, Gigi sensed his presence as his strong arms encircled her. His gentle kisses were just the beginning of a very pleasurable day. Later, they returned to the hotel as the sunset colored the sky deep orange and soft lilac, slowly shading to a velvety dark blue as twilight crept in. They walked hand in hand to their room.

The next afternoon, while Gigi was taking a nap, HJ met secretly with Mr. Hurd at his ranch on the hill in the Cahuenga Valley. Before he left California, he wanted a commitment to the right to purchase the first five hundred acres of his new town, Hollywood. Mr. Hurd listened attentively to what was being said. He promised with a sacred trust not to tell a single soul of the plans or the name of the future town. They agreed upon a very favorable price, which was, in Mr. Hurd's eyes, a sizable amount; and the deal was sealed with a handshake. With time, however, it became difficult for Mr. Hurd to keep the secret from his wife. With a slightly guilty conscience, he told her of his agreement with HJ. Little time passed before the word got out that Mr. Whitley, the town builder, had been around and was planning to buy land in the area. HJ worked out his plans for the new town that was soon to be put on the map. The only other people he told about his future plans were General Otis and Ivar Weid.

While having dinner one night General Otis informed HJ that he had heard that the Indian lands would soon be thrown open for white settlement. "I know you could never resist the thrill of being on hand," declared General Otis. "You go ahead with your plans for that town in the Cahuenga Valley as soon as possible, and make sure to protect your ideas. Now that you have decided on a name, I cannot wait to see you promote it, for everyone knows you can make any place flourish. People with money to invest watch every move you make, so beware, HJ. I know their tricks and ways better than you. I wish you would stay right here. Of course, I realize you have big holdings in the great Northwest, but prospects are more favorable here."

HJ and Otis parted, and they were not to meet again for several years. Gigi silently followed alongside her husband to the pioneer work in the great Northwest. This short space of time was filled with cares and trials for both of them.

After leaving California so reluctantly, Gigi found the train trip quite appealing. HJ imparted his knowledge of the sights as they passed through different sections of the country. She felt that now, at last, she was getting all of his attention, which pleased her a great deal. The scenery was composed chiefly of rich, rolling prairies interspersed with groves of trees that were watered by numerous streams. Those fertile and flowery plains seemed to extend on forever. Until now, Gigi had not spent much time talking to HJ privately, and she was glad that they were alone. That private time did not last. When they changed trains, HJ encountered many of his business friends going East.

Once again, Gigi had lost his companionship. She tried not to let it bother her. Instead, she gazed out the window at the scenery. After a while, she began to look around to see if some of the other ladies wanted to chat. Gigi noticed a woman with auburn-colored hair and an oblong face with small eyes. What stood out most was her little hooked nose. The woman had a stately air, and her manner of speaking was mild and obliging. Gigi was pleased when the woman smiled her way and invited Gigi to join her. The woman lived in California and was very fascinated with the story about their honeymoon adventure. She was intrigued to learn that HJ worked for the Rock Island Railroad and developed many towns across the western United States. Most of all, she was interested in his new town that he planned to name Hollywood. She asked the exact location of the land he planned to purchase.

Gigi was having a lively conversation when HJ returned with several important men and informed her it was time for lunch. "Be ready in five minutes, Gigi," he said.

They went to the dining car together. The waiter quickly served their meal. Gigi was anticipating a cheerful conversation with HJ about the woman she had just met.

HJ began to upbraid her. "Gigi, you have to be careful about speaking openly to strangers. You must take into consideration that your husband is an important man of considerable standing. From now on, I will choose your friends for you, Gigi."

Gigi tried to smile at him; but inwardly, she was perturbed. She was troubled, and she let HJ see it. In the next breath, she slowly said, "Now, dear, I wish to obey you as often as possible, but when your wishes interfere with my individual rights, I draw the line."

"Well, now, little woman, I want to tell you I am the head of this family, and I know best."

"My father's people signed the Declaration of Independence, and my Uncle Samuel instructed me to be just but not to let *anyone*, even a husband, take away my individual rights. There is no sin in life worse than being controlled to the point that I lose my identity. I cannot imagine anything worse than letting other people tell me what to do. I felt it only common politeness to be friendly."

"I will find out who she is, but in the meantime, stay close to me out in the observation car. I can talk to my friends there, and you will not be alone, dear. It is too bad that I have to leave you alone so much. Business must be attended to, and it has been so fortunate to meet with these men today. You understand, dear? Answer me."

"No, I am afraid I do not. I am too sentimental, and you know that this is our honeymoon."

That afternoon, Gigi occupied herself in the same coach as HJ. He felt quite content to see her sitting and reading while he spent the afternoon discussing his business plans. Leadership was a great responsibility; but at that particular moment, she wished he was just an ordinary farmer.

Gigi spent the afternoon reading magazines about the beautiful things she wanted for their new home: rich furniture, handsome paintings, sculptures, and a piano. She realized that it was not only possessions she wanted but also the joy that they brought. Gigi thought about the simpler things in life that brought an unconscious beautifying effect to a home as well. The songs of birds, the drifting of clouds, the twinkle of stars—all these things imparted a subtle and compelling peace in their lives. Gigi resolved to study them and have them influence her home.

For many years, Gigi had been a fan of Thoreau. Being a bit of a rebel herself, she loved his philosophy of marching to the beat of your heart. She went to Walden Pond and walked around it, trying to capture a sense of his thoughts and what he saw when he lived there. What Gigi learned from him was that no one could steal your ideals, dreams, or happiness unless you gave them the power to do so. And why would she ever do that?

Gigi reread his words in a magazine that day and thought about them. She would strive for simplicity, live humbly and with kindness. The norms of the times Gigi lived in required her to tread softly, taking the higher road in issues that concerned her marriage. Thoreau's words would direct her path:

> I learned this, at least, by my experiment, that if one advances confidently in the direction of his dreams, and endeavors to live the life which he has imagined, he will meet with a success unexpected in common hours.

The afternoon closed with a glorious sunset as Gigi was filled with thoughts about her future. As the day ended, she saw the magnificent colors of creation, offering her a unique feeling of God's presence. The calmness of the night fully draped itself across the plains as HJ finally made his way to her. She greeted him with a sleepy smile that overpowered him as he took her hand and said, "Gentlemen, this is my wife."

As they left the observation car, Gigi said, "If you have finished your business with those gentlemen, let us spend this evening alone."

As they headed to their cabin, HJ winked. He scooped Gigi up at the door to their sleeping cabin, carrying her in his strong arms into the suite. Carefully, he lowered her onto the bed. Their hearts raced with the click-clacks of the train speeding to the north.

HJ was up early the next morning and secured the best seats outside at the end of the train to view the scenery. He imagined that Gigi would enjoy fresh-baked scones, a pot of tea, and a bouquet, so he ordered them from the porter the day before. Gigi loved the great grain fields and wild game she saw. Some parts had vast sections of cattle, but Gigi did not find these parts as interesting. There were not as many hills and mountains in the Dakotas. HJ told her all about his new town, Dickinson. He opened the bank January 1, 1886. He hoped that their new home would be completed when they arrived. If not, they would have to stay at the little hotel in Dickinson for a while. He was sure she would not mind.

As they were finally nearing their home in Dickinson, Dakota, HJ said, "Are you all packed and ready? The next station is ours. Put on your best traveling outfit. I want my little wife to look her best."

At times, Gigi felt a slave to fashion. Keeping up the level of dress required to be called "respectable" was quite a feat. The number of clothes changes required in a day was often more than she liked. Styling her hair and putting on the many layers of clothing took nearly an hour. HJ smiled as Gigi appeared in a stylish, fawn-colored dress complete with a cape, hat, and shoes to match. To complete the outfit, she carried a stylish purse lined with a floral material and a handkerchief monogrammed with dainty needlework.

Chapter Four

"At last we have arrived, Gigi. See. The whole town has appeared to greet us," HJ exclaimed as the train jolted while coming to a stop.

It was a beautiful spring morning. As they stepped from the train, they could see HJ's bank on Villard Street. Although the breeze held a morning's chill, Gigi smiled, feeling the warmth of love from her future friends. The band serenaded them while friends, bank employees, and city officials affectionately greeted them. Then they were driven by carriage to the hotel.

Gigi decided to rest while HJ hurried to the bank to take care of business. Before he left, he ordered tea and had it sent to their room. The tea tray was delivered a short time later. To Gigi, there were few hours more pleasing than the hour devoted to the ceremony known as afternoon tea. She started drinking it with her mother when she was just a child, and it became a lifelong habit. Since this was not a meal but rather like a late afternoon snack, Gigi only sampled the finger foods to stave off hunger until their late-night dinner. The tea tray held dainty tea sandwiches, scones, and pastries. Relaxing, she wondered what lay ahead in their future.

Now that their honeymoon was over they would need to work on their marriage. Gigi was a loving, sentimental woman with little experience in dealing with men. She read many romantic novels and hoped that HJ's devotion to her would be the same as Romeo to Juliet. Although HJ loved her, he still expected Gigi to respect his time and privacy. During the times he was busy with work he wanted to be left alone; he hoped she would learn to honor this request. She realized he had been a bachelor for numerous years and work had been his entire life. Gigi would have to be patient, giving him time to adjust. It was imperative that HJ learn to make time for their relationship.

The next morning, HJ hastily finished his breakfast at the Dickinson Hotel and left Gigi at the table while he picked up the buggy for their little excursion. They went to see their new home. HJ was, of course, practically born on a horse. His experience building towns taught him how to be a master at driving a team. His face wore a contented look when he returned with the buggy. His hands held the reins tightly, with the whip easily within reach.

As they approached their Queen Anne-style home, she knew at once that she would enjoy living there. They spent nearly an hour exploring the home's many features. As they entered the house, they were welcomed by two reception rooms: a parlor and a sitting room. Both rooms had elaborate fireplaces. The dining room, kitchen, and the servant's bedroom were at the rear of the house on the first floor. Adjacent to the servant's room, although it was for family use, was a bathroom. The bathroom contained a tin-lined, square tub and a marble wash basin. It was a luxury, not to mention the first indoor bath in the city. HJ told her that he planned to order a Walker's range for the kitchen. It was a great improvement over the open hearth that some of their neighbors still used. This stove heated water that was piped directly to the kitchen sink and the bathroom.

Four bedrooms were on the second floor. The beamed ceilings were high enough for HJ to walk across the room without stooping, and all four bedrooms were of a reasonable size. Even the attic room at the top of the house gave plenty of room to store their future treasures. Their bedroom was placed at the southern end of the house with a balcony that overlooked the valley. It had an elaborate oak staircase, beveled mirrors, ornate window moldings, and spindle work at the doors. Gigi ran up and down until she could run no more.

Gigi sat down on the stairs next to HJ. "It is perfect. Nothing is missing."

As they sat there, they discussed the placing of the new furniture. They planned to have it moved into the house at the beginning of the next month. Gigi decided that she wanted to learn a little more about cooking before the maid arrived. Appearing ignorant about those things to a household servant was unthinkable.

As an added touch to make the day complete, HJ ordered a picnic lunch from the hotel. Before HJ went more than a few yards out the front door, he grabbed Gigi's hand and directed her to follow him down a little path.

They journeyed on until they found the perfect spot under a large tree overlooking the valley. There they sat, two lovers, with their bodies touching each other, gently feeding one another tantalizing tidbits from the basket: sandwiches, applesauce, ginger snaps, and a jug of lemonade. So profound was their love for each other that they needed no words to express it. And so they sat in silence, enjoying the sunshine.

Gigi finally broke the silence. "Do you love me?"

"You know I love you, darling."

There was more silence as they sat with their bodies touching, holding hands in the sunlight. Once more, her voice was heard. "Kiss me."

Leaning over, he pressed his lips passionately to hers. HJ pulled her even closer. She ran her hands up and down his back. Her spirited heart raced, the passion and love so intense, his heart intertwined with hers. The unexpressed feelings Gigi experienced were like flowers in a garden, taking root and blossoming into glorious emotions. He slowly eased her down on the blanket and looked into her eyes. The sunlight made her eyes sparkle. She smiled up at him, and he kissed her again. All thought was abandoned. It seemed the kiss lasted forever yet ended all too soon. They lingered in the moment, enjoying each other's presence. Gigi wanted the day to go on forever; but as the sun began to set and paint the sky vivid colors, they headed back to the hotel.

Mending clothes was the only responsibility Gigi was given the first few weeks they lived at the hotel. HJ chose to order the meals and make the necessary arrangements to make their stay comfortable. Up to this point, someone always did the mundane chores in life for her. She knew little about running a household, so the most important decisions about the new home were left up to HJ. Gigi was an entirely dependent person—no provisions to buy, no plans to make. HJ decided everything for her, and she was beginning to think that she could not be happy living that way. Gigi needed more adventure.

HJ believed that it was important to start things off on the right foot. He immediately informed her that people were very traditional in this part of the country. He wanted her to be a housewife, not taken by the new ideas circulating the nation.

She should think of him first at all times. He wanted her to spend her time reading, sewing, receiving guests, going visiting, letter writing, seeing to the servants, and dressing for the part as his social representative. That was a wife's duty. He let her know that he did not have a selfish hair on his head, but business would compel him to devote most of his time to getting his work done while he was still young. After all, he was working to support her.

HJ further explained, "God's design for humanity is for women to bear children and for men to do the work of the world."

Gigi started out by trying to please HJ but found it harder than she expected. When someone almost persuaded her to participate in some exciting activity of the town, HJ always found out. He quickly put a stop to such "foolishness," as he called it. It was while reading letters that Abigail Adams wrote to her husband that Gigi first began to think that things must change. Gigi decided to hold Abigail's words in her heart and make it her anthem: "Remember the Ladies."

As a married woman, Gigi concluded that she had no legal existence; she had no more rights than a slave on a plantation in Alabama. She took the name of her husband. She owned nothing and could bring no action in her name. The principle on which a slave and she were educated was the same. Slaves were taught what was considered best for them to know—which was nothing. HJ planned to teach her what was best for her to know—which was also little more than nothing. Socially and religiously, Gigi was what HJ chose her to be. As such, a slave and Gigi had much in common. How would she be able to teach HJ that she had the same sense of right and justice, the same love of freedom and independence that he had?

Gigi decided to make a list of dreams and goals she would like to accomplish by the time she reached age one hundred. It would help her become more adventurous and creative. As she crossed off the tasks, they would serve as a record of her accomplishments. Gigi titled the journal: *A List of One Hundred Important Things.* The list was in no specific order, just things she wanted to accomplish. She felt that if she could picture something happening, it would. Yet Gigi wondered, would she be able to see herself making a difference, causing the world to be a better place? Would she ever own a piece of property that was recorded in her name? How would she learn to be less worried about what others thought? Would women ever be allowed to vote or sit on a jury? On a more personal note, she pondered having children and hoped that she would be lucky enough to have a boy and a girl. Would her travels take her to exotic places where she could ride a camel into the desert? But number one on her list was to compose a song that became famous.

Gigi chose to be a faithful steward of her heart, doing whatever she could to honor the dreams it held. She could not separate herself from who she was or from who she envisioned herself being in the future. They were intertwined.

The new society Gigi entered in Dickinson offered more hardship than she had first anticipated. It was difficult for her to live among strangers, repeatedly being left alone while HJ spent most of his time attending to business. The whole town knew almost everything they did; in fact, everything they did seemed to be a town matter. Gigi had never lived in a little town and could not imagine why they were so interested in their affairs. At first, HJ was annoyed by their curiosity; but when one of his largest clients at the bank invited them over for dinner to discuss the purchase of their new stove, he was delighted. HJ found it simpler to perform future business transactions. Women's influence over their husbands was no longer a mystery to him. He used it to his advantage.

With the arrival of the new stove, Gigi tried her hand at cooking before the first maid arrived. The wood stove was hard to start up and even harder to keep going, but she was determined to impress HJ with her cooking skills. Gigi's first attempt was a failure. The cake burned on the outside and was raw in the middle. Gradually, she learned that the damper that opened into the firebox created only a small draft. Without a draft, the fire would flicker out. While baking, she had to keep constant watch on the fire; and even then the stove did not keep an even temperature. Every time the heat slacked, she had to throw logs, kindling, or corn cobs into the firebox.

The kitchen smelled warm and sweet from canisters of sugar, flour, and spices sitting on the counter. At last, Gigi baked an exceptional three-layered cake with custard in between and icing on the top. She placed it on the kitchen table, hoping that HJ would find it tempting to taste. To accompany it, she had baked some bread and a batch of applesauce. Gigi peeled and steamed apples and then mashed them. These were HJ's favorite foods. When she told HJ of her three successful ventures, he remarked, "You are definitely living up to your reputation as an excellent cook. This has been a true treat. I declare I have never seen better looking bread, or a more tempting cake, let alone that scrumptious applesauce I tasted." His praise was a great vote of confidence, for his approval was dearer to her and more difficult to win than from others.

Early one morning, as a treat, Gigi decided to make the most delicious doughnuts to impress HJ. They were made from a secret family recipe her sister had given her. Their friends who had tasted the doughnuts described them as heavenly, tender and airy, only fit for a queen. They were large, plump, and golden, with enough buttery taste to make your mouth water in anticipation of the next bite. An irresistible aroma drifted through the entire house, causing HJ's stomach to rumble.

After the first bite, he said with a second mouthful, "They are the best I have ever tasted. Please make a four-gallon jar full so they will last a long time."

Gigi had never seen him talk with his mouth full before. He ate with such relish that it made her smile.

Gigi got so busy frying that she did not notice that HJ had taken two of the large platters to the neighbors. When he came up the back steps, he was out of breath; and Gigi was a bit perturbed. She turned to run in the house, but he called, saying, "Gigi, please do not be annoyed at me. I was so proud of you making the delicious doughnuts and wanted to impress my friends. Before I realized it, I had given them all away. You would have thought they had never tasted doughnuts before."

It occurred to her how funny all the day's events would look to an outside observer. But as she laughed, she also was struck by the fact that the nickname she may soon be given sounded so completely odd. "What a great big boy I have married. Now they will call me the doughnut woman."

HJ knew that every moment of his time would be occupied with business, so he was passionate in getting everything completely settled as quickly as possible wherever he lived. He wanted all the pictures hung and everything in its proper place within the first forty-eight hours after the furniture arrived. To accomplish this undertaking, he hired extra staff to complete the job. Dirt and disorder made him positively uncomfortable. He did not want anything to distract him from his important

household was put together so quickly, Gigi
lf with too much spare time. Her life seemed
urance.

t sustained her in those first lonely years was
her faith. The gentle guiding hand of Uncle Samuel had taught
her that she would have the necessary answers to life's challenges. Uncle Samuel spent many years studying theology, and
his library had a number of books dealing with faith. As a young
adult, the Bible occupied many hours of her free time and gave
her much comfort.

Short walks in the countryside showed her the miracles of
nature. Lovely flowers with their varied colors and perfumes
were a joy to behold. Trees imparted refreshing melodies with
cheerful songs coming from their branches. At times, Gigi
would be homesick for her family. But sitting under a wide-
spreading tree and listening to the meadowlark send forth the
most charming greetings magically wove a spell about her. As
the song vibrated through the airy spaces between the leaves
and drifted out across the sunshine of the garden, it held her
spellbound. Dreams of a bright future in California flooded her
mind. She especially enjoyed her walk if she could find a small
bird sitting on a branch in the endless shade of a tree, throw-
ing its song into the air to dance with the sunlight and the cool
breeze. Generally when she finished her walk she felt refreshed.
Curious about her newfound friend, she studied him, his plum-
age, character, native abode, and why he migrated. From then
on, Gigi enjoyed walks in her garden that were brought alive
with the sound of chickadees, warblers, jays, and woodpeckers.

Gigi used these walks as a way of building a sanctuary in the
midst of her everyday life. She needed a way to refresh herself, to
keep loneliness at bay. This sanctuary was built in her heart and

mind, but it is no less real for that. The basic reason she did this was to find a way to deal with her day-to-day dealings with other people, especially HJ. She knew that you could not mistreat people one moment and then find peace the next. Gigi realized that there would be no peace without sacrifice and that, ultimately, there is no peace without justice. She felt that the way she lived her daily life was the key to finding happiness. Gigi found that nature provided a doorway to this spot.

Later that week, HJ and Gigi were invited over to the Dickersons' home for dinner. The Dickerson family was noted for their promptness, and their household management ran like clockwork. The dinner consisted of a delicious soup, followed by roasted chicken. But Gigi was most interested in the conversation after dinner.

HJ began. "Do any of you know Mr. Roosevelt's whereabouts?"

Mr. Hilliard replied, "I read about him in the newspaper. They say he is back in New York to stay. I bet he is getting married. He will probably sell off his interest out West and return to politics in New York or Washington. We need him back there."

"Well, I imagine with all the people coming to this part of the country and establishing large farms that soon the cattle business will disappear."

"Have you gotten your invitation to the round-up this October? It will probably be our last one."

HJ decided that he would make a special effort to be at the round-up that year. "Maybe you could show Gigi some photographs from our last round-up?"

The other guests and Gigi spent nearly half an hour looking at and talking over the scenes. They were extraordinary pictures of thousands of cattle being sorted out and the men who drove them to market. It was getting late, so HJ stood as a signal that it was time to go. Important work was scheduled for early the next morning.

HJ would have to work alone for a month at the bank. The bank teller was traveling East to get married. This gave him a heavier workload than usual. He made special plans to hire a night watchman because the teller would not return from his wedding trip before payday. HJ was nervous because the payroll was extremely large that month.

A few nights before the monthly payroll was to arrive at the bank, Gigi awoke from a nightmare, gripped by fear. The dream was particularly disturbing, so Gigi thought it wise to practice shooting her rifle on prairie chickens. The warning was a dark shadow lurking in her mind. On the afternoon before payday, a large sum of money would be delivered to the bank in the afternoon. Gigi suggested that HJ come home at one o'clock for a dinner of prairie hens and roasted potatoes, and then he could take his revolver back to work in case of an emergency. HJ was glad that Gigi could handle a rifle because he had been informed that some suspicious-looking men were in town.

Later that evening, when HJ came out of the bank at nearly ten o'clock, he was greeted by the sheriff, who said, "I have never seen so many strangers coming into town, but do not worry, we are prepared for any surprise. Make sure you check all the locks on your home. You never can tell what type of tricks they might try to pull. We plan to make our rounds tonight to make sure everyone is safe."

As HJ entered the house, Gigi said, "Now, HJ, I am going right to bed, and you should get some sleep too. You look so tired."

"All right," HJ apprehensively said. "I feel I should let you know, Gigi, I am going to put my revolver under my pillow and your rifle next to the bed in case we need them. The sheriff warned me to be extra careful tonight."

After trying the doors and windows to make sure they were locked, they went off to bed. At one o'clock, Gigi was awakened by a noise right under their bedroom window. A few minutes later, she heard coal in the cellar begin to roll as step by step, someone was climbing over it to reach the cellar stairs. She lay perfectly still while the intruder was trying the cellar door. Thankfully, it was locked. The blinds on the bedroom windows were closed, so she could not see outside; but she could distinctly hear footsteps going around the house, trying every window several times. Gigi softly touched HJ before awakening him. When he opened his eyes, Gigi whispered in his ear, "Someone is outside. Can you hear them? They are going around the house on the other side."

HJ was cautious as he stepped out of bed and onto the floor and then quickly snatched his revolver in case the robbers were armed. He warned Gigi to stand in a safe place, so she held her rifle and stood on the stairs leading up to the bedrooms. A deep, paralyzing fear gripped her as she reached the landing. Her pulse raced and then seemed to stand still.

The men outside began to swear at each other, one threatening to break a window. HJ held his revolver up. Gathering his courage, HJ ventured closer to the windows. He could barely see through the darkness. Just out of range on the porch, a large shape looming in the shadows made the hairs on the back of HJ's neck stand up. Gigi sensed the presence of something evil, as though she was going to die.

Suddenly, one of them yelled, "Run!"

HJ watched as several husky men mounted their horses, which were standing under a tree, and rode out of sight, followed by the sheriff and his deputies. Gigi placed her rifle in the corner as she sat down on the stairs. HJ rushed over to her, thinking she was going to faint; but she looked up at him and requested, "Stoke the fire in the stove, and I will put the kettle on. We will have a good cup of tea. I guess we will have to stay up the rest of the night until they are caught."

As soon as they finished their tea and toast, she tried to get HJ to go to bed. There was no way to communicate with the sheriff, so HJ had no way of knowing how things were at the bank. He hoped that the payroll was still safe. As soon as it was daylight, he was off to get some news from the sheriff and check on the bank. The sheriff told HJ the men had escaped by horseback and headed west out of town. What HJ did not realize was that the men hoped to get him to open the bank while Gigi was held captive in their home. Just a few days earlier, the men had visited the Dickinson Bank and studied its layout to be sure that every detail of the robbery was thoroughly planned. Fortunately for Gigi, they did not expect the sheriff to visit their home that evening.

HJ's thoughts raced as he arrived at the bank. He could not get the men on horseback from the night before out of his mind. He figured they must have been in a highly nervous state and that they were inexperienced. The men appeared to be spur-of-the-moment criminals whose irrationality might be compelled by any of a number of illogical motives. They did not appear to have a well-rehearsed plan. HJ figured they would probably attempt another robbery and try to take control of the bank. He decided that his overall objective would be to protect the payroll at all costs and had warned the hired guard to be on the alert. HJ was startled back to reality when he heard several men enter the bank.

HJ, seeing the masked outlaws, readied himself for their assault. The robbers shouted out warnings of violence, and they yelled loud instructions as they tossed canvas bags at HJ. One thief waved his gun, motioning for HJ to start unloading the drawers full of cash and valuables. As each drawer was opened, the gunman ordered, "Faster! Faster!"

As HJ examined them, he determined that they were not the really dangerous type, the true man-killer type, but they were objectionable creatures, would-be bad men, bullies who, for the moment, were having things their way. He realized that the men were beastly drunk, probably having quaffed a few drinks to bolster their courage, so HJ jumped over the counter and quickly grabbed the ringleader. He punched the man in the face three times before, to HJ's surprise, he fired his guns. The last blow sent the ringleader flying, and as he went down he struck the corner of the counter with his head. HJ took away his guns. He was not willing to take any chances. If the ringleader moved, he was ready to crack his ribs with his knees. Luckily, the robber was knocked senseless. His accomplices stood paralyzed.

Fortunately, the sheriff and his deputies heard the shots. They arrived a few moments later and arrested the other gunmen. As they hustled them out to put them in a shed, one accomplice began to cry, declaring that it was his first robbery and begging for mercy. HJ and the sheriff spoke and decided to ship the robbers off on the next train with a warning never to return.

All the excitement did not interfere with the arrival of good news. Promptly at 6:00 p.m., HJ received a telegram at the bank from Mr. Roosevelt.

Chapter Five

Teddy Roosevelt, one of HJ's close friends, had made time in his busy schedule to speak in front of the Dickinson Bank on July 4, 1886. HJ viewed him as the great advertiser. He preached as no revivalist ever preached. His speeches were vivid expressions that the average man yearned to hear. America was his pulpit. Men listened and believed.

At ten o'clock, just after Mr. Roosevelt had been escorted from the train to the bank, the parade began. The whole citizenry of the surrounding area turned out to watch civil war veterans, volunteer firemen, and local residents costumed in mostly patriotic regalia proudly march through town. The parade included a band playing a collection of patriotic music, including "America," "Yankee Doodle," "Buffalo Gals," and military hymns and marches. Following the band were some of Roosevelt's old pals, Sylvane Ferris, Bill Merrifield, Will Dow, and Bill Sewell on horseback. Many spectators, decked out in patriotic colors, were waving flags as the festivities began. With numerous participants, oodles of spectators, countless children holding candy-filled bags, and not a cloud in the sky, the Fourth of July parade was a booming success.

HJ awoke early on the Fourth. As he dressed, he had practiced his speech to introduce Teddy. His introduction was brief and impressive, only three sentences long. Still, he was able to explain the importance of the day and its notable speaker. It was clear that HJ understood the audience's interest.

As the applause died down, Teddy stepped to the platform to address his old cowboy chums. The life that these cowboys represented, one Teddy had played a part in, stood for so much to him. Roosevelt began his speech by warmly greeting the sizeable crowd. The speech he delivered spoke to their pioneer spirit. It discussed the ever-pressing issue of opening up the Indian Territory to white settlement. Indian Territory had become chaotic with civil unrest and intertribal conflict.

Before long, Gigi listened to his closing remarks.

"This government was founded on honor, religion, justice, and brotherly love. May the kind, ever-loving God above protect us. This is the fervent wish of your humble servant, who has had the honor and pleasure of being with you all this glorious day, the Fourth of July."

She later wrote the events of the day in her journal.

After his speech, Mr. Roosevelt told the reporter, "I am best suited for work in the political arena. I will soon be relocating back East."

HJ responded, "Then you should become president. You would be superb for the job!"

Mr. Roosevelt expressed no surprise at HJ's remark. He gave the impression that he would indeed become the president someday.

After a short time of handshaking and greeting, the crowd dispersed to the hotel for lunch. At the luncheon, all the leading citizens took part in giving speeches and toasting Mr. Roosevelt for the many accomplishments he had made in his political career and his writings. The luncheon had barely finished when Mr. Roosevelt bid HJ and Gigi good-bye and boarded the five o'clock train going to the East. As Mr. Roosevelt waved a hearty farewell, the crowd cheered and the band played a resounding chorus of "The Star-Spangled Banner."

Several of HJ's business associates boarded the train with Mr. Roosevelt. They were delighted to be given the opportunity to discuss politics as they traveled. Several of them tried to influence HJ to return with them to Washington and assist in the Indian affairs. Someone with great experience would be needed to address the question of opening up more land for settlement.

Now that the events of the day were finally completed, HJ and Gigi went home. They would always remember that wonderful Fourth of July celebration. Teddy's speech brought renewed hope to their community. Just before she fell asleep, Gigi thanked God for giving her the gifts of memories, hope, and most of all, love.

As fall approached, they found themselves busy canning their garden's bountiful harvest. Hannah, the cook, sang gospel tunes as she filled the mason jars. HJ was fond of canning time, and he seemed to request more than Gigi thought they could ever eat. He requested one hundred quarts of green beans, tomatoes, cucumbers, beets, apples, berries, and corn, stopping only when the basement was full.

Soon it was the middle of October and time for the fall round-up. HJ asked if Mrs. Hilliard and Gigi would like to drive out and see all the cattle cross the river as they were driven to Little Missouri. They had been invited to the Roosevelts' Ranch. Gigi would stay at the ranch while HJ was off with Teddy at the round-up.

They took the train to Medora and then traveled by wagon to the ranch. The fall colors were spectacular. They listened to the morning doves sing along the trail. As they approached the ranch, a cool breeze stirred along the Little Missouri, blowing in their faces the aroma of honey, a refreshing change from the hot days of summer. Teddy's Elkhorn Ranch contained eight rooms and a porch that ran along the east wall. It was shaded by leafy cottonwoods towering overhead. In the distance, there were shallow meadowlands and grassy plateaus reaching as far as Gigi's eyes could see.

Teddy, their charming and noted host, was standing in front of his cabin, waiting, along with his staff, Sylvane Ferris and Bill Merrifield, to greet them. When they entered the cabin, they were shown to their pleasant room. As the evening shadows were quickly approaching, they were given time to refresh themselves before dinner. Dinner consisted of venison and wild game, accompanied by tales of hunting trips and other round-ups.

As they sat by the blazing fireplace after dinner, Gigi surveyed the room. It contained the best of books, magazines from eastern cities, and newspapers from around the world. Teddy told a story about his experience hunting the dangerous grizzly bear. The walls were covered with bearskins, buffalo roves, elk antlers, wolfskin overcoats, coonskin caps, deer horns, and gauntlets made from the fur of otters. Knowing that danger quietly inhabited the woods around their home, Gigi vowed to rise early the next morning and practice shooting. Teddy promised to be up early to give her a lesson.

Teddy taught Gigi how to shoot straight, literally and figuratively. Every skilled hunter he knew honored the sportsman's code.

Gigi needed to develop patience and persistence. Accuracy would come with practice, but safety was imperative. He instructed her to be sure that she never touched the trigger until her sights were on the target and she was ready to fire. When she was hunting, she should not aim directly at the target but instead attempt to anticipate the animal's movements. With his lessons complete, Gigi took in a slow, deep breath and gently squeezed the trigger toward her. A single, clean hole marked the center of the bull's-eye.

Startled by the sound of the rifle's shot and her animated yelling, HJ looked out the door. He joined them and was delighted with Gigi's accurate shooting. She hit almost every mark.

HJ exclaimed, "Is it any wonder?" for there stood Mr. Roosevelt, one of the best marksmen in the world, giving her lessons.

Gigi remarked, "How could I possibly fail with such a noted teacher?" The visit with Teddy was memorable from beginning to end, but the highlight was the shooting lesson. Gigi was pleased to show off her impressive shooting skills.

That year's round-up district included Beaver Creek and the Missouri River. HJ and Teddy acted as overseers, observing the work more than participating in it. Since the starting point was far away, the men brought several ponies so they could easily cover long distances at a rapid pace. They needed several four-horse wagons to carry the blankets and mess kits. HJ would not need to ride such long distances, so he only took one horse. Jack was a beautifully marked paint horse with a star on his forehead. He was as fast as the wind and an excellent cow horse.

There would be fifty cowboys on the round-up, along with the ranch foreman. The men were lean, sinewy fellows, accustomed to riding half-broken horses at any speed over any country by day or night. They wore flannel shirts with loose handkerchiefs knotted round their necks, broad hats, high-heeled boots with jingling spurs, and sometimes leather chaps, although they often had their trousers tucked into the tops of their high boots. The ladies had gathered early in the morning at the river to watch the cowboys cross and their husbands head out.

Individually and in twos and threes, they appeared from every quarter of the horizon, the dust rising from the hoofs of the steers, bulls, cows, and calves they had collected. Two or three of the men were left to take care of the herd while the others changed horses, ate a hasty dinner, and then rode out for the afternoon work.

In the evening, they gathered at the appointed place with the cattle that had been collected. At night, Teddy assigned different men to keep a watchful eye, making sure that the herd was safe from rustlers. HJ enjoyed the exhilaration of the drive and the peaceful evenings of sitting around the campfire for an hour or two, telling stories and listening to the fiddle and harmonica being played. The weather was superb, and HJ never slept better. He found that sleep came quickly in the open air after a hard day's ride and away from the thoughts of impending business. He was surprised when he woke with a start, as he had dreamt that the herd was stampeding. Grateful it was only a dream, he rolled over and quickly joined the chorus of snoring among the other ranch hands.

In the morning, Teddy's cook, Mac, prepared breakfast long before the first glimmer of dawn. As soon as it was ready, around three o'clock, he uttered a long-drawn shout; and HJ was up in an instant. HJ grasped a tin cup and plate from the mess box and poured some coffee. He helped himself to two biscuits that had been baked in a Dutch oven and a slice of the fat pork swimming in the grease of the frying pan, ladled out some beans, and sat on a large boulder to eat his breakfast. He enjoyed the sunrise while devouring the delicious food. His appetite had grown with the vigorous exercise of the trail.

Fall round-up was a great way for HJ to end the summer and reconnect with his friends. There was something very special about friends and the bonds they shared. HJ leaned against an old tree and listened to amazing stories they told.

It was a bright day when HJ returned to the ranch. Gigi peered out the curtains as he walked up the path from the stable. His absence stirred a yearning deep inside her. As he swept her up in his arms, they were both silent in delight of the moment. There were no words to express the love she felt in her heart for HJ.

Gigi's journal shares, "He is my best friend and one true love. The day we became acquainted was not fate, but the beginning of two lives intertwining into a beautiful tapestry. Love is the only thing that makes my life worth living."

Unfortunately, HJ was oblivious to her need to be near him. After their long train ride home from Medora, Gigi hoped to spend some time with HJ. They had barely entered the house and only chatted for just a few short minutes when he decided to rush over to the bank and check on business. Gigi was left alone once again. At times, their marriage lacked the give and take and mutual love she needed. HJ had no time for intimacy. Business was calling.

Monday morning seemed to come early and Gigi spent her morning with Hannah, putting up melon preserves and sweet pickles. Hannah had arrived about three weeks after Gigi had learned to cook on their new stove. Hannah was a marvelous cook. Gigi's mouth always watered when she thought of her. In the afternoon, they made red currant jelly. Entertaining was so easy when Gigi was given credit for Hannah's creations.

By early afternoon, Gigi had tired of the project; so she said, "Hannah, I am leaving so you may have all the room you need to finish your plans for the housewarming dinner."

Gigi invited some friends over for a small housewarming party. Hannah suggested a Swedish meal that included fish. Gigi had no idea how to prepare such a meal. She began to think about what a friend had said of a Swedish dinner she once attended: "The only thing I remember about it was I could not eat one single thing that was served."

Gigi held her breath as their friends tasted the food. What a relief it was to hear HJ declare, "I do not think I have had a better meal in my entire life. The only thing lacking is four and twenty blackbirds baked in a pie. You have outdone yourself tonight, Gigi."

After dinner, the men retreated to the library to discuss business. Dick Hilliard was concerned that HJ was spending too much time and energy on his business adventures. "You will kill yourself and leave Gigi the most charming widow around," remarked Dick.

HJ strutted. "I promise you, Dick, I am going to use real common sense and not let anyone impose on me."

"Common sense, HJ? You usually do all the hard work of planning and building. You overtax yourself. When all is done, the great want-a-be folks put their stamp on your work, just giving you a little blarney."

"Well, it really does not matter who takes credit. The good Lord knows who did the work anyway. Having others pat you on the back does not make you more important. A man's self-worth comes from within and is a gift of God. I would rather have his praise in the end than praise from a man."

"HJ, you like the excitement. That is all there is to it. You are willing to sacrifice peace of mind, home ties, and your best friends to get it. You fool!"

After a pleasant dinner, the women sat in the formal parlor, recounting pleasant experiences of the last few weeks. They viewed the many housewarming presents. It was still early when they said their good-byes.

The next week was going to be busy at the Dickinson Bank, so HJ wanted to go to bed early. He had several meetings scheduled. HJ signed contracts for more buildings. To HJ, the most important thing in life was work. New people were coming into the bank every day, inquiring about prospects for business. HJ was in his element, and nothing seemed to tire him. People were astonished by his endurance. Gigi looked on as best she could to all his plans and activities. She found that she was unable to keep up with him—even in her thoughts.

Overcome by the kindness of their neighbors, Gigi beckoned HJ to sit with her as she opened the many remaining housewarming gifts. They were sweet little presents, almost too numerous to mention: a long tablecloth with a dozen embroidered napkins to match; a wonderful, silk, handmade bedspread; embroidered towels; six dresser scarves; and a whole set of linen doilies to be used instead of a tablecloth. Her favorite gift came from her faithful old nurse, Mariah. She promised Gigi's mother on her death bed in Mobile, Alabama, that she would never part with a certain handmade quilt until she gave it to Gigi. Her mother's handiwork was exquisite, and Gigi cherished it for over forty years. Each of the stitches brought back loving memories of her mother. HJ was delighted that they received a gift from

Mr. Roosevelt. To Gigi's surprise, it was the same expensive rifle that she had used at his ranch. The attached card read:

> My dear little lady,
>   This beautiful rifle was once used by the dearest one in the world to me. I know of no one on earth whom I would rather bestow it, and I trust that some day it may be used greatly to your advantage, Mrs. Whitley.
>   Your Rough Rider Friend,
>   Teddy

By Thanksgiving, the ground in the gardens surrounding the back porch was sodden and cold, the air fresh and damp. Feeling a little melancholy, Gigi opened the cookbook she had brought from Alabama and began to plan Thanksgiving dinner. She and Hannah would cook a turkey wrapped in cheesecloth and soaked in pounds of butter. With this, she planned to serve cornbread stuffing, green beans, potatoes, yams, and pumpkin pie for dessert.

Gigi invited some friends to help them celebrate. The snow that had fallen the evening before had a magical effect not only on the setting, glistening on the trees and cradling the house in a warm blanket, but on the spirit of the guests. When the front door opened, there was a sudden whiff of freezing air. A renewed sense of comfort on entering the toasty home gave the guests a feeling of being sheltered, welcomed, and cozy. Also, the inviting glow of candles greeted everyone. The scent of freshly baked pumpkin pies lingered in every room.

After a while, everyone went into the living room, full and content. They told stories about joyful events, and it took all afternoon to hear them. They got to know their neighbors better. Gigi learned who grew the best gardens and made the best pickles and preserves. She learned what time to go visit so as to be sure to get a free sample. No amount of money was as valuable as the laughter and joy shared around the table that year.

HJ's work had a magnetic lure that drew him away at dawn, so Gigi needed to find something to do in the long winter months ahead. She decided to organize a group of neighbors to make quilts. During the westward expansion, making quilts was a routine part of domestic life that filled the long hours of winter. Patchwork quilts were a well-established form of bedding. The group gathered on a regular basis at her home. They could complete a quilt in three or four sessions.

The quilting bee provided an excellent opportunity for the women to discuss the current news of the country, something they were not expected to do in the presence of men. Meeting around a mahogany table in the parlor, all six women contributed their thoughts to the discussions. With the men at work, the women felt safe in discussing issues that concerned them. Many of them read articles in magazines and newspapers that discussed women's rights. They discussed the idea of women on juries. Could they stand the stress of handing down verdicts?

An article from the *Philadelphia Public Ledger* and *Daily Transcript* stating, "A woman is nobody. A wife is everything," created a lively discussion. Many of them longed for the day when laws would no longer give a husband ownership of their wife and children. How many times had women wanted to say, "No, not tonight, dear," but were afraid of the repercussions of their actions.

Gigi's favorite article came from the *Massachusetts Courier:*

Affirming it their right to vote, to become teachers, legislators, lawyers, divines and do all and [sundry] the 'Lords' now do. They should have resolved at the same time that it was obligatory for the lords aforesaid to wash dishes … handle the broom … darn stockings … wear ear trinkets, look beautiful and be fascinating as those blessed morsels of humanity whom God gave to preserve that rough animal man.

Smiles grew across their faces. Even a giggle or two was heard as the paper was read aloud to the group. Was this really such an amazing concept for the world to accept? Although they never solved any social issues in their discussions, it was wonderful to feel free, if only for a moment. However, the ridicule women were receiving in the newspapers and magazines started them thinking. Addressing these issues was perhaps the first baby step to women's freedom. At their first meeting, Gigi had established two rules: no gossip was to leave the room, and no one was to be belittled. They spent their winter growing stronger and bonding. They laughed and cried together. Their sewing offered relief in ways they never expected.

The quilts had many pieces of fabric sewn together to form a picture or geometric pattern. Gigi was complimented on her ability to quilt decorative patterns. Her friends admired the intricacy of her designs, the vividness of her colors, and the amazing skill and speed at which she could complete a quilt. Gigi took great pride in her quilting. Additionally, quilting was a way to bring her mother within reach, a way to step back into the past. Quilting took considerable time and was an answer to prayer for those long, winter days in the Dakotas.

Each quilt was mounted on a large, wooden frame that allowed quilting from two sides. As a section of the quilt was completed, it could be rolled up around the frame to give easy access to the next section. The women generally took turns piecing tops for the group to quilt. Their little group was called the Rosebuds.

To make a strong bond with each other, the women decided to make six friendship quilts. They each embroidered a twelve-inch square. Each woman would embroider her name on a quilt block, and then the group would set the blocks together. These were pieced together to form the top and then quilted. No matter how long it took them to make the quilts, they all had the same purpose: to record memories of cherished friends. The quilts themselves were beautiful, each square a different design; but it was the signatures of the block makers that made each quilt special. Gigi felt that to own a quilt that so many women had worked on was a great privilege. Their warmth and beauty were enhanced by every loving stitch that adorned them. Her heart was gladdened as they sewed and talked. The bonds that were forming would last a lifetime.

The winter of 1886 was long, cold, and dreary and lasted well into April. As the rain drizzled constantly on their home and the unplanted backyard turned into a mud bath, HJ and Gigi occasionally talked about the hill in Cahuenga Valley with the beautiful view. It would be all right to be rained in there, romantic even. How cozy to be curled up on the settee, listening to the raindrops on the windows, watching the countryside turn green as spring arrived. But at that time, it was only a dream.

When spring finally came, the roses emerged from their dormancy along the driveway. The air smelled of fresh rain, the ground was damp, and the birds whistled high in the treetops overlooking the house. Gigi became aware that it was time for her garden once again. In the bright spring sunlight and with the help of the gardener, Gigi arranged long, straight rows of flowers. Her favorites were the pink, wild prairie roses and the bright golden sunflowers. How beautiful the blossoming perennials would look, nestled along one side of the garden by trellised sweet peas and staked tomato vines. She would enjoy wandering among the vibrant blooms, humming and daydreaming about the exciting adventures that were soon to come.

In winter, when the fireplace was burning brightly and soup was simmering in the kitchen, the house was decorated with deep blues and reds. Quilts hung on the backs of the chairs and settees. Candles burned brightly, as if to chase away the dark demons of loneliness. This was a time when solitude meant contemplation and contemplation meant a quest for wisdom, writing, and reading great works of philosophy and literature. But as soon as spring arrived and came with the promise of summer, the drapes were switched. The pillows on the settee were changed from deep hues to light colors with roses all over them. Food became fancier and lighter. No more sticky toffee pudding or heavy, dark breads. Gigi seemed to change all things when the seasons changed. Bed linens were white now, with deep, crocheted lace edgings and fine handwork. The down comforters were put away. Gigi's days were spent in the garden, playing in the dark, rich soil and watching the clouds overhead. The season changed, and so did she.

Around the shady porch, Gigi displayed a collection of fancy-leafed begonias. She loved the coolness of the porch, which was furnished with comfortable, wooden rocking chairs for warring off the oppressive summer heat. On Sunday afternoons, HJ and Gigi invited friends over to relax and pass the time by chatting and laughing about whatever came up. The men, of course, would discuss important issues such as politics or business while the women's discussions centered on the children, church socials, and poetry. As the day wore on, one might even catch a man slumped in his chair, dozing.

Even though the surface of their lives now had a familiar, very comfortable pattern, Gigi sensed darkness on the horizon. A chilling tune played in her mind with uneasy sadness, bringing the nagging premonition of tragedy into focus. To counteract her moodiness, she sat at the piano, flooding her head with the music from Beethoven, Strauss, and Vivaldi. *The Four Seasons* was her favorite. The music had such a soothing effect on her that she lost track of the lingering omen.

Chapter Six

With the first year of marriage completed, HJ and Gigi made many adjustments in their new life together. As Gigi entered the dining room to celebrate their one-year anniversary, HJ handed her a bouquet and a small jewelry box inlaid with mother of pearls. Inside, Gigi found a stunning, twenty-two-inch strand of lustrous sea pearls fastened with a solid 14K gold ball clasp. HJ gently fastened them about her neck. Chatting over dinner, they shared their dreams—thoughts of expanding their family. They reminisced about their honeymoon in California and discussed plans for their future.

For a special treat, HJ had asked their housekeeper, Hannah, to make a miniature replica of their wedding cake to be served after dinner. On this special day, HJ made Gigi's feelings and needs seem important. This one simple act made it easier for her to love him. Gigi began to tell him how she admired his humor, honesty, and business knowledge. He promised to devote more time to her and care for her for the rest of his life.

Later that night, as HJ sat reading by the fire and Gigi was upstairs getting ready for bed, his mind began to fade back to the deep, dark secrets of his past. Secretly, he hoped that since they were now trying to have a baby, he would be able to connect in a more intimate way with Gigi. Until now, what HJ did to survive was quite different from what he needed to do to live. He wanted to get off the treadmill of survival and refocus on life. He wondered if it was possible to live so defensively that you never got to live at all. For most of his life, he had held his darkness close to him. He had used it as his protection and even defined himself through it. Even more than his tragic experiences, his beliefs became his prison.

Life was meant to be shared. For his love to be genuine, it had to be heartfelt. It could only happen when he was honest about who he was and what had happened in his life. He needed to share his hurts, reveal his feelings, confess his failures, disclose his doubts, admit his fears, acknowledge his weaknesses, and ask Gigi to help him; but at that time, he could not muster the courage to reveal his secrets to her. At times, he wondered what good it would do. Even if she had not understood, she could have prayed for him. Why was it so hard for him to tell her?

HJ wondered how he could erase the memories written in his journal so long ago about his first wife and baby daughter's death. He had thought of destroying the journal; but it also contained many tender memories, memories lodged deep in his heart. He still enjoyed reading them occasionally and remembering the good times.

He had often warned Fannie that she must be sure that all the candles were put out before she went to bed and to keep the candles away from the curtains. When he came home late from work, he consistently found candles still burning.

Presumably, Fannie had gone upstairs and put the fussy baby to sleep. Exhausted, she craved the comfort of her bed. She shed her clothes, got into her nightgown, and turned off the kerosene lamp by her bed. She slid under the covers and had just fallen asleep when the wind blew the curtains against the candles, catching them and then the house on fire. The wind then blew sparks onto the barn. Cries from the baby rolled down the hall-way. As she stirred from her sleep, she suddenly smelled smoke. Darkness engulfed Fannie as she groped her way down the hall, attempting to rescue her precious child. As the fire grew, the smoke from the burning home began to suffocate her. Overpow-ering smoke filled the air as the fire moved up the curtains. The fire spread rapidly, blocking the stairway and leaving no way of escape. If it was carelessness, it was carelessness that had enor-mous and disastrous consequences, for the fire spread; soon, the whole house was ablaze. For HJ, it was as though the grass had withered and his two precious flowers had fallen.

Those painful memories had been subjected to selective amnesia, thus yielding but a few sentences in all his writings. Not so amazingly, this stickler for accuracy preferred to forget the sad events of his youth. None of the family ever found out how the fire actually started. There were no survivors to tell the story.

"Please come to bed, dear," Gigi said, her words breaking the spell and drawing HJ back to the present.

"I am coming, dear."

As he saw Gigi at the top of the stairs, he told her that he loved the way she looked that night, with her hair flowing down her shoulders. Kissing her gently as they entered the moonlit bedroom, his breath on her body made her warm inside.

As they slid beneath the covers, Gigi said, "I have been dreaming of holding you, touching you. The only thing I want to do is be with you, be as close to you as I can be. I have been missing your tender touch and your sweet smell. Hold me tight. Do not let me go until the sun comes up."

Over a year later, in 1888, the long-awaited day arrived when Gigi learned that she was pregnant. As soon as she got to her room, she went to her bureau drawer and took out a sweet little box, a gift that Mariah, her nurse, had given her many years ago. Mariah had wanted to be the first to offer a gift to her for the baby that was soon to arrive. It was a handmade baby dress, the most elegant she had ever seen. As Gigi showed it to HJ, he could barely speak.

"Is that—for our baby?"

He was so overcome that he sat on the side of the bed, weeping like a child. Gigi thought it had brought up memories of his daughter who had died in Texas. He never liked to talk about the painful event. Gigi silently folded it up, placed it in the box, and locked it in the chest of drawers. Gigi was touched by the solemn moment. Neither of them spoke a word. Each said a silent prayer, climbed into bed, laid their heads on their pillows, and began dreaming of the joy that would soon be theirs.

After a good night's sleep, they awoke to the aroma of freshly brewed coffee and cinnamon. They sat at the cozy little table in one corner that Gigi called her own, sipping coffee while enjoying a delicious breakfast of melon, cooked oatmeal, and brown bread. In the morning, Gigi preferred to sit there by the window rather than in the formal dining area. For a long time, they just smiled at each other contentedly.

Gigi began to think of the work that lay ahead. She needed to hire a fine seamstress who was experienced in needlework, as everything would need to be handmade. Gigi would purchase beautiful, fine linen; soft cotton for night dresses; and flannel. Then all the clothes would need to be embroidered with an amazing range of stitches. HJ sat, contemplating hiring a young Swedish girl who lived in town to help Gigi until the baby arrived. Then, as he sat thinking, he began to hum a sweet lullaby to her.

Like many young women waiting for their first baby, Gigi was nervous. She decided that every person had been born so there was nothing extraordinary about what was happening to her. Giving birth was a natural event. Gigi craved candy, but she could not get out and get herself any. One afternoon, a dear old lady called; and Gigi had been crying.

"Tell me, dear. What is it? Perhaps I can help you with all my experience."

She was so sweet and kind that Gigi replied, "I just cannot stop craving candy. It is all I think about. I keep imagining myself standing, transfixed before the windows of the confectioners' shops, fascinated by the luminous sparkle of candied fruits, the cloudy sheen of chocolates, the kaleidoscope of fruit drops—red, green, orange, violet. I coveted the candies themselves as much as the pleasure they promised me."

"Now, dear, do not get so upset. It will affect your unborn child," she remarked.

That was all news to Gigi, so she promised the old lady she would be more careful. The next morning, the doorbell rang and announced the arrival of a package for Gigi. Inside was the most delicious box of chocolates. Gigi was sure that HJ had sent it, knowing that she craved candy. When Gigi thanked him, he looked surprised. She realized her mistake, but it was too late to keep the event of the previous day a secret.

HJ's only comment was, "That old bitty will be in the bank telling everyone how foolish you were, crying for candy. This is just nonsense. How can craving candy affect the baby?"

"I have no idea."

"Well, I hope that woman was wrong when she told you that our child would be marked. I just wish it was anything but candy," HJ snapped.

Gigi fondly remembered the day the lady's guild surprised her with a baby shower. From the time she entered the room, her heart was filled with an immeasurable love for her friends. Mrs. Hervey suggested that Gigi take a seat in the center of the women to open the presents. Mrs. Hilliard read the cards so that Gigi had more time to take in the entire event. The gifts all had exquisite embroidery. The women of the lady's guild were expert seamstresses or had the necessary funds to hire one. Her precious baby would definitely be one of the best-dressed children in town. Gigi was finally becoming anxious for the baby's arrival.

The friendships that Gigi had with these women became the cornerstone of her life and a constant source of inspiration and amusement. It was like pieces of a quilt, stitched together firmly with love. Each piece was elegant, strong, and lovingly crafted. They shared an amazing camaraderie and seemed more like sisters than friends. They had introduced her to new music, books, and new ways of seeing the world. Her friendship with these women multiplied the blessings in her life and divided its problems. If Gigi were to list the gifts and treasures of life, friendship was on the top. Gigi was a rich woman not only in dollars, possessions, and wisdom. Gigi was rich with friends. She realized that friendship was a scarce commodity and women needed it more than they realized. It was precious to her.

It was like a biblical plague coming true, but no one realized it at the beginning. HJ said that it was horrible and that he did not like to talk about it. It all began the day a telegram arrived for HJ with disturbing news about Gigi's sister, Martha Jane. Not wanting to upset Gigi in her condition, HJ decided to wait a few days before giving her the news. He hoped to receive brighter news in the next few days. After all, influenza never made the list of deadly illnesses. To HJ, it seemed harmless enough. It came around every winter, and everyone got better sooner or later.

When the next telegram arrived days later, his face became ashen as he read the news of Gigi's sister's death. Seeing the concern on his face made Gigi remember a dream she had a few nights earlier. In the dream, her sister had sent for her and Gigi became lost in a fog and could not find her. Grabbing the letter from him, Gigi read it, and a most perplexed expression marred her face. Without warning, Gigi collapsed into HJ's strapping arms. Guilt-stricken, HJ lamented not giving her the first telegram; but deep down, he realized that he was protecting the life of his unborn child.

With a bit of reluctance, it was decided that Gigi should go to her sisters' home in Minnesota until the baby arrived. There was no reason to take a chance of her catching a disease that appeared to have no treatment. HJ arranged to finalize any urgent business obligations and join her in a month. Gigi soon settled in with her sisters, Elizabeth and Mary, just before Thanksgiving.

December of 1888 began with its usual frosty reputation. In fact, the first freeze had come in early October that year. It was a dismal morning, very cold and gusty, with the wind whooping in the chimneys and blustering against the windowpanes when

HJ walked in the door. Too surprised to speak, Gigi noticed that, as she embraced HJ, he appeared red with fever and his face was swollen. His voice was hollow and unnatural as he said, "If I could get in bed, I am sure I could sleep it off."

HJ headed for the bedroom, undressed, and immediately slipped into bed. After having a few sips of the tea that Gigi brought him, he quickly fell into a fitful sleep. Gigi darkened the room. When she turned to look at him, she saw his eyes surrounded with dark circles, completely sunken in the sockets. It appeared to her that his countenance had collapsed. His skin was discolored. He was covered with a cold sweat.

Gigi asked her brother-in-law to call for the physician. The doctor was unsure what had caused the infection. Perhaps it was an unidentified pandemic disease. He was aware of how lethal the disease was, as it had symptoms of the annual flu. He advised them to let HJ rest, and he promised to send a nurse to care for him. He advised that communications between families should cease as a precaution to isolate the potential outbreak of influenza. Gigi did not want to leave HJ's side, so she told the doctor not to send the nurse until the next day. By morning, it was apparent to the doctor that Gigi should also be sent to bed.

As the days passed, HJ's condition became very serious. He appeared to hang between life and death. Bacteria had swarmed into HJ's lungs, giving him pneumonia that would either kill him or, if God was so kind, let him live. Dr. Anderson stayed overnight, but all he could recommend was that HJ be kept as warm as possible and be given hot, raw alcohol to drink. Before he left the next day, the doctor decided to share this news about HJ with Gigi. "Get some rest. You will need your strength," he said, walking toward the front door to leave.

Almost as soon as the doctor left for the evening, the contractions began. Labor was very short. When the doctor returned the next morning at eleven, a faint sound greeted his ears as he entered Gigi's room. The nurse was holding a little bundle on a pillow, so tiny that its sounds could barely be heard.

Ross Emmett Whitley was born nearly a month early on December 15, 1888. Gigi was overcome with joy. It was such an emotional miracle, for at almost the same time as Ross was born, HJ began to get well. HJ, much to everyone's surprise, had called out, asking about Gigi only moments before Ross had been delivered. He was somewhat surprised with the news since he had not heard the baby cry. Now they had a beautiful little son that was theirs to love and adore for the rest of their lives. It was difficult to explain the closeness the birth brought them. For the first time in a long while, HJ felt complete, like the void from the past had been filled.

Gigi loved to kiss Ross's sweet button nose. There would be two more feet to make music, with his pattering about the nursery. For a while, Gigi saw less of her friends; but nothing held her interest like Ross. Gigi loved to spend hours watching her precious baby sleep, dreaming of the fine individual he would grow to be. Gigi gave him tender care, her strength, and her lifelong prayers.

HJ was tender with Ross, and he often sat in the rocker in the nursery and sang him sweet lullabies. There was nothing like the calming sound of lullabies to help Ross go to sleep when he woke late in the evening. HJ often sang, "Are you sleeping, are you sleeping, baby Ross, baby Ross?" This healed his heart, the broken spot left by the tragic death of his first child.

After a little more than two weeks and over the doctor's objection, HJ decided to head back home to work. Business was business, and he had to get back to get everything in shape for Gigi's return.

Change in his environment seemed to strengthen HJ; so by the time he reached their home in the Dakotas, he was feeling much better. As much as they were happy to be home, they were saddened with the news that many of their friends had died. It seemed that almost everyone that was exposed to the disease became ill about two days later. The disease struck young and old, strong and weak with a deadly blow. So many became ill immediately and were unable to get enough oxygen because their lungs had filled with fluid. They died within days, delirious with high fevers, gasping for breath, and lapsing into unconsciousness.

There is no love equal to a mother's love. No sacrifice was too great for her sweet baby boy. In the first few months of his life, Gigi felt that every moment spent with him was sacred. He had been so small at birth that the nurse was kept for a month to help care for him. Gigi was a tense, even anxious mother. Though she had few skills for caring for a premature baby, thankfully, her careful nursing and love helped him thrive.

The nursery was situated at the top of the house. It was accessed by a flight of stairs. Ross had a night nursery with beds and a day nursery where he played. A little wicker gate across the landing prevented Ross from tumbling downstairs. Here, his nanny, Augusta, spent much of her time washing and dressing him. Augusta played an important part in Gigi's life for many years. Gigi never had any interest in dolls or little children. She knew absolutely nothing about handling or feeding a baby. Augusta sang him lovely lullabies; and when he was older, she played games with him. One of Ross's favorite toys was Noah's ark, which held many carved, wooden animals.

Gigi wrote in her journal September 26, 1889:

> We are having a heat wave and I am unable to sleep. It is four a.m. I went to the porch outside in the hopes of even a slight breeze to refresh myself. I am sorely disappointed. As time passes I hear Ross stirring upstairs and inform the nanny that I will give him his breakfast today. I get a bowl of applesauce and a soft biscuit from the evening before. I let him just bite off a piece of the biscuit whole; he thought he was quite smart using his teeth. He is saying "da-da" all the time now. I wish it were "mama." His favorite word is "dog." Sunshine, our dog, is sociable and always comes out to greet Ross with kisses on his cheeks. It was very baffling to me what a close friendship they have developed and how gentle and protective Sunshine has become. Ross imitates different noises I make at him, kissing, and clicking his tongue. Ross's hair is coming in dark brown and his eyes are sparkling blue. He is such a beautiful little boy. I thank God for such a precious gift and pray he will give us the wisdom on how to raise him.

It became more difficult to handle Ross as he developed his own personality. By the time he was twenty-two months old, Gigi found it challenging to understand why her once sweet and innocent son was now boisterous. He did not understand no and, at times, could be very naughty. He fell on the floor, cried until his face reddened, and banged his fists on the floor. Their home became chaotic and noisy, full of great tenderness and loving indulgence. Fit to be tied, Gigi got a sugar plum out of the old-fashioned sugar bowl and gave it to Ross. The bowl had once held treats for her when she was young. Gigi wanted him to be at his best when callers came. It was the only way she could keep him quiet. Nothing had such a wonderful effect as one of those little balls of sugar that he could suck on for the next hour. Gigi kept them ready for immediate use. Ross loved candy and was always quiet and well behaved for her guests.

Friends told Gigi that she was spoiling him. HJ thought that she should just let the nanny do her job. Why spoil the child with so much candy? Reluctantly, Gigi began to turn his upbringing over to the very competent nanny, Augusta. She suspected that Ross was just going through a phase and it would fade away as he matured. Unfortunately for Ross, from the beginning of their marriage, Gigi was, at times, treated like a cherished, spoiled child. HJ expected her to bring children into the world, but he did not expect her to bring them up. That was the duty of the nanny.

After the birth of Ross, Gigi anxiously pondered the approach of a new chapter in their lives. She heard HJ discussing the opening of the Oklahoma Territory with many of his railroad associates. The prospect of unimaginable business ventures was highly interesting to him. It was fortunate that he had completed his contracts in the Dakotas. Gigi was looking forward to moving to a larger town where prospects of a more cultured life could be found. At first she had no thought of danger or misgivings on the subject of retaliation by the Indians, for her fears had all been dispersed by constantly receiving assurances that the soldiers would take care of any disturbances that the Indians might cause. She had no thought of danger or misgivings on the subject of savages, as up to this time all the Indians she had met were kind. Her fears had been all dispersed by constantly received assurances of the Indians' friendliness.

She became alarmed after having several frightening dreams about the Indians attacking. The tribes may have been helpful initially to travelers, but a newspaper article stated that hospitable feelings turned to resentment as the Indians' way of life began to decline. Lately, she had heard too many stories where fierce warriors, determined to keep their freedom, swept down in hordes, showing little compassion. An Indian attack was swift and merciless. Without notice, unsuspecting settlements were ravaged. After a savage raid, the Indians often tortured their captives and scalped and mutilated the dead. In many instances, the withdrawing attackers took women and children captive, a fate worse than death. This was her greatest fear.

Chapter Seven

On April 22, 1889, the same year the Eiffel Tower opened in Paris, HJ was one of the first capitalists and men of enterprise at the opening of the original Oklahoma Territory. Over 1.9 million acres were allotted to settlements. The unassigned lands were laid out in 160-acre homesteads. Only white men were allowed to participate. HJ was in Guthrie, Oklahoma, on the day of the opening. As the hour for the opening approached, HJ gathered with some friends to wait on the border while mounted soldiers stood on guard to turn back intruders.

HJ said, "I know exactly where the town should be. I have surveyed the area many times on different trips out West. There is no question in my mind where it should be."

The government had warned everyone not to enter the lands or risk forfeiture of their claims. Everyone ignored the warning, including the soldiers who were there to enforce it. Steam-driven locomotives came plunging down the quiet, cottonwood valley, unloading over ten thousand people by nightfall. Only one little frame building, the United States Land Office, handled all the recordings. People slept in tents if they had one. Many laid down on the cold April ground supperless and with no covering except the drapery of a star-studded night. Twenty-four hours before the legal opening, the hills of what was afterward Guthrie were covered with snow-white tents. Town lots were already staked out, and public meetings were held hours before high noon. Men came from every state for homes. At noon, bugles sounded and guns were fired as a signal that the land was open. HJ had already staked out the piece of property to his liking. He was one of the first to register his property at the tiny office that was soon overrun with people.

This was the spot where he was instrumental in building a marvelous town. During the next seven hours, nearly ten thousand people settled in what became the capital of the new Territory of Oklahoma, Guthrie. What was typical prairie grass in the morning became one of the nation's largest cities west of the Mississippi River by nightfall. Guthrie was truly a miraculous city. Each man had been given the opportunity to find a new beginning. The new society was composed of elements from the four points of the compass. Eastern exclusiveness was merged in Western democracy while Northern conservatism joined Southern hospitality in a spirit of harmony that, up to that time, had not been found in any other area of the United States. Refinement, education, and society were the three elements that unified the framing character of the Oklahoma Territory.

HJ was quickly involved in feverish promotion of his new land holdings. He built and owned the first brick block building in the territory, which housed the National Loan and Trust Company at 202 West Oklahoma Avenue. HJ's one desire was to raise Guthrie to the proud position of a thriving metropolis. In addition, he owned several other brick and stone buildings in Guthrie. At the time, they were the best buildings in the territory.

At the organizational meeting of the Chamber of Commerce held on July 20, 1889, at the city buildings, HJ was elected president. The secretary then read the constitution and bylaws, as prepared by the committee; and upon motion, they were unanimously adopted. A motion was made and seconded that all parties desiring to be members should sign the roll. This motion was unanimously approved as well.

HJ enjoyed being a small business owner, as he liked the respect he earned from his peers. His business success had come at a high personal cost. It consumed most of his time and energy, including precious evenings and weekends. He did not have much time for family or friends. He never asked Gigi if she was willing to make the many personal sacrifices necessary for his business to be successful. He felt that it was her duty to do so.

Progress was gaining momentum, and towns sprang up like weeds along the Rock Island Railroad and the Northern Pacific Railroad Lines. HJ built over one hundred of them in Dakota and Oklahoma territories. In Oklahoma City, HJ built several brick block buildings. HJ was manager of the land development department of the Rock Island Railroad in Oklahoma Territory, Cherokee Strip, and Texas between 1885 and 1894.

In Oklahoma, HJ helped found towns like El Reno, Kingfisher, Norman, Stillwater, Chickasha, Medford, Enid, and Ellendale too. He was designated to be the first governor of Oklahoma, but he refused the nomination. HJ hated political bickering and refused to deal with all the nonsense. What he despised most were all the social gatherings, where things became too personal. HJ preferred work to socializing. Instead, he became the president of the Chamber of Commerce. Gigi was furious. Why did he always let others receive glory for the work he did? Gigi had put up with many years of hardships only to see the glory of her sacrifice slip through her fingers.

It was while Gigi was in Oklahoma City that the mood became tense. Gigi and Ross had moved to Oklahoma City to be with HJ. The air was hot, and the wind was rising. The war dances the Indians were participating in had become so unruly that the government had requested reinforcements be sent to the fort. The Indians had been extremely restive and had continued their dances for over a week. Many had put on their full war emblems. The agency on the reservation became alarmed; and one evening, just at dusk, a war "whoop" rang out.

Everyone hurried into the street to listen to the report from a rider who came rushing by, frantically shouting, "The Indians are breaking loose! Fortify the hotel! Unless reinforcements arrive by midnight, we will all be killed."

The men hastily collected firearms and barricaded the hotel. Many sat silently, praying as time slowly passed. Gigi took Ross upstairs and lay awake all night, exhausted by the strain. The guests of the hotel were kept awake that night by strange noises. They grew louder and louder and seemed like drums beating and guns firing. The night was still as dark clouds hung low over the town. Gigi wished that the sound was thunder, but there was no lightning or storm coming. She lay in bed, listening as the sounds grew louder. Terror seized her. Gigi's breaths were erratic, her chest was tight, and her heart was pounding out of control.

Why was HJ gone when she needed him the most? He was in Guthrie, taking care of what he considered important business. But while Gigi complained a lifetime about being left for important business, deep down inside, she knew that she had found something special in HJ that she had not seen in any other man.

A frightened woman and her children could be heard crying down the hall. The piercing war cry grew nearer and nearer. The dreadful noise seemed to come from all sides, even from the sky. Everyone was sure that a band of Indians, bent on revenge, was approaching. All hearts beat fast in fear.

Gigi later learned that after scouting the woods to the northwest, the captain of the newly arrived reinforcements ordered the lead horses to take their positions. He then commanded the skirmish line to advance, and the men went forward seventy-five or one hundred yards; and then they dismounted, lay down, and commenced firing at the warriors approaching across the wide front. The captain, fearing for the safety of the horses, took part of the company from the right flank down into the bottomland and deployed the men along the bank of the river to protect them. After some long-distance fighting, the Indians charged; but the heavy firing of the troops caused them to fall back and later surrender.

The noises lasted all night long, sometimes coming nearer, sometimes dying away in the distance. The townspeople waited in dread. At last, toward daybreak, the dark clouds slowly lifted. With the first light in the east, the sounds ceased. When the sun rose, clear and bright, Gigi regained her courage. Everyone at the hotel felt truly blessed when they learned that reinforcements had arrived in time to put down the uprising. They had all feared that if the Indians had made it to town, they would have burned the hotel, along with its inhabitants, to the ground.

Gigi was delighted when she received word from HJ that the National Loan and Trust building's construction was complete and that the bank was now open for business. HJ was the president, George D. Orput was the manager, and JW McNeal was the treasurer. Once more, they would live as a family. After buying tickets for the train, Gigi and Ross boarded; and Gigi selected an empty seat next to the window so that Ross could see the sights as they traveled.

Dust blew in lazy drifts as HJ waited for them on the train platform just outside Guthrie. The train slowed to a halt amidst the squeal of breaks and puffs of warm steam. A high, echoing whistle interrupted HJ's thoughts; and he leaned out from the platform for a better look at the arriving train. He scanned the milling crowd, looking for them. The crowd thinned, and still he did not see anyone remotely resembling them. He had barely finished scanning the crowd when a slim figure carrying a small child stepped onto the platform and smiled in his direction. He ran to them and wrapped them in his loving arms.

"Well, dear, here we are in Guthrie. I have a carriage waiting for us."

It was almost four o'clock when they entered their suite on the second floor of the Guthrie National Trust and Loan Company. They would reside there until a home could be built. Ross and Gigi were hungry after the long train trip, so it was decided that they would take their first meal together in Guthrie at a nearby restaurant. The town was still rather primitive. HJ had to hire a boy to keep the flies away from the table. Ross was so interested in watching the young boy swat at the flies that he did not eat. Instead, he sat laughing, which was a most welcomed sound to HJ's ears. Ross's laugh was pure, innocent glee. After a hearty dinner, HJ took Ross around to shake hands with his friends and business acquaintances. Gigi was glad to have a chance to eat, but she found it difficult to escape the flies.

After many trials and delays, people became desperate for the government to enact protective legislation for the new territory. To aid in the organization of the Territory of Oklahoma, HJ was sent as a nonpolitical representative by both the Republicans and Democrats to Washington. He assisted in framing the first laws of the territory. His stay lasted three months, and the citizens of Guthrie were amazed at how quickly the legislation came from Congress. It was due entirely to his influence and efforts that the first territorial capital was located in Guthrie. He was in Oklahoma at the time it was opened for settlement and was well informed on affairs there.

HJ regarded the condition of things as critical. As he spoke to Congress about Oklahoma, he said:

> There are numerous challenges over homestead settlements in the country and lots in the cities and towns. Honest settlers are at the mercy of professional contestants and lot jumpers. The public temper is as great as it can bear. A number of murders have been committed. Some of the best men in the country have been shot down while protecting their property. Many homes have been burned and numerous crimes have been committed for which there is no law to punish. The farmers throughout the country have about given up the work on their homesteads to see if any protection will be given them. It is probable that any improvements that may be made will be swept away by a general outbreak of the bad element that lives in Oklahoma. The settlers feel that their only protection is a shotgun or a revolver. I believe that unless law is extended at once over the country there will be a general uprising that will bring alarming and disastrous results. You must act today and place the olive branch

between the nearly two thousand contestants whose blood is worked up to a doubly dangerous temperature.

As HJ spoke, he had an appearance of a sovereign, jovial-looking king, bright-eyed and robust, with a voice that roared and a phenomenal air of being a lion in person. HJ believed that the laws that were in place in some states should be applied at once to Oklahoma so that criminals could be prosecuted and the honest man protected. He spoke with great passion and conviction, pleading with Congress to move before things became worse. HJ was influential in assisting in the perfecting and passing of Oklahoma town site bills in Congress. He had been so instrumental in the opening of the territory that he was assigned to a post to direct allotments for the Indians.

While HJ was in Washington, Gigi and Ross went to Philadelphia to visit Uncle Samuel Ross. HJ felt that it was too dangerous to leave them unattended for such a long time. Gigi had nearly become an invalid because of all the stress she went through living on the trail to please her strong-minded husband. Gigi was not equipped for pioneer life. The doctor said that she needed to rest. HJ decided to send her back East once again.

Although Gigi enjoyed the company of her uncle, late at night, after Ross was soundly asleep, to soothe herself, she would read the letters HJ had written. Her favorite one said:

Dear Gigi,

It has been so very long, but when I shut my eyes I still remember everything. I miss your kiss and the way you make me feel so loved. I never thought we would ever be apart for such an extended time, but now it has been way too long. I just want to hear your voice. I miss seeing Ross, and I am sure he has grown more than I can imagine. I know our life together has not been perfect, but I hope you know how much I love you. The way I feel for you does not go away. I thought after being gone so long you might fade away from my mind, but still every day I wake up dreaming of our time together. I love you with all that I am and all that I will ever be. I desperately hope that Congress will soon approve the necessary legislation so I can return home to you, my darling.

Love always,

HJ

He returned home when the laws had been enacted, and things looked more favorable for Oklahoma. When, at last, he took up his work, he made up for lost time. As his reputation circled the territory, he was offered any price he might name to add a guiding hand to the district. HJ was considered one of the greatest developers in the United States, even at that early stage of his career. Future generations would benefit from his struggles and hardships, whether they knew it or not.

Gigi was saddened that no one thought of the environment they were invading when the new territory was opened for settlement. The new settlers had no regard for the surroundings they were destroying. Many towns and cities had sprung up and erased much of the wildlife that had called that area home. Gigi wondered why people did not place their daily behaviors in an environmental context; their decisions were literally thoughtless. She wished that they would realize that the land and natural resources were *not* limitless. Reading Emerson and Thoreau had taught her that all creatures and natural objects were created by God and had inherent worth. At night, Gigi would pray that God would keep man from destroying the land that she dearly loved.

HJ and Gigi had been invited to the Underhills' home for a fine dinner. The meal was superb, prepared by a fine cook and served by an excellent staff. This was not a difficult task when one had the heart and purse for such an endeavor.

After dinner, the men withdrew to the smoking room. Since HJ did not smoke, he walked in the garden with the hostess and Gigi. It was a sultry August night, and the gardens were enchanting. The full moon shone above them as the scent of roses filled the air. They were so inspiring that Gigi recalled the ode that Robert Burns had written about them. An hour later, the business moguls were relieved to have HJ's attention once again. They wondered if he was trying to shirk his duties in building two new towns along the railroad. If HJ would promote the two towns, they all agreed that the towns would come to life. HJ was flattered by their praise and eagerly began to explain his plans for them.

The first thing HJ would do was plot the layout of the land. He had already arranged for the railroad to build a fine depot. HJ would be in charge of supervising the installation of streets, trees, water, and lights. In addition, he had planned to build the first homes and donate land for the schools. Realizing that the town was still incomplete, he suggested opening a bank and a hotel. HJ promised that he would start the surveyors to work as soon as the site for the two towns was complete.

It was remarkable how quickly the area changed. With completion of the train depot, materials, groceries, and all sorts of goods were shipped rapidly and inexpensively by rail. No longer did everything have to come over land by wagon. The accessibility of these materials helped the towns grow even faster. New businesses were added along the main streets nearly every month to meet the needs of growing population.

A few years later these same businessmen walked down the main street of their new town. HJ boasted, "Look. Guthrie now has a general store, hardware store, drugstore, furniture store, harness shop, boot and shoe store, hotel, printing office, blacksmith shop, wagon shop, farm machinery dealer, livery, grain dealer, flour mill, lumber mill, machine shop, woolen factory, photo gallery, millinery shop, bank, church, school, doctor, two land agencies, and a bakery."

It is admitted that the building of the Rock Island Railroad west from El Reno was one of the largest factors in the development of that portion of western Oklahoma, including the counties of Custer, Roger Mills, Beckham, and the adjoining territory. The people of that section seemed to follow the progress made by HJ, building towns along the railroad. As HJ and Gigi prepared to move on to California, she knew that the best of his work was yet to come.

Chapter Eight

When Gigi said farewell to the Dakotas, it was a sad parting. She replayed the happy memories of the many friends she was leaving. Although Gigi knew that she would still be friends with them, it was not going to be the same. It was difficult for Gigi to accept that they had to go their separate ways. One day, she went for a walk to gain some perspective. Gigi sat in her usual secluded spot overlooking her favorite meadow. It was a place where she could think. As Gigi looked over the meadow, it reminded her of her friends. Like flowers, friendship in life end and begin, over and over again, in a cycle. Gigi realized that while some of her friendships were ending, new ones would begin. Although there were moments when things seemed dead for a season, everything would grow again. Flowers would represent the good times they had and, when Gigi was lonely, the good things that would happen again.

But when Gigi, who was now twenty-five, bid good-bye to the Oklahoma Territory, it was different, for she had not had a chance to make close friends with the people she met. HJ would not settle in one place, leaving little opportunity to make as many friends. HJ's activities took him from one place to another; there was no possibility of a stable home life. Having a young, delicate child made it additionally hard on her.

Gigi's diary recorded the Whitley family's arrival to California:

> January 17th, 1893. We are here in California at last; a dream come true. Finally our family will settle down and perhaps new friendships can be made. I used to think that friends were the people that I could laugh and talk with. Friends are the people that touch my heart. I could spend hours with them doing nothing at all and it would be the best time of my life, just because I was with them. They are the people I share my secrets with, cried with, and laughed with. They did not judge me. They accept me exactly as I am. We are tied together with the golden thread of memories, tears, laughter, and smiles. Friendship is the greatest gift one can give. I find that the times with my friends are the best times of life. Now that we are settling in California I hope the lasting bonds I long for can be forged once more.

Gigi read that women fared splendidly in the Californian society that was taking shape. California showed a special appreciation for women and their role in fashioning this new territory. In part, she felt this was because there were, at first, so few women at hand. But, beyond this, men of the frontier appreciated the courage and physical strength displayed by their sisters, wives, and daughters in dealing with the hardships of early California life. Men could no longer pretend that women were delicate or powerless when they proved the opposite every day they spent on the frontier. Gigi was very impressed that California's first constitution recognized the special contributions made by women by guaranteeing the right of married women to the control of their own property. This inspired her to believe that she could make her own mark in this new, developing land. Perhaps for the first time in history, women would be given the proper position they deserved.

HJ took Gigi and Ross to the Westminster Hotel on Main Street. He felt that the Westminster was one of the finest hotels in Los Angeles, and Gigi immediately agreed after entering the ornate lobby. The service in the main dining room, Los Angeles's finest, had the reputation of being the most leisurely and stateliest on the West Coast. HJ felt that it was the place to see and to be seen. It was the place where a business transaction could easily take place.

After a few days, HJ started back to Oklahoma to finish some work. He was in the process of selling his banks, businesses, and properties. He would be there nearly a year before he returned to them. Gigi only prayed that HJ would think as much of her and their beloved son as he did his business. He was her best friend and her only real emotional support. Gigi desired his love and affection. Somehow, the act of making friends with the residents of the hotel kept her loneliness at bay.

Gigi tried not to think about him; but it was impossible, especially late at night. In the hours of darkness, her loneliness swelled, consuming her with pain and a need to create something more than just a diversion. While the world around her slept, Gigi wove dreams and fantasies that made her feel strong and whole. Gigi exorcised her pain by writing in diaries, certain that HJ would come and live in California in the near future. Gigi would not hear from him unless he telegraphed or wrote a short letter. Since his business required him to travel extensively, she had no other way to contact him. Ross missed Papa and would often ask for him. The only thing that Gigi was thankful for was that the Westminster was a family hotel conveniently located near the park on Sixth Street.

While HJ was in Oklahoma, he contracted typhoid fever, and rose spots appeared on his abdomen and chest. Additionally, he had a very bad spell of black erysipelas, leaving him out of his mind for some time. His survival was miraculous, considering that there had been over forty deaths that year in the town of El Reno where he lived.

HJ's heavy responsibilities in Oklahoma and the continuous strain of business brought about a breakdown in his health. Work had been a challenge. HJ knew that it would be a struggle to see tangible results completed on such a hectic timeline. He worked long hours. His business required him to be outside, supervising employees during the day and doing the long hours of office and detail work at night and in the wee hours of the morning. Now all he felt was pressure. On the advice of his physicians, HJ came to California in 1894 after resigning his position as secretary of the Chicago Rock Island and Texas Railroad Company.

It was with a better understanding of married life and a lighter heart that Gigi began her new life in California. Those trying beginning years of their marriage had vanished. It seemed easier to appreciate her strong-minded husband. HJ wished for them to live together. "I will be home soon to look out for you," he wrote. "You must expect to spend the entire first night home alone with me without any visitors. I want you completely to myself." Principled as HJ was, this letter seemed to steam itself open.

Once in California, he soon employed his talents in local productive enterprises, although his business interests elsewhere continued. His greatest task and the scene of his best work was yet to come in Hollywood. It seemed providential to read in the newspaper that the first showing of a moving picture took place at the Kinetoscope Parlor in New York the very same year HJ made California his home. By 1895, the first film to use actors, *The Execution of Mary Queen of Scots,* was shot in West Orange, New Jersey.

When they were settled in their new California home, there would be nothing to interfere with their blissful and joyous lives. He had repeatedly told Gigi that he wanted to make her the happiest little wife in the world. HJ planned to get her a piano and a riding pony and promised to consider bringing her a box of candy as a surprise now and then. Gigi laughed to herself and then began to hum a happy tune as she dreamed of their life in California. Their home on Flower Street would be the home that Gigi had dreamt about for many years.

Heavy rains had come that winter, bringing everything to life. The added beauty in the surrounding hills and valleys was so intense that they took a few short days to just linger in the enchanted peace it brought. The trees had clusters of fruit while the hills and valleys were blanketed with gorgeous wildflowers. HJ would rise before dawn and pick a bouquet to bring to her with her morning tea. Was it any wonder that HJ and Gigi spent most of their time out among the hills and valleys surveying the landscape? Gigi hoped that she would be able to call the loveliest of spots her home.

He, in his mind, was building a lovely town that would amaze the world. After a much-needed rest, HJ decided to set down some temporary roots in Los Angeles until he could finalize his purchase of the Hurd Ranch in the Cahuenga Valley. He purchased a magnificent, three-story home at 839 Flower Street, between Eighth and Ninth Streets. Gigi prized the massive front porch, filling it with a happy jumble of wicker rockers, potted plants, and reading material. The hanging fuchsia baskets were treats for her beloved hummingbirds. It was a perfect spot to sit and watch the children play. Inside, Gigi placed her collection of contemporary furnishings, oriental rugs, a piano, and original artwork. While Gigi was setting up their new home, HJ was going over plans for his new town.

HJ had unquestionable knowledge on how to develop towns by now. As a civil engineer, he had designed and supervised the construction of roads, buildings, tunnels, bridges, water supplies, and sewage systems. Civil engineering, considered one of the oldest engineering disciplines, encompassed many specialties. HJ had an excellent understanding of the major specialties within civil engineering. These included structure, water resources, construction, and transportation. HJ had seen cities and states built up and then decline again, especially when they were built on advertisement and hot air. When a slump came, many lost everything. Towns and cities were wiped out. This served as a serious lesson to HJ; therefore, he recognized that there must be some substantial reason for the town to remain besides a basic infrastructure. HJ planned to attract creditable business ventures to his town. He was interested in finding some industry that could be developed in Hollywood that would furnish occupations for many of the young male inhabitants.

It would take some time to negotiate the land deals related to Hollywood. HJ was an excellent tactical player and could keep his nerve under trying circumstances. This quality manifested itself to the greatest extent when doing a business transaction. To HJ, a sale was purely a mental transaction, a meeting of the minds of a seller and a buyer. He realized that, rather than selling merchandise, it was the service he offered that played an important part in the transaction. People bought things not for the things themselves but for the service those things performed. There was not a single purchase made that did not take place first in the consciousness of the buyer long before it took shape in the form of a contract. So, regardless of what he was selling, what he was really selling was his ideas. Likewise, it was apparent to HJ that the more unique the items he carried were, the more attractive the purchase became to his customers.

To supplement his income in the interim, HJ founded HJ Whitley Company, located at III North Spring Street in Los Angeles. A second store was opened at 21 Rue de Paradis in Paris, France. Having ample capital, he was enabled to commence business on a solid basis.

HJ developed working relationships with a variety of people, including customers, merchants, staff, bankers, and professionals such as lawyers and accountants. He could deal with demanding clients, an unreliable merchant, or a cranky employee. He made decisions constantly—often quickly, independently, and under pressure.

Starting and managing HJ Whitley Company took motivation and talent. HJ spent over a year researching and planning the new business. He re-evaluated his business goals and then used the information to build a comprehensive business arrangement that helped him reach these goals. Developing his plan helped him think through some important issues that he might not otherwise have considered. HJ's business plan had two basic goals. It described the fundamentals of his business idea and provided financial information that showed that he would make a sizeable profit.

HJ Whitley Company was more than a jewelry store. To reach a wide range of clientele, HJ sold teapots, cutlery, silverware, silver novelties, bric-a-brac, cut glass, gold goods, French clocks, cuckoo clocks, canes, umbrellas, opera glasses, leather goods, and watches and had a repair department and provided engraving and mail orders. His clients appreciated fair treatment and superior goods at low prices. HJ would tell people, "There are no finer goods kept in any store in California than are sold over our counters."

HJ even put beautiful flowers from Gigi's garden in the windows to draw more attention to the store. The shelves were imported French marble. The ceiling of the salesroom was handsomely frescoed with cupids floating among the clouds against a blue sky, and a dainty rococo design in gold ran around the arched corners. The floor was mosaic tiling. To the left of the entrance and in three other parts of the store were cozy corners where patrons could make themselves comfortable.

The patronage of HJ Whitley Company grew by leaps and bounds. HJ prided himself on the fact that each item in the store had been bought for cash directly from the leading manufacturers in America and Europe. HJ and Gigi traveled to Europe at least once a year to purchase a vast variety of goods. Since HJ bought directly from Eastern factories, he was able to cut out the cost of a middleman. The result was a savings of twenty to thirty percent, which he partly passed on to his customers. Because of the enormous amount of purchases the store made and HJ's ability to barter, he was able to buy diamonds at rates substantially less than those procured by Tiffany's in New York. Building a competitive edge into the fabric of his business was crucially important for the stores' long-term success.

He would guarantee that each stone was free from flaw and perfect in both cut and color. HJ loved helping his customers find just the right purchase. He depended on one simple principle for the store. At the end of every work day, he would tour the shop; and after inspecting the day's sales, he asked a single question: "Can I put my name on the work that has been completed? If not, I will have to work harder." He knew that if he could put his name on the work, then he would exceed his client's expectations. The ultimate compliment came when his clients would refer their friends to the store. He let his work speak for itself. HJ had a steady stream of customers that never seemed to end. That was the only way he did business. Quality work was the reason for the referrals.

HJ hired and retained truly excellent employees, not just reasonably competent ones. He felt that a highly competent and truly enthusiastic employee was at least two and sometimes even three times as valuable as a person of average skills. To create a stable and happy workforce, it was essential not only that his employees believed they were being fairly treated but that his business was worthy of respect. Employees who liked their work would respect him on and off the job. Customers were loyal to an upbeat business and were more likely to recommend it to their friends. The gentlemen HJ chose to be the directors of the company were of the highest standing both morally and financially. They were GJ Griffith, RH Variel, Robert Hale, and John Leuakenbach.

The store was far grander than anything else on the West Coast. It also far surpassed anything Eastern cities offered, in Gigi's opinion. Her major reason for loving the store was the frequent trips it required to Europe. On these trips, HJ was the attentive husband she longed for. After a dinner alone in Paris one night, Gigi recorded in her diary:

> I am overwhelmed by HJ's love. His words bring warmth
> to my heart. I know that he loves me but to hear him

say, "I just wanted to let you know how much I love all that you are and will be. Without a doubt you keep me together. You truly are my love, my soul mate, and my best friend. You give me strength to be a man of high calling. You have seen me at my worst and still take me as I am. I thank God for you every day because I know you are heaven sent; you are my angel. The years will be a test, but nothing will keep me from loving you or from being by your side. I love you more than you could even know. You are my world.

It was hard to remember those sweet words. As soon as HJ arrived home, he raced back to the same familiar highway he always traveled: the road of big business. Business, always so important, never left enough time for their family. HJ frequently came home for lunch and brought men with him. When he did come home, he wanted a short lunch and no time to be wasted.

"We must be able to talk freely," he said.

To accommodate his request, Gigi had a silver bell put beside her place at every meal. When Gigi rung the bell, the servants came in to serve them or took plates away. They would stay in the kitchen until she rang again.

They wanted more children; but after not becoming pregnant for so many years, they thought that Ross might be an only child. Then, finally, Gigi became pregnant again. Like many women, Gigi was very nauseated at the beginning of her pregnancy; but she did not pamper herself too much. Gigi continued with her usual life until the final days of labor.

The pregnancy was quite normal. HJ and Gigi received a precious gift, their daughter, born in Los Angeles on December

14, 1894. Ross was told that she was his special birthday present. Gigi spent a few minutes admiring her baby. She had a red, ruddy complexion and light hair. She looked a lot like Ross, though she was a little chubbier than he was at birth. Her face was round and sweet. Gigi loved her tiny features, especially her precious nose. What would her future be? They had difficulty choosing a name. They finally decided to name their daughter Grace. There was something in her appearance that reminded them of HJ's sister. So, arm in arm, they ascended the broad stairway that night as they went to bed, very happy with Grace's arrival.

Ross was six years old the day after his little sister was born. She was a great delight to her big brother, and he begged his father to take him to the jewelry store so that he might help support her. HJ wanted to encourage his son's business endeavors; so, on the weekends, when Ross was not at school, he set up a little table with tie pins for him to sell as souvenirs. Everyone was quite amused to see a small boy working so diligently. Ross enjoyed his father's praises for his outstanding sales.

At two, Grace was chubby and rosy, with golden, silky hair, her big, round, blue eyes peeping from beneath her bangs. She was constantly on the move and afraid of nothing. Grace was always looking to climb higher, jump farther, run faster, and sing louder than her brother. When they were out of the house, Gigi worried that Grace would wander away. It just seemed easier to leave her home with her nanny.

Grace turned shy and somber at age five. The only time she really smiled was when she was dancing. She loved being dressed up and allowed to come down to dance for a group of gentlemen who applauded and laughed as she pirouetted before them. HJ would pick her up and hold her high in the air. He showered her with love. Whenever she was with him, she was perfectly happy. Regrettably, with his busy work schedule, his time with her was minimal.

Gigi tried to have afternoon tea at home every day so that she could see the children and read them a story. It did not work very well, especially with Grace. When Gigi tried to have lunch with her, she refused to stay seated at the table, so Gigi returned her to the nursery to eat with the nanny.

After trying several different things, Grace and Gigi finally found common ground in the arena of music. Gigi played the piano, keeping her eyes fixed on Grace, whose glorious voice floated out on the morning air, filling the whole world with the sweetest melody. As Grace danced about the room, a peaceful, dreamy look stole across her fine face. Gigi's thoughts were lifted up on the wings of the music. It was magic. The music seemed to heal, soothe, calm, and relax the many tensions that their lives held. They sang and played music because it was just so easy for them. Grace sang songs to her dolls and cats with the voice of an angel. Playing music in the evening seemed to help Grace settle in for the night.

Exhausted from tense work, HJ needed a break. He came home in the late afternoon tired and restless. He bathed; wrote up some notes; and lay on the bed, resting. HJ's ears roared, and he could not sleep. He kept a pace that would have been punishing for a man half his age. The crushing workload and his mounting frustration all left him on the verge of physical and emotional collapse. HJ believed that all he needed was a good rest. In keeping with current therapeutic trends, he decided to do his convalescing in Europe, where the scenery also would provide opportunity for him to enrich his architectural expertise. He planned forays to public gardens and the Paris exposition. He would relax and make purchases for the HJ Whitley Company. The children were left in the competent hands of their nanny.

They arrived in New York at the end of spring in 1897. Early in the morning, they set sail with the tide for England. Always eager to make friends in a short space of time, HJ had gotten to know many members of the ship's crew. He learned many things from the sailors and all the crew of the ship. HJ found it fascinating to learn the operation of different industries. He had been told that the boat was making wonderful time, the weather was fine, and that in a day they would reach England.

Gigi was extremely excited to be at the Diamond Jubilee that celebrated the sixtieth anniversary of Queen Victoria's rule. HJ and Gigi were a part of history in the making. On June 22, 1897, it was a bright and sunny day, quite a peculiarity in London. They watched the parade from the hotel window as it was situated on a main street where all the sights for the festivities could easily be seen. Gigi read in the newspaper that an estimated hundred thousand people had turned out. They lined the whole route. People crowded together, having stood since morning in hopes of catching a glimpse of the queen.

The magnificent procession was a delight to their eyes. The royal pageant included representatives from far across the seas. First, the Indian rajahs passed by. They were followed by African chiefs, officers, and men from the armed forces in Borneo, Hong Kong, West Africa, and Jamaica. Gigi was speechless when Queen Victoria rode past, sitting in an open carriage drawn by six white horses. No mortal on Earth rode in such style as the Queen of the British Empire.

After all the excitement in London, HJ decided that he needed some time to relax. They headed to Edinburgh by train. They saw churches and castles until HJ refused to see any more. Yet he never tired of sitting at one of the little tables at a pub. HJ peered through the window and watched the waves crash on the shore. He recalled Scottish history with the locals. They took drives through the countryside to view gardens and the natural landscape. Gigi loved the sight of a Scotsman in his kilt. One of the locals, Alistair Johnstone, wore his kilt to dinner as a treat for her; and Gigi was delighted to get a chance to really take a good look at it.

Early one summer's day Gigi welcomed the morning light and the freshness of the sea breeze. HJ and she casually climbed to the top of a hill that overlooked the Firth of Fourth. They watched the foam-covered waves topple over each other and then slide back into sea.

"I worship having time to share the beauty of this place with you, watching the seagulls dive toward the sea as they find their breakfast," HJ remarked. "I am here because I want to be. It is what I should do more often. I do not understand why I let work steal me from you. I trust you cherish this time as much as I do. It is what I want. I sit here and we talk, and I think there is nothing more precious to me than you. I just wish men understood women better. Our driving forces seem so different."

As HJ revealed his interest in her, she became calm and relaxed. His heartfelt interest for her well-being allowed her to feel loved. A slight smile formed on her lips as she tenderly remarked, "I love being with you too. I wish you were not such an important man with so much responsibility."

As HJ listened intently, Gigi sensed that he heard her and understood. They sat together, enjoying the sunshine as it danced on the waves. Gigi rested her head on his strong shoulder as they breathed in their surroundings. HJ discerned that Gigi liked what he had said. They sat a while longer, and Gigi began to think of Wordsworth's "By the Sea":

> The gentleness of heaven is on the sea:
> Listen! The mighty Being is awake,
> And doth with his eternal motion make
> A sound like thunder—everlasting.

As HJ and Gigi rose to return for their Scottish breakfast, Gigi clasped HJ's arm and smiled. "You are a good man with a loving heart. I will try to remember what you have said when you are away at work. It is my decision. I will just learn to understand the demands that business places on you."

In Paris, HJ went to the old exposition grounds. The buildings had not weathered well, but enough of the fair remained to give HJ a reasonable idea of what the exposition had looked like. He studied its architecture. Evidently, the site was still popular; and a long line had formed at the base of the Eiffel Tower. This time, they traveled to eleven countries in their three months away. Of course, no trip would be finished without the purchase of a new wardrobe, which included hats. As much as Gigi loved the museums, bookstores, theaters, and shops that Europe furnished, she still missed California's climate and scenery. Gigi was always ready to go home.

When they were done with the trip, HJ arrived home, refreshed and ready for the next challenge. During the remaining years of their marriage, they observed much the same routine. When HJ needed a break from the stresses of work, they would take a trip to Europe or the Orient to relax.

Much to their surprise, when they returned home, their sweet baby Grace cried and cried when she saw them. She did not like their new clothes, especially the high, silk beaver hat her father wore. Gigi decided that it would be best to store it away as a keepsake of the most wonderful trip HJ and she ever had.

Gigi was very excited and a little frightened when she heard that they would soon be moving to their new home in Hollywood. Moving to a new town was like walking out into the unknown. The familiar landmarks and friendly faces that Gigi had known would be gone; but with HJ's voracious appetite for success, she knew that she would be in for an exciting adventure. One of the amusing things that Gigi looked forward to was identifying all the unusual quirks that the locals possessed— ones that, after living in a town for a long time, most people no longer notice. Gigi wondered whose nose would stand out in the crowd of faces.

Chapter Nine

HJ finalized the deal with Mina Hurd to purchase the Hurd Ranch on April 11, 1899, for the price of $22,500 in gold coins and their home on Flower Street in Los Angeles. Negotiating its purchase had become complicated with the death of the first Mrs. Hurd. The second Mrs. Hurd had emphatically convinced her husband not to sell the ranch. Then he died at the end of 1894. Fortunately, a dip in the economy eventually caused Mrs. Hurd to reconsider HJ's offer. HJ, the magnificent magician with words, persuaded her to give in. HJ and Gigi's new property ran along Prospect Boulevard (now Hollywood Blvd.) between La Brea and Cahuenga. A few short words and a handshake had bound the contract from 1886.

Their Hollywood holdings now amounted to 480 acres. The land occupied the same alluvial plain as Los Angeles, lying thirteen miles west of the city's center and eighteen miles from the Pacific Ocean. HJ was encouraged that others had already begun to use the name Hollywood for the new town he was now ready to develop. Ivar Weid told HJ that he had shared the name Hollywood with his neighbors, the Wilcoxes, many years before. That is why she had begun to use the name. Telling Daeida Wilcox Beveridge to keep the name a secret only ensured that the name spread like a wildfire, branding the town forever.

That hill would become HJ's crowning achievement. On it, he laid out what was known as the Ocean View Tract extending north of Hollywood Boulevard on to Highland Avenue and beyond. The land was composed of two hills, Whitley Hill and Whitley Heights, that directly overlooked Hollywood. Highland Avenue ran through the center of the two hills.

His new land lay in a frostless belt that made it possible to grow a wide array of tropical fruit and winter vegetables. Most important to Gigi were the daily gentle ocean breezes that tempered the heat of summer and cold nights of winter. HJ marveled that he was able to grow pineapples in his backyard. He employed the very best floral and landscape gardener, one that had worked for Madame Modeska. Strolling through the garden was like walking through a kaleidoscope. One's senses were bombarded by brilliant hues of purple, orange, yellow, red, pink, and white blooms. The garden imparted calmness and harmony. The choice variety of plants the gardener introduced were rare and costly. The parklike backyard was perfect for entertaining.

The ceiling downstairs was beautifully frescoed, and all the walls were tinted striking colors. To make their lives simpler, a servant's quarters with a bathroom was added. Gigi insisted that the house be freshly painted, as fading paint drew the luster from any fine home. She selected a fine shade of green to be accented with dark trim. What a striking effect the magenta window and doorsills had on their home.

In the early hours of the evening, the light from oil desk lamps from inside the house and the voices of laughing children would mingle and dance beneath the glittering stars. As soon as they moved into the new home, Ross developed an avid interest in the study of nature, particularly collecting beetles, moths, and butterflies. Gigi believed that Ross was influenced by her love of nature as well. On warm summer nights, as the big dipper slid slowly across the evening sky, he would hang up a linen sheet against the wall on the porch off his bedroom and put a lantern in front of it. Bugs and insects of all kinds would swarm toward the light in large numbers. Soon, the sheet would be covered with crawling life. On one single evening, he collected twenty or more species of bugs. Ross loved the sounds of the crickets, but his favorites were the katydids that could be heard with their dual rhythm, "katydid … katydid." Under the veil of darkness, he lay awake at night, listening to them play wonderful tunes.

The new home was a child's paradise. There were an infinite number of places to play. Ross and Grace both adored the play-house that HJ had built for them just up the hill near the stables. Ross's governess read to him as he worked on his bug collection. She was very kind and would often play chess with him. Ross thought that he was very good at playing because she would usually let him win.

While the children played, HJ, as always, continued his busy work schedule. HJ began to plan the city's infrastructure. One day, HJ and Gigi drove over the rough roads to make plans for engineering new ones. Actually, they could barely be considered roads—just narrow, deep gorges with perpendicular sides.

Fortunately, HJ was an expert driver and was able to secure a span of strong, well-trained horses. Elick and Jim, he called them. HJ used an English carriage that had the driver sitting up higher than the passenger. This enabled him to have a better view of the road. One morning, they went off to survey a narrow path. HJ grabbed the reins and urged the horses onto the road heading out to the hills. The road began to grow increasingly bumpy. Gigi felt that if it got any worse she would have to jump out, as it was almost impossible for her to hold on. She yelled for HJ to stop; but, apparently, the clamor of the horses drowned out her cry. HJ was so busy watching the team jump over the hollows and scamper up the hillside that he forgot all about her. The wagon lurched as it hit a pothole in the road, tossing her from the backseat. Her head struck the side of the wagon as she fell; and after a few stars, everything went black. Gradually, the road became smoother, and HJ got a breathing spell. He looked back; and to his amazement, Gigi was not in the carriage. He called for her but heard no answer.

HJ managed to secure the team and rushed back to find Gigi lying flat in a hollow space, unconscious. It was quite a precarious task for him to gather her in his strong arms and carry her to a comfortable location, where she could rest until he could determine if she was all right. She gave a little sign and gradually opened her eyes, waking with a severe headache. Raising her hand to her temple, Gigi was surprised to find a cool handkerchief placed there. She tried to rise but fell back, overwhelmed by the dizzying pain. Opening her eyes, Gigi saw HJ standing over her.

His deep voice echoed, "Well, you have finally come back. I was starting to worry."

As fear overtook her, Gigi again tried to rise; but gentle hands pressed her back.

HJ said, "You are not ready to get up yet. Better stay there for a while."

Gigi was relieved when she found that she could move her hands and arms without pain. About that time, a young man rode up and offered Gigi some water from a jug he had hanging from his saddle. HJ's hand raised her head, and Gigi felt the jug touch her lips. Gigi drank a little, and her dry throat felt better. Her headache seemed better, so she tried to sit up. HJ's strong hands helped her to rise. Gigi found that she could see and saw a man sitting on a beautiful chestnut horse. Focusing on his face, Gigi saw blond hair under a beat-up hat and a pleasant face with tiny crow's feet at the corners of the eyes.

He smiled and said, "Feeling better?"

As the traveler and HJ began to talk, they realized that they had a lot in common. They sat down and discussed a way to put the road through. Once Gigi was rested and able to continue the trip, the traveler showed them a more agreeable route to return on. The traveler happened to be an expert surveyor and was soon employed by HJ. Together, they designed a new public works system for Hollywood. This project would last over a year. Years later, they put in the roads that ran all the way to the San Fernando Valley.

The early settlers of Hollywood complained that it was almost impossible to drive from any part of the valley to the city of Los Angeles during the rainy season because of the bad condition of the roads. From time to time, a little work was done here and there; but an organized effort was not made to put the valley roads in proper shape. There appeared to be a spirit of jealousy among the residents, which made progress difficult. If the county attempted to do any work at one end of the valley, the residents of the other end would immediately complain of favoritism. The little work that was done was then stopped to avoid the conflict.

Instead of having the best roads in the county, as Los Angeles did, Hollywood's roads were known as the worst. This, of course, was before HJ got involved. In the later part of 1898, HJ correctly predicted that the valley would immensely benefit from a good system of roads and a foothill branch of the electric streetcar line. They could be built from the city to the sea. First,

HJ gave the railroad his attention. For eight months, he was required to leave his business for weeks at a time, devoting his energies to this project.

When HJ began to investigate the prospects of an electric streetcar line through the Cahuenga Valley, he did not anticipate the many problems he would find. He had promised Gigi that if she would move to Hollywood he would have a modern electric streetcar at their front door within a year.

The nearest electric streetcar line was in Los Angeles. There were only a few dirt roads in Hollywood. It was a two-hour ride on horseback from Los Angeles to Hollywood. The roads ran through several ranches, with the Wilcox Ranch at the east end and the Mull Ranch on the west end.

HJ and Gigi, along with some other friends, met at the offices of Sherman and Clark to discuss the construction of the new electric streetcar line. While the men discussed business, the women went down the street to a candy shop for afternoon tea. They ordered tasty buns and cakes that were served on beautiful, hand-painted, blue china.

The men agreed to meet in a week to finalize the deal, and HJ was put in charge of organizing the funding for the new streetcar line. The major concern would be to convince Madam Hancock to give an easement for the cars to run through her property. Her husband had secured the land while he was in politics and had left it to his widow and two small children. Fortunately, Madam Hancock had heard of the many wonderful things HJ was doing for the community, so she agreed to grant the easement. She hoped that this improvement would be a financial benefit to her small family.

Hollywood Boulevard would run east and west, and HJ chose it to be the main thoroughfare for his new town. It portrayed

Hollywood's character: small town simplicity and sophisticated luxury. The shops, office buildings, and small hotels would make it the central business district; yet it was also an esplanade where people could stroll along to look at splendid window displays. Attire worn on the Boulevard was formal and colorful.

HJ remodeled the Hurd ranch and improved the dirt road to the large stable at the end of his land holdings. Mr. Hurd originally opened the road on the corner of Prospect (Hollywood Blvd). HJ thought that it would be fitting to name it Hurd Avenue. His neighbor, whose property adjoined the road, thought that it should be named Wilcox, after her deceased husband. Mrs. Beveridge threatened to sue if she did not get her way. HJ decided that it was not worth the time or money to battle over such a trivial matter; but still, he felt that if she wanted to name the road, she should have put it in herself. He agreed to record the street's name as Wilcox, as long as she granted him access to lay half of the street on her property.

As New Year's Eve and the end of a decade quickly approached, it gave Gigi the opportunity to look forward to the future while reflecting back on the past. Every year, when she entered the holiday season, beginning with Thanksgiving and followed by Christmas and finally New Year's Eve, she found herself grateful for her many blessings, looking forward to new adventures. Gigi made resolutions to do better in the new year. This year, Gigi confessed, she was a little awed, like many other folks, by the number of zeros in this year-end benchmark: 1900. It made her reflect on how quickly the world around them was changing.

Chapter Ten

The first years of the twentieth century brought amazing changes to Hollywood: the urban electric streetcars, the automobile, the telephone, the electric light—the catalog of new inventions seemed endless. "Peace, Progress and Prosperity" marked the headlines at the end of the 1800s. The prophecies made by newspapers of the inventions to come in the next hundred years were fantastic, beyond belief. Edison invented moving pictures that projected on the screen. Hollywood was the perfect spot for filming moving pictures, with its unending sunlight, progressive thinkers, and magnificent open spaces. By 1900, the typewriter, the sewing machine, and artificial rayon fibers became normal purchases for many people. New inventions and how to use them led to new thinking in Hollywood. Women of all classes felt the dynamic atmosphere of change as much as men. They saw astonishing things—the first zipper; the first all-electric kitchen, which included an automatic dishwasher; and a box claiming to contain everything a cook would need to make pancakes, under the brand name Aunt Jemima's. There was a new, oddly flavored gum called Juicy Fruit and caramel-coated popcorn called Cracker Jack.

By 1900, there were a hundred thousand people living in the city of Los Angeles and several other thousands in the outlying communities that were surrounded by farms. HJ knew that his town needed something to efficiently link it to all the surrounding areas. At last, people could farm part-time and commute to good-paying jobs in the cities. The effect of the growth of the outlying towns was tremendous. These roads and the Los Angeles Pacific Railroad line would be more than a means of commuting. It could be used to haul freight, including tons of sugar beets; provide entertaining tour routes; and even a means for hearses to carry the deceased to undertaking parlors in Los Angeles.

HJ continued working on his plans to fashion an elite hillside community in Hollywood designed after the beautiful villas of Italy. He was optimistic that the up-and-coming society of Hollywood would find the Mediterranean ambiance captivating, as many of them had European roots. He wanted to design the hill so that each resident was guaranteed a view of the valley and, hopefully, even a peek at the ocean. Neighborhood streets would meander around crags, offering never-ending panoramic views.

Late in the afternoon of September 6, 1901, at the Buffalo Exposition, President McKinley was murdered by Leon Czolgosz. Mr. Czolgosz stood in line, wearing an innocent expression and dressed in a dark suit. He waited for more than two hours in eighty-two-degree heat for his turn to shake hands with the president.

The news of the murder was on the streets almost as soon as the tragedy happened. Gigi heard the piercing shouts from the newsboys on the street. She ran to the curb to snatch the paper, unable to believe her ears. On hearing of McKinley's death, she saw even strong men cry. Abraham Lincoln's death had been dreadful, but it had not seemed quite so insane because America had just ended the Civil War. Even their friends who had held McKinley in slight contempt had not hated him enough to want him dead. To hate him seemed ludicrous. He was not slain for anything in his character but simply because an anarchist felt that all government should be destroyed.

Gigi thought to herself how strange the world was. It was amazing to think that McKinley had been the first president to ride in an automobile and campaign by telephone. We had made so many advancements, yet we were still shamefully uncivilized.

Although saddened by the news, HJ was delighted to know that his friend Teddy Roosevelt would now become president. Keeping McKinley's cabinet allowed Roosevelt a smooth transition from the vice presidency. Changes could be made as things settled down. Roosevelt had too much originality to follow another's plans for long. HJ supported Teddy's new policy, the "Square Deal." Teddy had asked all Americans for their support on attacking "serious social problems" facing the nation. His platform included legislation to allow the regulation of big business, broader control of the railroads, and conservation of natural resources. HJ felt that he would have followed those same avenues had he become president. He wrote a quick note to Teddy, congratulating him on his recent presidency.

In 1901, while sitting in office chairs around the executive desk in his downtown office, HJ formed the Los Angeles-Pacific Boulevard and Development Company, along with his old-time friends General Harrison Gray Otis and George Hoover. Over a snack of freshly baked raisin cookies he brought from home and coffee, the men decided that HJ would be the president and principal owner of the company. HJ owned the land that the company would soon be developing. For three long hours, HJ solicited ideas and laid out the foundation of the new town.

HJ insisted that what he had in mind was something far grander than any other town in California. He described for them a vision of a dream city. HJ assured Otis and Hoover that by agreeing to help, they would be joining their names to one of the greatest undertakings of the century. HJ would personally direct the design and construction of the new town. From the moment HJ finalized his purchase of land in 1899, he began discussing the project with his friends in the Los Angeles business community. Although there were several small businesses in the area, most of Hollywood was still farm frontier.

There was no mystery to forming this corporation. In its simplest sense, it was merely a license to do business in a particular manner. HJ filed the articles of incorporation and had the secretary issue the stock. The company was capitalized for $100,000. It was a closed corporation, which required the shareholders to agree to operate the business pursuant to a shareholder's agreement. The executive board of directors consisted of: HJ Whitley, president; MH Sherman, vice president; FH Rindge, vice president; Clem. S. Glass, secretary; and Thomas Keith, assistant secretary. The corporation was comprised of a small group of very powerful men who banded together to improve that particular part of the world and who, from their combined efforts, produced the foundation of Hollywood. This was a business venture of monumental faith. Each of them possessed the traditional virtues of hard work, patriotism, personal responsibility, optimism, and trust. It can easily be said that many of the techniques, plans, and know-how commonly accepted as standard procedure today were first pioneered by HJ.

In the words of his new business partners, HJ was "a grizzled, six-foot, heavy-handed, shrewd acquaintance that we are quite eager to do business with. He was a likable man, insightful and disciplined with a straightforward manner that helped him win in business—the kind of man who made good company."

It was his extraordinary combination of imagination, intensity, and magnetism that drew his partners to his ideas. The newly formed corporation acquired three hundred acres from HJ, which ran between La Brea and Cahuenga. Acting in the capacity of the president, HJ laid out the Ocean View Tract, setting the standard for residential development north to the foothills.

Using his experience from the past, HJ convinced the board to begin construction of a hotel and the incorporation of a bank. Bordering the west and east corner of Highland Boulevard, the stucco hotel and brick bank building fronted onto a dusty, unpaved road. This road would eventually become Hollywood Boulevard. More than a mile of the land fronted the Boulevard. The area was graded and finished with curbs and sidewalks. Also, Highland Avenue was graded, graveled, and curbed. It would open up a new outlet to the San Fernando Valley.

For the first time, grading was completed by electric lights. The electricity was obtained from the railroad line. There was such a demand for gravel cars on the trolley line that the grading had to be done at night. Poles were erected and wires connected to the rail lines. The light produced was sufficient for the work to be completed.

HJ wanted the area to be posh. No residence could cost less than $3000. Multiple dwellings were barred from the area. The adjacent hillside area north of Franklin was developed several years later by HJ as Whitley Heights, becoming a haven for silent screenwriters, actors, and directors who sought privacy close to the studios.

After a strenuous time of getting the streets completed, the great developer, HJ, gave his attention to building the first wing of the Hollywood Hotel. HJ selected a skeleton organization that would carry on the activity necessary to get Hollywood started. In 1901, HJ's Hollywood syndicate placed newspaper advertisements for carpenters and laborers; and soon, workers with teams of horses began excavating the land. Masons set the foundation and laid the exterior walls while carpenters erected the interior frame. The street clamored with the wheeze of handsaws. Nothing brightened HJ's day more than dealing with somebody, anybody, who took pride in their work or went the extra mile.

The overall attributes of the town HJ envisioned concealed a billion smaller obstacles that most of the directors had no idea existed. HJ negotiated with the railroad about delivering steel, stone, and lumber to the construction site. He managed the delivery of supplies, goods, and articles sent by transcontinental shipping companies. He worked to improve the police force and fire department. He found a way to remove the tons of manure generated each day. HJ realized that the tiniest details would shape the way people judged his town. His vigilance extended even to the design of the hotel's stationery.

"It may not occur to you how very important the matter of hotel stationery is," he wrote to Otis. "It will be very largely distributed throughout the world and is one of those trivial things by which people judge the artistic standards of the Hotel."

Thirty applicants applied for the position as hotel manager. With Gigi's help, he decided to hire Mrs. Anderson and Mrs. Stewart. They had already established a successful reputation catering dinners and weddings. The women signed a seven-year lease in which the first two years were rent free. The only payment received from the women was five hundred dollars, which was used to purchase linens. The rest of the expenses were covered by HJ. In a short time, it became burdensome to carry the entire expense of the hotel; so HJ sold half of his interest in the hotel to Mr. Hoover. The following year, HJ decided that he preferred working with the hotel rather than managing the bank. So he and Mr. Hoover swapped shares of stock. Mr. Hoover became the bank president, and HJ once again controlled the hotel.

All these were mere distractions compared to the single most important task HJ made: the selection of an architectural firm that designed the buildings and oversaw their construction. HJ declared that Hollywood, unlike any other before it, would be primarily a monument to architecture.

In appreciation of the support of the stockholders, HJ invited the stockholders to the hotel to celebrate. The banquet was held on December 18, 1902. Otis, for his part, knew that HJ had been a leading force in the creation of Hollywood and the business genius of the project. He was decisive, frank, and cordial. He spoke under a level, blue gaze that Otis found assuring. In private communication, Otis and Hoover agreed that HJ was a man they enjoyed working with.

By the time the new company paid its fifth and final dividend, approximately three years after the company was formed, the group of financiers received $1.72 for each $1.00 they invested. Those who were familiar with Hollywood's growth realized the ability of the Hollywood Hotel to attract desirable people to the new town. One of the chief factors of its success had been its superior service.

It was the beginning of Hollywood's golden years. The Hollywood Hotel was designed and built on the corner of Prospect (now Hollywood Boulevard) and Highland Avenues as an emblem of glamour and elegance for travelers and businessmen alike. It was a large and quiet country resort nestled amid the fruit groves that covered more than four acres. It was located in the center of the civic and social life and would be the home of many movie stars over the years. Having traveled abroad, HJ incorporated his extensive acquisitions and appreciation of architecture into both the hotel's decor and its Moorish and mission design. The residential feel of the hotel's design was highlighted by white, plastered walls; a red tile roof; and a lobby featuring European antiques and oriental rugs. It was a sanctuary for travelers who longed for tranquility offered by formal gardens and landscaped patios. The hotel was also a popular public gathering place. The Hollywood's rates were from $3.50 to $6 a day or $21 to $35 a week.

Among the amusements the hotel afforded were a pool, billiard tables, and a paved tennis court. Because of his competitive nature, HJ often enjoyed a friendly tournament with the guests. Hollywood had the only bowling green in the West. HJ, who was a devotee of the ancient Scottish game, would enjoy a game with friends whenever possible. This sport had flourished in Scotland during the 1840s. The Scottish developed a set of standardized rules for the game, rules that had changed very little. He also had a weakness for a quick nine holes at the nearby golf course. In the evening, there was plenty of music and dancing.

Within less than three years, HJ would be compelled to expand the forty-room hotel by adding an additional 104 rooms, which took another three years to complete. With frontage of an entire block on the magnificent Hollywood Boulevard, the Hollywood Hotel stood amid a profusion of tropical plants and flowers. The wide verandas, with their easy chairs, afforded a place of rest and comfort to weary guests and lovers of fresh air. California sunshine was in ample supply, and many travelers would pass their idle hours enjoying it. The hotel was open year-round, which gave travelers an opportunity to enjoy Southern California as a summer resort. It already had a reputation as a winter paradise. The intersection of Hollywood Boulevard and Highland Avenue became the hub of the area, mainly due to the Hollywood Hotel.

HJ wondered if the rest of Hollywood could be transformed as easily. What kind of leadership would be required? A host of architects, community planners, craftsmen, road builders, and landscape designers moved to the area to change the physical appearance of the region. From the start, HJ understood that the people he attracted to the area would make Hollywood the most inspiring town of the century. It was not the transformation of things that mattered. In the near future, it would be clear that the dream, the visions, and the multitude of planning HJ had done would have a stunning impact on Hollywood's social and economic landscape.

HJ put up lighting posts to light their home and street. He obtained the electricity from the Los Angeles Pacific Electric Railway Company as soon as the cars began running. Their home was the first electrified house in Hollywood. Although the staff could easily take care of the home's eighteen kerosene lamps, an electrified home with incandescent lights was the wave of the future. Also, HJ always felt uneasy having fire in the house.

It was an enormous expense to change the gas lamps to electric fixtures; but in those early days, everything had to be done in order to advertise his new town. Little Grace, who was held in her father's arms, turned on the first electric lights in Hollywood.

"Well, now," her father said, "we will have a party!" HJ invited everyone to their home for evening refreshments.

The opening of the Ocean View Tract marked a historic milestone in the life of HJ. It was to be his last great development enterprise. It was mostly a myth, in Gigi's opinion, as she was sure HJ would never retire. HJ felt that he had no choice but to be a dynamic man all of his life. Destiny had paved his path.

Knowing the task that lay before him, HJ picked out a number of associates he knew could and would stand with him shoulder to shoulder. The practical management was, however, in his hands. Through his efforts, the water and electric works were put in for the first time.

HJ hosted a party, inviting all the important businessmen in the area, to promote his town's expansion. The event allowed him to announce the grand opening of his new subdivision, Ocean View Tract. Dinner for more than a thousand was prepared for the opening. The feast consisted of barbequed mountain turkeys and many other appetizing dishes.

The community came to see the first four-block area of homes that brightened the evening skies. HJ covered the cost with no outside help. He wished that his mother could have been there to see his accomplishments. There were times in his life when he longed for her presence. She would have been vith his work. Long ago, he had told her that he would

to live up to the family Johnstone clan crest. The John-
sto... ...an crest consisted of a winged spur enclosed in strap and
buckle. Upon the crest was inscribed the motto, "Nunquam non
paratus," which is Latin for, "Never unprepared." HJ was a man
ahead of the times, always prepared for the new adventures that
lay ahead on the horizon.

HJ succeeded in interesting a number of wealthy and influential newcomers to purchase lots in his choice residential section. A number of escrows closed during the first few months.
Houses sprung up here and there like wild mushrooms in the
forest. These homes proved to be a splendid investment. The
view from the southwest-facing windows gazed onto the expansive valley below and extended toward the Pacific Ocean. Gorgeous homes with terraced patios made this new area a unique
and highly desirable community. Each home had an appealing
interplay of levels, textures, and furnishings. The homes were
complete with rambling gardens. Among the purchasers were
MM Harris, AE Adams, RR Buzard, CD Crocker, CE Bire-
ley, Dr. JH Martin, PB Chase, Judson Williams, and Leonard
Pogsen.

HJ witnessed, with much pleasure, the rapid increase in
value of real estate as a result of his enterprise. Before the electric streetcar lines were built, Hollywood was known to one out
of ten citizens of Los Angeles. It seemed to be off the traditional
line of travel and was almost undiscovered by visitors and sight-
seers. Property was not in demand. The few people who were
living in Hollywood appreciated the beautiful valley. However,
to get others to go there was only accomplished once the electric
railroad line was completed.

Property that formerly went for $400 an acre now transferred at $800 an acre or more. HJ knew the truth of the adage, "To make money, you must first spend money." To encourage Hollywood's rapid expansion, he donated reservoir sites and wells worth $100,000. He spent large sums of money to open up Sunset Boulevard. Whenever HJ saw a desirable improvement lag behind his anticipated date of completion, he was prompt to put his hand in his pocket and lend it the necessary financial aid.

HJ was loyal to his business partners and tried to assist everyone whenever he developed. Many men watched his every move so that they could benefit themselves by buying the adjoining property. They would hold it without doing anything to improve it, knowing full well that HJ had the golden touch. He had planned to benefit himself, but those who had watched his untiring work and his strenuous efforts often fared better than he. Even in trying situations, he had wonderful endurance, patience, and perseverance that allowed him to accomplish things that seemed impossible for one man to carry out. They used to say, "HJ is equal to twenty men."

To help accommodate people purchasing smaller homes, HJ planned to open a street between Wilcox and Whitley, which he would name Annandale Place. It was to be lined with small cottages. He chose the name Annandale as his family was in line for the title of the earl of Annandale. HJ filed a claim for the title but found that there was still one male who was older than he who could claim the title. This relative had no children, and HJ planned to try for the title again once this relative passed away. His never-ending business commitments seemed to keep him from this task.

At the same time HJ was developing his land, Mr. Hudson was subdividing his place across Prospect Avenue. It was subdivided into small lots for building purposes. The main street in the subdivision was Hudson Avenue. They owned about seven acres. Gigi thought that it was a crime to cut down all their beautiful orange groves, but HJ felt that the additional development would help his sales.

In 1901, Paul DeLongpre, the famous French painter of flowers, obtained a lot to build his family a home. HJ advised him to take a mortgage on it so he could build.

"I will advance you $300 a month if you need funds to live on until your business grows," HJ offered.

Sitting at the office desk that was piled high with stacks of papers, HJ and Mr. DeLongpre signed an agreement with the understanding that when the new Balloon Route of the Pacific Electric was established, Mr. DeLongpre would allow groups of tourists to visit his home free of charge. This agreement lasted for nearly three years. The tourists would pay for their round-trip tickets on the Red Car in Los Angeles, which permitted them to go through the DeLongpre gallery and gardens. Many of the new residents of Hollywood would be attracted there by DeLongpre's fame and a chance to see the new town of Hollywood. After viewing the gardens, the tourists were taken to the pavilion at Whitley Heights to see the panoramic view from the hills overlooking the magnificent valley below. This would eventually become the site of the famous electrically lit Whitley Heights sign.

HJ planned a surprise birthday party for Gigi. He had arranged to have Mrs. Anderson, the hotel manager, invite them, saying, "Come have dinner with us at the hotel at six thirty. Bring HJ too. Some of your old friends that you have not seen for a while are staying here. I hope you will wear your new dress from Paris. I would just love to see it."

Grace enjoyed helping Gigi get ready for the party. Gigi went to the closet and found her new dress. She slipped it on and looked in the mirror. It fit her perfectly and made her look very feminine. Grace sat on the bed, looking through Gigi's jewelry box. Gigi brushed her shoulder-length hair and then pinned it up. Grace handed her a pair of diamond earrings with a matching necklace. Gigi dabbed a little French perfume on each of her wrists as she stepped back to look at herself. HJ's face lit up when he saw her. He glanced at her with a shy smile.

Wearing his evening attire, HJ was a man to be stared at. His self-confidence was an advertisement of success.

As they walked in the hotel door, a large crowd of friends yelled, "Surprise!" The excitement sent a shiver down her back. Gigi's eyes flashed in amazement. At promptly seven o'clock, the doors to the dining room were thrown open to a most glorious sight. The candlelit tables were placed in a *W* shape and had red rose garlands strung down the center, flowing in waves of beauty. Each couple was seated by a waiter—men on one side, ladies on the other—as an orchestra played lovely contemporary tunes.

Placed at each seat was a special birthday greeting to Gigi. In between the courses, various friends stood up to read them. Some were funny comments about birthdays gone by; others had a serious note about birthdays with family and friends. Each touched her in their own special way.

It was a February birthday, and the dinner followed that theme. The first course was a lettuce salad with heart-shaped croutons. This was followed by London broil served with parsley buttered potatoes. What birthday dinner would be complete without ice cream and chocolate cake? The orchestra continued playing lovely tunes during dinner, and many guests could not resist dancing late into the evening.

Gigi received a lovely copy of the *Mona Lisa* painting and *The European Tour*, a book by Grant Allen. Later, when they closed their home to travel abroad for seven months, the book was very useful. At the end of the party, all of the guests held hands and formed a circle. The orchestra played the parting tune, "Auld Lang Sine," as the guests sung along.

After the electric lights were installed in their home, after the surprise party, after everything, Gigi looked forward to the time she would spend alone with HJ. Gigi went into his study dressed in her nightgown. As always, he had two cups of hot tea waiting; and they settled on his couch, her feet nestled in his lap for warmth. They discussed the trials and tribulations of his day. There was a fire in the fireplace and the scent of gingerbread lingering through the house.

Gigi enjoyed those moments most of all. She was probably the only person to see HJ at his most relaxed, when his stern features would gradually soften and he would stretch out his legs toward the fireplace, sipping his tea and rhythmically stroking her leg with one hand. They spoke leisurely about the events of the day, the antics of some of the more annoying business transactions he had completed, and the promise of some new ones that were on the horizon. He spoke of his frustration with the general public, how it would be so much easier if everyone had the same high standards he had. Before long, they would head upstairs to a peaceful night's sleep, dreaming of the changing world around them.

Gigi had a deep love of trees and did not want Hollywood to change to the point that they were lost from its scenery. It was in the summertime that the trees seemed to sing to her. Her happiest and most peaceful days were spent reading and writing under their green foliage. When exhausted by the summer heat, Gigi would reflect upon the many events of the last year. Her imagination enabled her to crystallize what needed to be done to promote the new town.

At her advice, HJ picked out and had planted over ten thousand trees and shrubs to beautify the young town of Hollywood. HJ valued plants, trees, and flowers not for their individual attributes but rather as colors and shapes on a palette. Roses were not roses but flecks of pink or red modifying green. He used their colors to accent his architectural designs. Most of Hollywood's streets had been graded and graveled, allowing the tree-lined driveways to give an effective parklike scenery. Nearly every road was aligned with trees—peppers, pines, palms, magnolias, and other choice varieties—the growth of which in three years was nothing less than wonderful. There were hill roads too, skillfully graded, winding up to plateaus from which superb views of mountains, plains, and the ocean could be seen. Also, there were bridle paths cut along the steeper slopes with flawless skill, due to HJ's superb civil engineering skills. The planting and development required a staff of over three hundred men.

Before he even contemplated the building of Hollywood, he found a water source. HJ would use this source to nourish the new trees. It was amazing the impact the trees had on the natural scenery of the area. Gigi noticed many of the fashion designers beginning to implement flowers on their hat and dress designs. HJ's idea was to make the streets so attractive, especially Hollywood Boulevard, so that the place would advertise itself. He charmed the newspaper men, especially the small editors, who helped him advertise this upcoming development project for free. They wrote amazing stories about the many improvements he had made. HJ was a great motivator and communicator. His extensive travels abroad to study landmark boulevards, along with Gigi's encouragement, made him realize how important beauty was to man's everyday life. This undertaking was quite impressive and laborious since the trees were watered by horse-drawn tanker wagons, a process that continued for over a year.

One night, HJ came home from a Hollywood school meeting and found that he could not sleep. He lay awake in the dark and listened to the faint sounds of the night. The events of the meeting raced through his restless mind. Unable to shake his heavy mood, he awakened Gigi, as he wanted her to walk up to Whitley Heights with him.

"I cannot sleep. Those stubborn folks have voted against the school bonds again. I have spent nearly a year and a half trying to convince them that it would not ruin them to pay taxes for a school. As the population grows, others would help defer future costs. But still, every time I thought they were going to vote for the new school bond, someone would go around the valley and talk people out of it. How can a city grow if it does not have a high school?" he crossly said.

HJ had to have been at the limit of his endurance or he would not have awakened her. So, in a few minutes, Gigi was ready for their customary tramp up to Whitley Heights. They would walk up Whitley Avenue and then over the rough road toward Grace Avenue. When they reached the top of the hill, they sat down to rest. Then Gigi said, "We can count the lights and think of all the beautiful things that will happen to these hills someday when you begin to develop them."

That helped to get his mind off his worries. They counted just seven lights. As they sat there on the hill, surrounded by wonderful peaks and brightly shining stars, Gigi felt the wonderful influence of God's handiwork. It was as though they were in another world.

HJ finally said, "Mama, I wish you would figure out how to get rid of that annoying codger who keeps convincing everyone to vote against me. He cares only about his own pocketbook and not the good of the community. He is an ignorant, stingy man that does nothing but make trouble."

"I will pray to have him removed from this town. And, furthermore, I have the faith that it will be done."

HJ began to laugh and said, "Well, if you are successful, there are a few more people I would like to have you pray over."

They sat talking for hours about the many other wonderful things HJ had planned for Hollywood. Around 2:00 a.m., HJ put his arms around Gigi and gave her a sweet kiss. Gigi was always able to clear his head. After a few more minutes, they walked home and went to bed.

Many times, HJ told Gigi that he thought how fortunate he was to find a wife who understood him so well, who had faith in him, and who encouraged him. He felt fortunate that she shared his home, helped increase his fortune, and inspired his success.

Several weeks later, the next meeting of the association was called. It was raining that night, and HJ asked Gigi, "Do you think he will be there?"

"Oh yes, but it will be the last time you see him," Gigi cagily replied.

HJ's face beamed as he heard the news. Then he turned around quite seriously as he said, "What is going to happen?"

"I cannot tell you yet, but I know he will be gone. Just last night, I dreamt that I read his obituary in the newspaper."

Well, the same old business happened. They voted against the school bonds. When HJ came home, Gigi was waiting at the door to greet him; but he did not look as serious as he had after the last meeting. Everything else at the meeting had been quite harmonious. The old man was there, and HJ said, "He looked quite gleeful as he voted against those school bonds."

It came as quite a surprise to HJ when he heard that, as the old codger started home that night, he caught a severe cold. In less than a month, he died from pneumonia.

HJ realized that many new residents were immigrating to Hollywood. Plans to complete the Panama Canal meant that even more would come in the future. HJ felt that for Hollywood to expand in a sound and progressive manner, the city needed to provide facilities for the education of the younger generations. How else could they become useful citizens? He would not quit until Hollywood had a high school.

To celebrate their return from a three-month tour of Europe in the spring of 1901, Gigi hosted the first big social event ever held in Hollywood. The party was held at the Whitley mansion, which was set on spacious grounds surrounded by orange, lemon, and deciduous fruit orchards, flowers, and ornamental trees. The tree-lined lawn was accented by a background of rolling hills and distant purple mountain ranges. The interior of the home was decorated with beautiful flowers of every variety artistically arranged, including long stalks of waxy yucca blossoms. The beautifully decorated and tinted walls were an effective setting for the wealth of color. The dining room was a veritable study in California fruits, especially of its semi-tropical production. A large bunch of bananas hung from the fireplace; and the mantel and buffet were banked liberally with oranges, lemons, and spicy pineapples. The table held bowls of figs and bronzed walnuts. HJ used every event to promote and draw people to Hollywood, showing off what his land had to offer.

An additional draw that Gigi used to entice people to attend the party was inviting Governor and Mrs. John L. Beveridge (Governor of Illinois) to their party. HJ had known them for many years. Gigi was delighted they came, as it helped bolster her standing in the currently developing society of Hollywood.

After they said good-bye to the final guest, HJ and Gigi slowly walked back to the house under the starlit sky. The band was softly playing a final tune. Gigi was uplifted by the music and the good time she had at the party. An old feeling swept over her. It always came with the music and having HJ at her side. It was as if she were far away from everything. Her head was among the stars; and strange, beautiful thoughts that Gigi had no words for danced in her head like shining will-o'-the-wisps. HJ bid good night to the staff and then whisked her to their bedroom.

Besides having parties, HJ and Gigi found that they could also visit with friends at the park. Every Sunday in the summer, they had an early dinner. Around three o'clock, the family, along with the nanny, hurried down the dusty trail to Westlake Park. Arriving at four o'clock, they were in time to hear the band play Gigi's favorite tunes. They came to enjoy the soft summer evenings; the green grass; and the honey sweet fragrance of the flowers in bloom, encounters with friends, and the music.

Westlake Park was set in a beautiful and expansive grassy area. It had a small lake that was dotted with boats. HJ and his friends climbed up one of the surrounding hills to catch a glimpse of the vast views of the country between Los Angeles and the ocean. These walks gave HJ a chance to discuss business with those who were interested in finding out how things were shaping up in Hollywood.

Young couples strolled about over the grass, chatting as they walked. Romping children raced about, organizing themselves in games of "Kick the Can," marbles, or "Tug of War." The children would simply use tree branches for sticks and everything from a ball of yarn to a tin can for a ball. Naturally, one of the greatest amusements for the children was their own imaginations. Countless games and various activities were created each weekend. Tired and ready for sleep, Gigi found the trip home tiresome, as there were few buildings on the way and the scenery was rather sparse. Gigi realized that with a little time and with HJ as the mastermind, the entire area would be something magical.

As years passed, Westlake Park became the political forum of the community. Their friends would climb up on the bandstand to deliver their political speeches. Sometimes the topics would be controversial, and heated arguments would ensue from both sides. Eventually, one argument turned into a fist fight, resulting in the city council putting a stop to such activities. The bandstand was torn down, no more concerts were given, and discussions were forbidden. All the seats were removed until the election was over. Peace returned to Westlake Park, but the gatherings were never as good—as far as Gigi was concerned—as they had been in the early days.

Gigi discovered early in their marriage that unless they attempted to see a few people at regular intervals, they would never see anyone informally. So once every two weeks or thereabouts, a few of their friends, usually four couples, dined together. They put formality behind them on these evenings and sat in random order around the table.

One of the first gatherings was an informal evening at the Otises' home. HJ; Gigi's sister Ella; and her husband, Thomas; and Gigi had a first-rate time. They played "Charades" with four other couples. Their friends divided into two groups. Having decided on a word, the first group created one-minute acts to describe the word. Both HJ and Gigi enjoyed this game, as it gave them an opportunity to converse with their close friends while laughing at each other's acting antics. Thomas was a real comedian. HJ's competitive nature only allowed him to win if he saw that winning the game would not hamper any business transactions. As they rode home that evening, Gigi remarked about how much she had enjoyed the evening, especially the friendly competition.

One week after Gigi said good-bye to Ella, she received a loving letter from her thanking them for their hospitality. She invited them to visit Thomas and her as soon as possible. Thomas sent a box of strawberries as a treat for Gigi since he knew that she was fond of them. The freight was free since he worked for the railroad.

The housekeeper and Gigi began to make preserves. How lovely the jars looked filled with fresh fruit. The aroma drew HJ into the kitchen. As an added treat, Gigi decided to pop some corn for HJ. He was given the task of shelling the corn.

When HJ suggested making popcorn balls for the children, Gigi remarked, "Who will make the syrup?"

"I will," said HJ to their surprise. Then he had a story to tell. "Back in my hometown, when I was just eighteen, I wanted to earn some money. I took a position in a candy store and became such an expert at making candy that, when the opportunity arose, I purchased the store. I cornered the candy market with my new recipes and had all the business in the area. One day, I noticed how fast my teeth were decaying and realized that I was consuming candy by the pound. My dentist bills had sky-rocketed. When I tried to cut down on my candy diet, I found it impossible to test the batches I had just prepared. I asked some employees to do the testing and soon found that they were giving samples to their friends, which cut into my profits. It disgusted me, so I sold the business and took a solemn vow never to eat candy again."

At last, Gigi knew why he never wanted to give her candy.

Chapter Eleven

HJ belonged to two select men's clubs, the Los Angeles Athletic Club and the Jonathon Club. Their members lived and worked in Los Angeles, Hollywood, and other nearby settlements. They were men of means, well-educated, and prominent in the business community. Members chose from a wide variety of activities that offered adventure, social mixing, and business connections. Their membership rosters read like a "Who's Who" of the city, with names like Valentino, Fairbanks, Chaplin, Chandler, Doheny, Slauson, and Whitley.

The Los Angeles Athletic Club was the city's first private club. It was located in the downtown core of businesses that included saloons and shooting galleries. It created an American-style club for the "best men" of the community. Ladies were welcome at social events and exhibitions. HJ could easily afford the initiation fee, which was five dollars, and the monthly dues that were set at a dollar. Colonel James B. Lankershim, whose family owned a good portion of the San Fernando Valley, was a member of the club. This contact was instrumental to HJ when he formed a syndicate to develop the San Fernando Valley.

Physical exercise was essential to HJ's moral and bodily welfare. He enjoyed the company of men and the hearty business discussions he had with them. These men also had notable careers. General Harrison Gray Otis, upon arriving in California, became the publisher of *The Los Angeles Times*. Harry Chandler, because of ill health, came to California, where he was hired to be the general manager of *The Los Angeles Times*. Several years later, Chandler married Otis's daughter, Marion. General Moses Hazelton Sherman built the Pacific Electric Railroad. Otto Brant was the vice president and general manager of the Title and Trust Company. They had all accumulated huge personal fortunes and enjoyed the prospects of making more.

These clubs gave HJ a chance to discuss business in a relaxed atmosphere. When he got home, he felt refreshed. Perhaps the best part of his day was sitting in the lounge, relaxing in the company of good friends.

Saturday started like any other day. It had rained the night before, but the sun was up that morning. It was quiet, yet Gigi sensed that there was an underlying vibration waiting to explode. Freshly brewed coffee and the sweet smell of freshly baked bread mixed in the air like a foreign perfume.

HJ returned from a long day at the office, and he was in no mood to discuss women's clubs. He did not believe there was any relevant value to the many new women's clubs that were currently springing up in his new city. Part of Gigi thought that she should have waited for a more opportune day to tell him. Still, she was more terrified of being trapped and alone than telling him her plans. Her freedom was always very important. Gigi could feel her courage drain as she told HJ that she was planning to join two or three clubs. His immediate response was, "You stay away from such things. My friends will get after me if they see you leading their wives astray. You are too innocent and do not realize how this will complicate our lives. A woman's place is in her home. You stay away from them!"

With her eyes blazing blue fire, Gigi replied, "Well, dear, you have a different way of looking at social affairs than I do. I am sure my joining a few clubs will not impact our lives that much. This is just a simple way for me to make friends and influence people on our behalf."

As HJ did not say anything, Gigi thought everything was settled. HJ just sat very quietly, and he seemed to doze off from fatigue. Gigi decided that while he was resting she would run into the kitchen to get a cup of coffee and buttered toast. Since it was the weekend, the maid was out for the evening and the children went to bed early.

When Gigi returned to the parlor, to her astonishment, the chair where HJ had been sitting was empty. Gigi called him, but there was no answer. She was a little surprised; although, by this time, Gigi was accustomed to HJ getting a notion to do something in his mind and just doing it. Gigi put down the tray on the little stand next to the chair and then picked up her book and began to read.

A half an hour had passed when she looked at the clock. Feeling somewhat concerned, she dashed upstairs. All was quiet—not a sound, and no trace of HJ. Her concern mounted. There were no telephones in town at that time; and after eight o'clock, the electric cars stopped running into Los Angeles. Gigi felt some relief in knowing that the maid would soon be home from socializing with friends, but worry still pumped through her body. Waiting. Worrying. At last, Gigi heard a key in the door and ran to see who it was.

"Why, madam," Nora cried, "how pale you look! No doubt you are worried over that businessfied husband of yours. He sent you a note."

She took the note and read it silently to herself.

> Dear Gigi:
>
> I forgot a very important business engagement and it was near time for the streetcar to pass our station. I got Tom to hurry and take me over there. So I am sending this note back to you so you will know why I rushed away so hastily. You understand, I hope. I am just a slave to business.
>
> HJ

Gigi trembled as she read the note. Crumbling it in her hand, she turned to Nora; and then she said, "I am going to bed. You do not need to get up as early as usual, as Mr. Whitley will not be here for breakfast. Eight o'clock will be early enough."

To her, the point that HJ was attempting to clarify was clear: women were different; they were physically, emotionally, morally, and intellectually inferior to men. His actions made it clear that he wanted Gigi to use her talents in her sphere, the home, to be the Victorian "angel in the house." Gigi was to contribute to the greater good of the family as the men used their talents in the business world for such a goal. Gigi felt that his outdated views helped explain her present obscurity in society.

Many years later, her grandson asked her how she felt about it all, if it left any bad memories for her, if it had affected how she felt about him.

"No, dear. That was just the way things were then. Society played an enormous role in the lives of women. Freedom has always been a precious jewel one must fight for."

The afternoon light was falling soft and sweet as HJ came slowly along the road that led to the house. Three days had passed without any word from him. Then, on the third evening, he came walking up the path with his arms full of packages. They were things Gigi would like, his way of apologizing for his actions. Gigi, along with the children, went into the parlor off the kitchen, waiting for their surprises. Ross and Grace quickly opened their gifts with shouts of laughter.

"Oh, Papa, it is just what I have been wanting," Grace squealed.

Gigi also loved her new diamond and pearl necklace. She was glad that HJ gave the children books as well as toys. Her favorite was *The Children's Garland: From the Best Poets*. But the best present was yet to come. HJ understood Gigi well enough to give her a sideways smile as he told her of his plans to have a telephone installed at home so that she could call him any time.

"I am having them hurry up about it, and I want you to send the first message to my office. I have also decided that you might try joining the Shakespeare Club and see how that goes. I figure there will not be too many complaints about supporting cultural events, and it will possibly help increase business. We will give it a try and see how it goes."

Gigi realized that HJ was trying to make amends, which was what she wanted. He could be gracious and thoughtful, yet his willful self-centeredness caused her pain. It was part of his personality and sometimes hers that caused much conflict between them.

In reality, Gigi won a very significant battle. Gigi was grateful that Anne Hutchison paved the path for her. Anne was the first true club woman. She was brilliant, progressive, and more advanced in Gigi's opinion than many ministers or magistrates.

The men in society persecuted her because they did not understand. Even her friends eventually became traitors to her, being afraid to stand by her in that time of an untried women's movement. Unfortunately, Hutchinson went down in defeat; but a small crack in the door of society occurred. The seed had been sown. Gigi knew that the club women of her day were a powerful force for men to reckon with. Hollywood actresses would become one of the foremost leaders in the upcoming Women's Movement.

The women's clubs Gigi joined were focused on self-improvement. A few were even devoted to reform. All of the clubs encouraged their members to take up leadership roles, to organize, and to speak. This helped promote a new generation of potential leaders. They began to realize that in order to transform society, they would need their own organizations to do so. Gradually, they became more visible, outspoken, and organized as they worked to improve social problems in their local neighborhoods.

Over the years, Gigi joined several clubs to fill her days while HJ was busy with his important work. The Hollywood Women's Club held weekly meetings that included music, literature, public affairs, card games, and celebrity luncheons. One treat for Gigi was when Mary Pickford came for lunch with her very nice husband, Douglas Fairbanks. She just finished filming *Through the Back Door*.

One of the first major projects for the club was raising funds for the library. Some of the ladies were considering possible sites for the library. Gigi racked her brain for the names of fellow townsfolk who could be called upon to raise money or at least to become subscribers. Gigi made a motion at one meeting to choose the chairman of committees from the club. She learned that to make things successful in a growing town, it was important to include everyone. If the people worked for the library, they would be interested in it. Gigi felt that there ought not to be any exclusive groups in a town this size. Everyone needed to roll up their sleeves and get to work. To further promote the library, she gave a book reception at the Hollywood Hotel, collecting over two hundred books. Not to be outdone by her, HJ helped organize a baseball game between Hollywood merchants and real estate men, collecting close to sixty dollars.

Gigi then worked with the committee to procure a $10,000 donation from Andrew Carnegie for construction of the library building. Being of Scottish heritage herself, she was of the opinion that Mr. Carnegie was a benevolent, noble man. The single-story English-style library was opened a few years later and boasted having over two thousand cardholders. With the completion of the library, the women eventually recognized the need for a clubhouse of their own. The women built the clubhouse on the corner of Hollywood Boulevard and La Brea.

Gigi's early clubbing proved beneficial to her dear friend, Carrie Jacobs Bond. Perhaps it was their love of music that drew them together. Carrie moved from Chicago to California because it was one of the few places she felt that a woman could find acceptance. HJ, at Gigi's request, built one wing of the Hollywood Hotel to accommodate musical concerts. Hollywood was rapidly achieving notoriety, yet HJ still felt keenly the gossip from Los Angeles that his city had few cultural assets. His underlying fear was that Hollywood might be considered second class. No one topped Hollywood in terms of business drive. Yet the upper echelons still sensed that the city lacked cultural development. Carrie's performances waved a giant white banner in society's face. HJ suggested that Carrie could live at the hotel free of charge for a year. In return, she would perform many of her famous tunes: "The Bird Song," "I Love You Truly," "But I Have You," "When My Ship Comes Home," and many other tunes she composed. At last, Hollywood had its first cultural ambassador.

Carrie began writing and publishing music in 1890. California was one of the few states that had a more liberal attitude about women being in business. Carrie decided to move her publishing company, The Bond Shop, to Hollywood. In her lifetime, she would compose over two hundred songs. Gigi felt that her most notable songs were "A Perfect Day" and "I Love You Truly." As a favor to Carrie, Gigi agreed to introduce her to President Roosevelt. From this introduction, Carrie was invited to sing for the president at the White House.

Gigi aspired to have the lyrical gifts that Carrie possessed, ones that gave her the ability to communicate a variety of emotions in her music. Carrie realized that if Gigi would help her have performances at the hotel, she could greatly advance her career. So Carrie asked Gigi if she thought that was possible. Gigi was delighted with the idea and invited many of her friends to the first performance to hear Carrie sing and play her compositions. Carrie composed "The End of a Perfect Day" while she was their guest at the hotel. Gigi felt that it was such a lovely song.

Gigi worked hard to get her many friends and club members out in the afternoons and evenings to see Carrie perform. The gatherings were a success. It was not an easy task to get her friends from Los Angeles to come so far. The social columnist began to write about these events. It was a sign that Hollywood was gaining notoriety. Carrie performed her songs so professionally that by the end of the year she established a reputation as an accomplished composer of parlor music.

Gigi found it interesting that, once Carrie's reputation was established, one of the "social ladder climbers" suggested that a birthday party be given in Carrie's honor. Daeida Beveridge would pay for the party only if the first piece of cake cut by Carrie should be given to her. When they heard the story from Mrs. Anderson, the hotel manager, both Carrie and Gigi laughed so hard that tears ran down their cheeks.

Carrie commented, "Just think. If it were not for our friendship, Mrs. Beveridge would not even give me the time of day, and now she wants a piece of my birthday cake."

When days were long and stressful, Gigi would sit at her piano, playing the wonderful tunes that Carrie shared with her. Their friendship gave them an unwavering ability to face whatever came their way. Carrie's music and art captivated Gigi, and she collected every one of her songs. Gigi gave Carrie the opportunity to conquer many daunting obstacles that a woman faced in society at that time. Yet their personal bond had been strong enough to allow for their differences. Their lifelong friendship enabled them both to live a life of triumph and faith.

Early in life, Gigi had been taught not to discuss her husband's affairs with any other living person. Men usually possessed the gift of silence, and they expected the same of their wives. But not HJ. He talked, and they occasionally quarreled over the long hours he worked. He said that the long hours he worked were not really hurting anyone. But they hurt Gigi because their children were not getting enough of his attention. Gigi felt that most businessmen worked long hours not because the business needed them to but because they had a great passion for what they were doing. Sometimes Gigi thought that HJ had the tendency to let important things slip from his attention. She did not want this to happen to their children. Gigi asked him to look closer at his tasks and see if he could delegate more to his employees. "Giving more responsibilities to your staff might allow you to get home earlier." His usual comment was, "I am working to support you and the children. I wish you would try to understand my responsibilities." He was, however, adamant that Gigi should never say anything against him to others, no matter what she thought.

Fortunately, Carrie offered her an outlet for her frustration. Carrie would listen and only offer advice when asked. She never criticized Gigi for her actions—only supported her. Their bond might be considered even closer than natural-born sisters.

They spent many hours of their free time together, laughing and talking. They shared their hopes and dreams. Carrie shared wisdom and advice with Gigi. They blessed and encouraged each other. Carrie was Gigi's friend, mentor, and encourager. Together, Gigi hoped that they could weather successfully any storm or difficulty the future brought. Gigi knew that if she ever had to walk down a discouraging path, she would not have to walk by herself. Carrie would be on the path, cheering her on, praying for her, walking beside her, or waiting at the end of the path with open arms. Gigi had no idea the incredible happiness or tragic sorrows that lay ahead, but Gigi knew that Carrie would be there to help. She was a friend who knew the song in Gigi's heart and could sing it back when Gigi forgot the words.

Chapter Twelve

HJ came home from work quite early to inform Gigi that the doctor advised him to take a much-needed sabbatical. His strenuous work required continuous concentration and left him exhausted. But, as usual, he found it difficult to leave his work behind.

"Well, dear, I think that doctor has some common sense, even if you do not. When do we go?" asked Gigi.

Preparation began immediately for their 1902 trip to Egypt and the Holy Land. They went to a steamship company's office that day and made a selection of time tables. Anxiously, they sat down and went over them. Even if HJ had found the elixir of life, Gigi did not think he would have felt any better than he did as he planned their upcoming trip.

Grace was so excited when she was told about the trip that she jumped and clapped her hands as she danced around the room. HJ told Grace that he would help her pack. He showed her that by packing a bag neatly, she would have more room for her belongings. Grace, the ever eager pupil, was engaged in an activity she loved: being with her Papa.

Ross preferred to stay at school with his friends and said, "I do not like traveling with such haste."

They left their estate in the competent hands of Nora and Gregory. As HJ said, "Gregory will take care of everything while we are away." They closed up the house, and the extra hired hands helped Gregory keep the grounds. They needed to arrive in New York in only a few short weeks, so the maid was paid extra to help pack.

Like a boy bolting out of the last day of school, HJ began his trip. The journey would last several months. It seemed as though the worn-out and very tired man enjoyed the traveling right from the start. The trip gave HJ the opportunity to become better acquainted with Grace. She was one of the most joyous children you could imagine. Everything was a delight to her. HJ had been so busy working that he did not really know her. As he sat resting one day, he smiled while he watched her play. His careworn face possessed a much younger expression.

Then Grace, who was eight years old, suddenly got up and kissed her father and said, "I love you, Papa."

She climbed into his lap, and he listened to her tell him about all the wonderful things she had seen on the trip so far. Grace's attention was totally on her father. Her conversations were a chorus of, "Father says this," and, "Father says that." As Grace saw it, her father's role in life was to charge out into the world, seeking success. He returned only occasionally to share his precious time with her. When he was there, she felt blessed.

The only rushing they did was from one train station to another until they reached their ship, which would carry them to Egypt. The quick trip only lasted five days. They wanted to arrive before the hot summer weather began. It was early spring, and they were able to take the trip with ease.

It was late afternoon when they finally arrived at the hotel in New York. After loading the trunks on the steamer, the steward informed them that they needed to board the ship at least one hour before its departure the next morning. The ship would sail promptly at seven. HJ had no time to visit his friends or business associates that night.

Upon entering the hotel lobby, a clerk refused to let them go any farther, stating that no animals were allowed in the hotel. Grace then handed her new teddy bear to the clerk who suddenly realized it was only a toy. It was one of the first ones made in honor of President Roosevelt. They all had a great laugh, and Grace loved her little bear even more because of all the commotion he caused. They went to bed early because they would have to leave at five the next morning. Everything was quiet, and slumber soon came to the three sleepy travelers.

The next morning seemed like such a tussle to Gigi. The trunks were taken to their first-class stateroom. They had an interconnected suite with Grace. Knowing how much they enjoyed hot baths, HJ reserved a suite with bathroom facilities. Hot water was delivered by the steward at the appointed time since faucets in the cabin produced only cold water. The rooms were of French design, resembling some of the rooms in the Palace of Versailles. They felt like they were staying in a very exclusive hotel.

They sailed on board the brand-new transatlantic liner, the *RMS Cedric;* and their journey would last seven to eight days. The first-class dining room resembled a king's palace. Meals were served on fine china. They dined at the table of the captain, Herbert James Haddock. Grace loved dining every day with her beloved Papa. He would allow her to order whatever she wanted, and she often ordered more than one dessert. She wished that children would have been allowed in the smoking room. After dinner, HJ spent several hours there with the other gentlemen, discussing business.

HJ and Gigi had a good night's sleep. The ship was so steady that it was almost the same as being on land. The two deck stewards were quite nice and allotted them steamer chairs in a select part of the upper deck. Gigi loved the elegant lounge and music room on the boat deck. The green and yellow color scheme really complemented the mahogany paneling. The stained glass skylight overlooking the room was majestic. Her favorite spot to sit was in the observation lounge, where she could devour her books without being disturbed. Gigi felt that it was her first glimpse of heaven.

To sit on a quiet deck while hearing the water kissing the prow of the ship was, to HJ, paradise. He loved to rest, rocked gently by the rolling sea, in a nest of velvety darkness. His only light was the soft twinkling of the myriad of stars in the quiet sky above. His music was the sound of the kissing waters, whose magical tunes cooled his weary mind. Give him that, and he had happiness in all its perfection.

HJ hoped that a short leave from his work would inspire him with a novel business idea. At first, he was disappointed to find that things had not changed from long ago. So he resolved to relax and enjoy the gorgeous sights as they sailed up the Nile at sunset.

As he sat there, relaxing, the cotton fields caught his eyes. He wondered how they differed from the fields back home. He decided to study Egyptian planting techniques. He figured that the best way to do that was to visit a cotton field. The next day, Gigi was not surprised when she saw a band of men following him around the fields, discussing the different aspects of the cotton business. HJ hoped to find new methods that might be used to grow cotton in California. Before he left Egypt, he used his friendship with President Roosevelt to convince several American diplomats to become interested in his project. He was so persuasive that the cotton growers allowed him to export all the cotton seed he desired.

As soon as the soil was ready in California, HJ had a field planted in cotton. He was surprised by the negative response he received from the local farmers, who were heard to be whispering, "HJ has gone plumb crazy...He cannot make that grow in California!"

HJ just waited patiently until the cotton grew so tall that you could not see a man walking through it. The cotton begged to be picked. Then he said, "I told you so." Egyptian cotton became a wonderful new industry for California.

Egypt was a land whose culture faded back into the mists of the distant past. Its recorded history goes back more than four thousand years. Gigi found it sad that the invading Muslims burned the great library in Alexandria, destroying records of an even more ancient civilization. History recorded that Plato studied Atlantis there. The grounds included lecture areas, gardens, a zoo, and shrines for each of the nine muses, as well as the library itself. Gigi imagined herself browsing through the millions of documents it contained from Assyria, Greece, Persia, India, and many other countries. The knowledge it held was inconceivable. How could anyone have such little regard for the truth? Gigi read that the Caliph, who ordered the library burned, said upon setting it afire, "They will either contradict the Koran, in which case they are heretics, or they will agree with it, so they are superfluous." It was said to have taken six months to burn all the writings.

After two days of wandering through Alexandria, they were anxious to see the Great Sphinx and the pyramids. The Great Sphinx had been carved from a single piece of stone and enhanced the mysteries of Egypt. The face of the sphinx was thirteen feet wide, and its eyes were six feet high. It was believed to be one of the oldest remaining structures. As they traveled under the deep blue sky through the yellowish sand, Gigi could see this strange, great face with its gaze directed into the distance. She looked at it and tried to understand it. Gigi was swallowed up in its glance—a glance that spoke of mysteries beyond her power of comprehension. They stood, looking in awe. There was something very mystical about it, conveying to her something almost spiritual. As Gigi stood there, the silence was on a scale she could never have imagined, silence that loomed large and forced her to understand, to pull sacred memories of the past.

How divine it was to be a woman in ancient Egypt. Egyptian women seemed to have enjoyed the same legal and economic rights as men. The queen was considered the mortal manifestation of female power while the pharaoh represented the power of the male. The roles of the pharaoh and the queen were explained as one aspect of a system of complementary dualities. While reading Egyptian stories and folktales, Gigi discovered that they revolved around the need to reconcile opposites. The Egyptians realized the need to maintain balance between males and females.

HJ told Gigi that he was fascinated by the pharaoh's image. Impressively inspired, HJ sat, contemplating the wonders of Egypt. He was intrigued that the Egyptians enjoyed hunting with boomerangs. Boomerangs were such clever devices—as deadly as a gun. A smile of true joy spread across HJ's face as he pondered the idea that the boomerang traveled from Egypt to Australia. Was it correct in Genesis where it said that the earth had divided at the time of Peleg? Or did each group develop this hunting tool independently? HJ mused over the thought and decided that the Bible must be correct. The Bible was such an interesting book—the most wonderful book in the world; yet so few seemed to read or understand it. The sound of the guide speaking caught HJ's attention, and he looked over to see that Gigi and Grace were headed back to the donkeys. When they returned to the hotel that evening, HJ shared his thoughts about ancient cultures with Gigi as they lay in bed, waiting for sleep to overtake them.

They took donkeys over rough roads to the wonderful pyramids that were built millennia ago. Gigi's donkey had no name, his master said, so she called him Samson. Grace rode next to her father, enjoying the magnificent stories he told of the ancient world they came to see. His stories were filled with tales of pharaohs, treasures, and intrigue. They were full of sharp observations and fine details. His stories were not only in the words but were brought to life by his gaze, laughter, and tone of voice. As they saw them on the horizon, Gigi thought that, from a distance, the pyramids looked like enormous anthills almost hidden in the brightness of the day. The roads were desolate, and Gigi felt a debt of gratitude to their guides. HJ studied the marvelous structure before them. The pyramids were truly one of the wonders of the world.

They arrived back at their hotel as the shadows lengthened and the intense light of the cloudy sunset began to spread across the valley. The light crept like a tide up the buildings, staining them the color pink. Their journey ended the next day; yet another would soon follow in its path.

Upon their return from Egypt, HJ and Gigi picked up Ross in Long Beach. Grace spent many hours telling Ross of her wonderful trip. There was a special bond between them. Her tales of Bible stories and events long ago stirred a hunger in young Ross, who decided to join the class for Easter confirmation.

HJ loved to call Hollywood home. He felt happier there than any place he had ever lived. While Hollywood might not have had the grand sights, the historical places, and the great antiquities that he saw in other countries of the Old World, he still marveled that he lived in a city unsurpassed in natural advantages of beauty and climate. It was one of the best-built and most prosperous cities in the world, not to mention free of beggars.

Traveling down the busy streets in Egypt, HJ was appalled that they were infested with professional beggars. He saw many lepers, in all stages of the dreaded disease, lining the streets. The lepers were simply ghastly in their misery. There were men, women, and children of all ages and conditions. The few filthy rags that hid their nakedness presented no shape of any garment or any color since they were so dirty and ragged.

HJ was glad to get home and away from such suffering. Hollywood could not boast of Rameses II and it had no pyramidal piles of stone or ancient temples, but it had what counted more. After all, in this life, a city that was prosperous, free, clean, beautiful, and unequaled in high-quality people was a wonderful place to live.

HJ was disturbed to hear the gossip spreading around town like a swarm of locusts. He had been told that many selfish people tried to take credit for the work he accomplished. HJ and Gigi had named Hollywood many years ago on their honeymoon. Why did others try to take credit for the extensive work HJ had done? He spent many long, sleepless nights poring over his business reports that brought wonderful changes to Hollywood. Before he had gone to Egypt, his life was sleepless nights, endless cups of coffee, burning the midnight oil, and digesting a whole town's infrastructure into his brain. He did not understand how people who had never lifted a finger to assist him would plot to take credit for his work while he was away because of poor health.

These betrayals, which would have sunk a lesser man, were shrugged aside. There was no sign of complacency. It was just one of those things. As cheery as ever, deeply suntanned, evidently rested, HJ was a picture of self-confidence. To combat any annoyance that might have attempted to creep in, he became determined to make the town even more attractive. At his own expense, he planted trees and flowers. He requested that every vacant lot be cleaned at once. If the owners did not respond, he said he would do the work himself and send them a bill. This made a tremendous change in the appearance of the little village.

Failure was not an option for HJ. If he failed, his honor would be tarnished. He was blessed with beautiful selective principles that wealthy men are famous for. Even as a boy, he thought that people who stole were scoundrels. He thought that people who would lie were rascals. He understood the importance of obeying laws, especially ones pertaining to licenses, fees, and other government regulation. He would not even pick an orange off another man's tree if he did not have permission. Few doors were closed to him because of his nature. Everywhere HJ turned, there was someone—a friend, a businessman, a fellow club member—telling him that they all expected something tremendous from him.

The Hollywood Hotel had taken nearly three years to build and driven him to the brink of physical collapse. Now HJ was being called upon to build what amounted to an entire express-way system not just for Hollywood but for the entire Los Ange-les basin. By traditional building standards, the challenge seemed an impossible one. HJ knew that it could be done because it had to be done, but the challenge would be monstrous. He saw that the challenge had two fundamental dimensions: time and money. His new highway would forever change the character of urban life. Horses and buggies would disappear, being replaced by automobiles and streetcars.

The clouds came up in the night, and the morning was overcast and gray. HJ was eating bacon and eggs and reading the newspaper when an article caused him to reflect on the new boulevard he was seeking funding for. It hung heavily on his mind for several days until he came up with what he said was the perfectly engineered path for the road to follow. He could figure in his head the calculations needed for the road. Some men just have a special knack. Men respected him for his abili-ties. It would have the tracks of the Pacific Electric Red Car in the middle. Plunging through high hills and over deep ravines, it would afford one of the most scenic routes in Los Angeles. It would be an exceptionally wide road with two lanes on each side.

HJ went to the city council almost every day, trying in his magical way to convince them to support his project. He walked with confidence and dressed well, displaying an impression of wealth and achievement. He was there to secure funding for the road. A giant metal clock on the wall seemed to be encouraging him like the benevolent god of success, each heavy tick tock a rhythmic note of their upcoming approval. Victory lingered in the air. HJ was one of the first to propose the idea of a boulevard from Hollywood to the ocean. Turning on his down-home charm, he delivered his famous line: "It takes a humble man with a strong hand to make a magnificent Boulevard."

He was so wise that he just made suggestions and let council members think that they came up with the idea themselves. No man liked to be sold on an idea. They would prefer to believe that they were acting on their own accord. He never requested the money to build the new boulevard; they offered it to him. He planned to have it begin in the city of Los Angeles and run to the ocean through undeveloped land. He selected a scenic route, a beautiful path that would end at the Pacific Ocean, where one could watch the sunset. The new boulevard would be named Sunset. The boulevard would be twenty miles long, and he estimated that it would cost about $250,000. "I am consistent. I never give up," HJ said. "And that is why my plan came together."

In 1902 and 1903, HJ began suggesting to the residents of Hollywood that many of their problems could be solved by incorporating into a city. He suggested that the new city be called Hollywood. As he spoke before numerous civic groups, he was an impressive figure, erect, elegantly dressed in a three-piece suit, imparting a highly polished presentation. His words were as enticing as a cool glass of lemonade in the desert as he stated:

> It has a core residential area and clearly laid out streets that make it perfect to become a city. If we incorporate into a city we will have increased service levels without increasing expenditures, improved road maintenance without increasing spending, superior traffic enforcement and law enforcement, better local control without limitations of

County policy, gain local control of planning for ultimate growth, improve citizen access to local government and improve local government's responsiveness. Hollywood should be incorporated.

Nothing stimulated HJ more than a challenge, especially one that people said he could not accomplish.

Daeida Wilcox Beveridge was opposed to the idea and attempted to stop the incorporation by collecting signatures on a petition opposing the issue. Whenever he heard her name, HJ thought that her artificial intelligence was no competition for her innate stupidity. Why was she such a busybody? HJ's passionate appeal fortunately outweighed others' objections, and the majority felt as he did. Later that year, at an election held on November 14, 1903, the residents of Hollywood voted to incorporate as an independent city. The vote was eighty-eight for incorporation and seventy-seven against.

The most pressing problem at that time was the control of sheep being herded through the city from the San Fernando Valley to the railroad station in Los Angeles. To solve this problem, the eight-member board passed an ordinance outlawing the driving of herds of horses, cattle, sheep, goats, hogs, and mules through the streets of Hollywood unless they were accompanied by competent men.

Business of an objectionable character was discouraged. Saloons and its kindred evils were unknown in Hollywood. HJ recorded on the deeds of trust that these types of businesses were not allowed. Both the Home and Sunset telephone companies had local exchanges, and the service costs were the same as in the city. Incandescent street lights were liberally used, producing striking effects along the rolling grounds of the foothills.

The name Hollywood became so popular that several ambitious tract-openers outside the city applied the name with various prefixes to their lands. They did this in order to tap in on HJ's success.

While HJ stayed busy that year, Ross attended his first whirl-wind week at Harvard Military School in North Hollywood. The school had been established in a barley field (now the corner of Western Avenue and Venice Boulevard). From the early morning shower to lessons, meals, games, prep, and lights out, Ross's life was now controlled and ordered by the masters of the school. To Ross, it was a place to learn, a place to play sports, and a place to make friends. Going to Harvard was Ross's choice as well as theirs.

His natural charm and whimsical manner attracted girls, to whom he warmly responded. He felt that girls were a foreign species, like his tiny insect collection, to be examined and handled with care. Gigi trusted that he would not be examining them too closely.

Chapter Thirteen

The Whitley household was located on the corner of Hollywood Boulevard and Whitley Avenue. It consisted of a cook, a housemaid, a governess, a butler/gardener/chauffer, and a laundress. The house was spacious, with high ceilings and many large rooms. Gigi furnished the downstairs in a very formal way. There was a lovely marble mantle and gorgeous chandeliers. Gigi even convinced HJ to order special china from France, Havilland, which he had monogrammed with a *W*. The dishes were etched with a gold border. To accompany the new china, he ordered a four-drawer set of silver. Grace loved the little salt spoons. When HJ and Gigi were out, she would sit and use them to feed her new kitten treats.

The library was filled with a standard set of books in addition to some of Uncle Samuel's religious books. Besides books pertaining to business, a good deal of fiction came into the house, as HJ was an avid reader. It was astonishing how quickly he could complete a book. Some of his favorite writers were Dickens, Scott, and Thackeray. He reread their books several times. When HJ visited someone's house for the first time, he always looked at their bookshelves. Relating to people seemed easier when he knew the types of books they read.

HJ was a severe judge of what his children read, wrote, and how they expressed themselves. He held them to the highest standard of conduct. Unfortunately, this resulted in a very rigid life for them. He expected them to conform to the conventional pattern of high society. To counteract HJ's sternness, Gigi gave almost no discipline. Perhaps she felt a little guilty for neglecting the children and spending so much time preparing for parties and events. At times, HJ would even treat Gigi as his grown-up child, which greatly compromised her ability to discipline the children.

HJ and Gigi settled into their routines of married life. HJ slept on the left side of the bed, and Gigi preferred the right. Gigi loved fluffy pillows; HJ preferred his hard. For breakfast, he drank several cups of strong coffee while Gigi preferred a cup of tea, lightly sweetened with sugar. One thing they did share was the daily newspaper.

The popular drift toward tropical and semi-tropical plants was alluring to Gigi. She loved the outdoors and insisted that HJ allow her to make their home a showplace. Gigi instructed the gardener to plant over two thousand plants and trees. Two of the more interesting plants were coffee and pineapple.

To make the move from downtown Los Angeles into their new home complete, Gigi decided to have a housewarming party. Although they had lived in the home for several years, it was now one of the first homes to have electric lights. It would be a special treat to have an evening affair since few of their friends owned homes with electricity. On a Saturday evening, a party took place in their beautiful new residence. It was a small party since the town was small and there were only a few families there at that time. In fact, only a dozen houses could be seen from their house. HJ increased Gigi's monthly household allowance so that no expense would be spared to make the evening a success. It took Gigi some time to write the three hundred invitations and deliver them. Gigi mailed those tiny, well-written invitations to her city friends and went by carriage to personally deliver them to the homes nearby so she could meet her new neighbors. Thankfully, Gigi employed a very competent housekeeper to take care of their home while she spent her entire day promoting the upcoming party.

Gigi's housewarming gown was beautiful. It was a deep shade of copper with beading that was almost a coffee color. The bodice of the gown featured a high neckline with a cream-colored lace lining extending beyond the collar. She chose a dress with a fitted bodice because she had a tiny waistline. The sleeves were long and curved and decorated with a beaded appliqué. Her hair was upswept and adorned with colorful satin ribbons and dainty flowers.

The orchestra was located in one of the large, unfurnished parlors, which made it convenient to dance in. An evening breeze waltzed on the notes of the music flowing from the house. The distant mountains turned to jagged black silhouettes surrounded by a dull orange sunset. An elegant supper was served in the spacious yard amongst the flowering gardens. The menu consisted of baron of beef, brown gravy, nips and tatties, coleslaw, celery, bread, butter, jam, coffee and milk, cake and pie. The supper was exceptional, and Gigi was pleased with the shower of compliments she received. The sky was crowded with stars as their numerous friends left. Their friends wished them many years of joy and happiness in their new home.

HJ was very enthusiastic about what he did to make the housewarming party a success. He arranged a deal with Moses Sherman and Eli Clark to have a special train run from Los

Angeles to Hollywood. Traveling by streetcar was far less stressful for the guests than traveling by buggy. The guests arrived at the party dust free and relaxed.

Wonderful accounts of the housewarming party filled the newspapers. After its great success, they opened their doors to the newly formed high society. Gigi decided to establish a weekly calling day in her schedule and kept track of all the newcomers to Hollywood. When newcomers had been in their new homes for two weeks, Gigi would put on one of her fancy dresses and make a house call. She would stop in front of a neighbor's home, admiring their flowers from her buggy. The lady of the house would come out and ask her to visit. Gigi would then invite them to meet her other friends and family members at an afternoon tea. Even though this tradition started with her mother long ago, Gigi felt that it added a bit of culture to Hollywood. Gigi served the tea in the garden. For post-meal merriment, her guests gathered in the living room to listen to a string quartet play lovely Scottish-Irish melodies. Their country home became the showplace for miles around.

Gigi invited the women of the Ocean View Tract to a delightful reception at the Hollywood Hotel on Monday afternoon, April 23, 1903. Over fifty women attended the luncheon. She hoped that many lifelong friendships would begin that day. Gigi believed that if they could develop a spirit of common interest with each other, it would help the town of Hollywood grow. The bits of gossip that Gigi heard that day were especially interesting. HJ intently listened to the stories that evening.

Gigi encouraged the new residents by giving them a little pep talk. "I think this fine Western country is going to have a wonderful effect on all of us. There is such freedom, loyalty, and kindness in the heart of people here in Hollywood. You know what scientists say: 'It is the real America.' I feel sure we are going to have such a good time together shaping this new society."

In appreciation for all the work Gigi did in the community, the ladies of Hollywood gave her a farewell party on April 25, 1903, at the Hollywood Hotel. She planned an extended trip to the East. The day was most delightful to her. At the banquet, Col. GJ Griffith presided as toastmaster. In his introductory remarks, he paid a most gracious tribute to the ladies. As a finale, the Reverend A. Porter entertained the guests with a musical program.

HJ left his office early as exhaustion from work covered him like a spider web trapping a fly. As he entered the house, he called for Gigi; but she had not returned from visiting a friend in Pasadena. For a moment, a pang of jealousy crept into his heart; and he tried to push it away. HJ told himself that he should get some sleep, but he could not force himself to close his eyes. He began to brood; he panicked and lost control. He knew that the panic he was feeling was really the fear of abandonment. He let jealousy cloud his judgment.

HJ raved and tore around. Grace locked herself in her room until Gigi came home at eight that evening. HJ impatiently watched the arrival of every streetcar. It was the first time that he had been home from work before twelve for ages. When Gigi got off the streetcar, HJ's mouth tightened to a thin line of anger as he shouted, "Where have you been with that man?"

Gigi bristled as she said, "That is silly. You know I have been over to see Mrs. Black."

HJ took hold of her and said, "You cannot fool me that way."

Too afraid to speak, a large, hard knot lodged in Gigi's throat. Gigi managed to free herself from him and ran as fast as she could into the house. His eyes looked frantic, like a trapped animal's eyes. His jealousy prevailed over his good sense. Grace sat looking out the window in fright.

When Gigi ran upstairs, he followed. Gigi went into the bedroom, closed the door, and locked it. HJ thumped and pounded on the door so hard that Grace began to cry. Gigi was so nervous that she softly opened the window and then unlocked the door. She then got out on the roof. Carefully, Gigi crawled around to Grace's room and climbed in the window. HJ kept pounding and pounding for some time until he finally tried the door handle and found that it was unlocked. He went in and looked all around for Gigi. He then went to Grace's room to ask her where Gigi might be. As he pounded on the door, Grace cracked it open. Grace started crying as she told him, "Mama is on the roof! She is going to fall."

HJ suddenly came to his senses and picked up little Grace and said, "Mama will be fine. Go back to bed."

Gigi was so upset that HJ put her to bed and sent for the doctor. After everything settled down, HJ went out and walked up the hills. He did not return until midnight. The next day, Gigi received two dozen roses and a two-pound box of chocolates. The note read, "I cannot explain my actions. I only know that I love you and cannot stand the thought of sharing you with anyone. I promise this will never happen again."

That was the only time it did happen. HJ never revealed why he acted the way he did, and he died with it unexplained.

HJ anticipated the result of the vote before he read about it in the newspaper. There were lively discussions about the pros and cons of alcohol, and HJ believed that it was in the best interest of society to keep them from harm's way. Los Angeles breweries and wholesale liquor dealers spent considerable amounts of money and energy in an effort to swing the election their way. As he read the morning paper, he was not surprised with the outcome. On January 30, 1904, the voters in Hollywood decided, by a vote of 113 to 96, to banish liquor from the city, except when it was being sold for medicinal purposes. Neither hotels nor restaurants were allowed to serve guests wine or liquor before or after meals. Ministers celebrated, and those who supported the sale of alcohol were nowhere to be seen.

Quite a transformation took place in the appearance of the little village of Hollywood. Many changes transpired since HJ first beheld it. New boulevards were established. All eyes turned toward the new town with pride and jealousy. The papers could say nothing but praise: "Sunset Boulevard," they wrote, "is finished at last, and it is coming into great favor. If Mr. Whitley never does another thing in his name, this will stand as a monument to him for all time to come."

Getting the right-of-way for the streetcar line was no easy job. HJ realized that it must be done in a roundabout way. People on the route hindered the progress for weeks at a time with their unreasonable demands and selfishness. No one seemed to care about the good it would do the community but just how it would help their pocketbooks. HJ used to say it was worse than getting the right-of-way through the Indian land in Oklahoma.

The Examiner ran an article that credited HJ Whitley, EP Clark, and General MH Sherman with construction of Sunset Boulevard. Mr. Stansburg was hired as the contractor to perform the work. He had over three hundred men and 250 teams of horses working day and night. Mr. Stansburg said that under his contract, he moved more than 7 million cubic feet of dirt.

In May 1904, the grand opening of Sunset Boulevard was a spectacular event. HJ was thrilled when he learned that over two thousand people attended the celebration. People drove there in an assortment of vehicles, eagerly awaiting the signal to start down the new street. At one o'clock, the Soldiers Home Band began to serenade the crowd and the parade started. The procession included people on foot and horseback, in carriages, automobiles, and packed into streetcars. To add a festive feel to the parade, American flags flew from homes and businesses throughout the route. The roadway was smooth and easy to drive. HJ took pride in designing one of the best highways in the United States. A small fortune had been spent to cut through the hills, quite a monumental feat. The parade wound around curves, and people waved to onlookers as they passed by. They were thrilled to be one of the first to use the new road.

HJ and Gigi were invited by their friend General MH Sherman to ride in a private car of the Los Angeles Pacific Electric, the Mermaid. When the parade reached Hollywood, the vehicles passed down Prospect Avenue (currently Hollywood Boulevard) to the Hollywood Hotel. When the parade ended, HJ and Gigi were invited to the residence of General HG Otis, the owner of the *Los Angeles Times*, for lunch. Refreshments were served on the porch of the residence. The house was delightfully decorated for the occasion.

It was arranged that HJ would be the first to address the crowd. He was taken by carriage to an elevated podium across the street from the Otises' home. HJ paused for a moment in optimistic assessment of the crowd before him. Every bit of the lawn and street was occupied by men in black and gray. Many of the women wore dresses in multiple hues—emerald, crimson, sapphire—and hats with ribbons and flowers. Sunlight fell between clusters of swiftly dancing clouds, revealing a scene that was festive and cheerful. HJ's speech was the shortest of all: "This is but the beginning. We hope to see the boulevard lined with shrubbery and lighted by electric lights, which will extend from Santa Monica to the new million-dollar government building in Los Angeles." A roar radiated through the crowd as HJ drew a picture of what was to come. Several other speakers followed HJ, attempting to take credit for the work.

HJ and Gigi were saddened when they received the news that Eliza Otis died. Although her illness lasted more than a year, it was hard to see a friend lose his beloved wife. HJ tried to keep his emotions from surfacing and wished that he could figure out some way to miss the funeral. He hated anything dealing with death. All his important business associates would be there, along with the reporters from the *Los Angeles Times*. This was something he could not afford to miss.

The funeral was on Tuesday, November 15, at 1:30 in the afternoon at "The Bivouac." HJ and Gigi sat in the third row. HJ sat silently as one small tear ran down his cheek.

Sitting, observing him at breakfast, Gigi realized that over the last few weeks, since the completion of Sunset Boulevard, HJ's attitude had changed. He was reserved, distant, and not as friendly as he usually was. She ascribed it to him being overworked and fatigued. He met his business associates at night for dinner, hashing out compromises over steaks and cigars. Work was so busy. He wasted so much time on pointless meetings to keep everyone happy. What was troubling to HJ was the gap between the magnitude of work to be completed and the smallness of individuals—the ease with which everyone was distracted by the petty and trivial, their chronic avoidance of tough decisions, their seeming inability to build a working consensus to tackle any big problem. Gigi could tell that he felt it would be even more hectic in the next few weeks. HJ was overworked because he was a victim of his own excellence.

Gigi saw it as her job to make sure that HJ knew how destructive this pattern of work was to their family life. She wanted to make sure it was as painful for him as it was for her.

"You have got to stop or it will kill you," she shrieked.

"I know."

"You have got to."

"I know, I know."

Her voice rose. "You aren't listening to me."

"Yes, I am."

"No, you aren't." Gigi stood over him, glaring, looking down on him like a conscience.

Finally, he would get up and escape to his work.

"That woman," he would complain, "could nag a flea off a dog."

Sometimes Gigi got so wound up that she would come out on the porch to press her point, and HJ would climb onto the streetcar to get away, all the time saying, "I hear you. I hear you." And then HJ would be bouncing down the road, safely away; and his guilt would vanish into the air as thoughts of upcoming business filled his mind.

Chapter Fourteen

While he was finishing up his work in Hollywood, HJ organized a group of businessmen who formed a new syndicate. The syndicate was headed by HJ. He decided to buy land along the Santa Fe Railroad at a place called Corcoran Junction and open up a town site. As the president and largest owner in the Security Land and Loan Company, he successfully financed the thriving farming community of Corcoran. The outstanding productivity of the area encouraged HJ to purchase 32,000 acres of land.

The large land holdings and extensive improvements were to be looked after by Roy Milner, HJ's personal secretary. One drawback was that Roy would be away from the office more. Sometimes, late in the evening, HJ missed Roy's companionship as well as his expertise with office equipment. HJ only typed with two fingers. The truth was that he hardly noticed when his young secretary was gone. In fact, he was often so engrossed that he barely noticed Roy even when he was standing at the desk right in front of him.

Before long, a brick hotel had been erected in Corcoran. HJ realized from experience how significant a hotel was to a new town. Where would the new residents stay until their homes were completed without it? HJ stayed at the hotel, where he met with men whose minds were on investments and real estate deals, talking business into the late hours of the night. Because of prohibition, every deed inside the town would state, "No liquor may be sold." The syndicate would end up employing over one hundred men to carry out different aspects of the town's expansion.

HJ and Gigi were gone for about two weeks up north. HJ was sure that they would find natural gas in Corcoran. It would supply power for the new factories. So he told the farmers to go ahead with their planting. He was planning to start one of the finest nurseries in that section of the county.

They had just finished breakfast when Roy rushed up onto the porch of the hotel, jerked the door open with a crash, and slammed it shut behind him and rushed into the dining room to tell them the news. That April morning in 1906, the residents of the little town of Corcoran saw water in its large ditch being thrown violently from side to side. Even the ground under their feet seemed to shift and tremble. The next day, they heard that several hundred miles to the north, a great earthquake had taken place in San Francisco, and the shock rocked the country as far south as Corcoran. HJ and Gigi were stunned when they heard the news. They could scarcely believe that more than four and one-half square miles of San Francisco was burned and crumbled, becoming like a desolate desert. Nearly two hundred thousand people out of San Francisco's population of 450,000 were left homeless by the disaster. Many of HJ's friends at the Southern Pacific and Santa Fe Railroads immediately closed their ticket offices and gave away tickets so that all who chose could escape the scenes of destruction and desolation.

Unfortunately for Corcoran, the San Francisco earthquake caused water to keep coming down from the mountains, filling the ditches for two months and bringing water all around the homes. It was after five when they first noticed the strange occurrence. The evening light was prowling down the street and through the window. HJ and Gigi could see a silver line off in the distance. It was found to be the edge of Tulare Lake, constantly growing larger. Eventually, the water could be seen within a few feet of the hotel's steps. Luckily, this was only a problem for a short while.

The land in Corcoran was sold for approximately fifteen dollars an acre. The initial problem with the Corcoran area was that there was not enough water to irrigate the land on a regular basis. To solve that problem, alfalfa was planted in tulles around the rim of the lake. Eventually, tall, protective levees and dikes were built to control the water source. Once this was done, the growth of Corcoran was steady.

HJ was quite successful in promoting sugar beets in the Corcoran valley. He was instrumental in organizing the construction of the sugar beet factory at a cost over a million dollars. However, HJ felt that his largest contribution to the area was the introduction of cotton. Corcoran became known as the "Farming Capital of California." The valuable information he gained on his trip to Egypt was instrumental in this undertaking.

After HJ had completed his business in Corcoran and saw that the town was beginning to thrive, he returned to Hollywood. Finding additional land for sale, HJ purchased it, planning to develop it as the town grew. Additionally, he decided to open the streets between Wilcox and Whitley. He planned to build small cottages on these streets for people who could not afford larger homes. Gigi was sad to see large groves cut down but realized that progress was a driving force of its own. Wanting to make a lasting statement on the quickly growing community, Gigi asked HJ to give many of the streets in Whitley Heights family names.

Gigi was concerned because night after night, HJ got out of bed when he thought she was asleep. Sometimes Gigi heard him walking up and down the hall; sometimes he went downstairs to read. In the morning, she found books left open by his chair. In the course of the winter, he got through most of the dark, old books he kept in his bookcase. Some nights, HJ did not come home at all or could not. Gigi was never sure whether he was with a business associate or walking off his anxiety in the streets. He was so strained and so uncommunicative that she dared not ask him what was bothering him. Gigi was left to endure in silence, realizing that she was no help to him. He was like a life-size, primeval grizzly bear hibernating for the winter. Gigi resolved that all she could do was pray.

It did not help Gigi's mental attitude to brood over not seeing HJ. Business demands were so heavy that he stayed away in Corcoran for nearly two weeks. He begged Gigi not to be impatient with him for his lengthy absences from home.

"You know how much work I have right now," he said with more than a hint of frustration.

"This is about more than your work, HJ," Gigi said. "If I lived in the three-ringed circus, as you do, I would not be able to get my work done. That is what has me so worried. You seem to be your own worst enemy. You have become a glutton, putting more on your plate than you can possibly handle, and the overload is killing you. You insist that you have family values, but then you structure your life so as to ensure that I get less and less of your time."

HJ never seemed to get, or want, a break from his busy life. HJ knew better. His family values were tarnished and worn. He betrayed them more often than he cared to remember. But there was so much to do. His only remedy was to appear with his arms loaded with gifts and offer warm touches and soft kisses. Some people would call it a complicated existence, would wonder why he did not do it right all the time and spare himself and his family the sorrow. The answer is that if he had, he would have been someone else.

To stop the cycle, Gigi resolved never to let him distress her again. Gigi sat at the table, enjoying the tasty luncheon her faithful housekeeper prepared. Instead of brooding or feeling sorry for herself, she read one of her favorite books as she ate. When lunch was over, Gigi smiled and thanked the housekeeper for the care she bestowed. The housekeeper was a warm and caring woman who enjoyed seeing the whole family gathered around the table. Now, with both the children away at boarding school, she could not understand why HJ gave all his time to business and ignored Gigi.

Gigi, at last, realized that to feel positive feelings of love, happiness, trust, and gratitude, she would have to release and heal the anger and sadness she stored over the years. To heal these negative emotions, Gigi, once more, drew her strength from nature. She was determined not to let negative sentiments ruin her health, so she filled her days by enjoying the garden, trips to the ocean, long walks about the town, and parties. In the early evening, as a special treat, if Gigi knew HJ would be late at work, she would make a cup of tea. Then she headed to the bathroom and would start the water for a hot bubble bath. Gigi liked the way a bath relaxed her—a perfect spot to read her favorite romantic novel. Surrounded by dozens of lit candles, Gigi slipped into the warm water. It was the perfect way to pamper oneself. In the confines of the tub, Gigi lived in the dream world her books presented. It was a perfect world. As her emotions began to rise, she felt better.

1906 was a busy year for Theodore Roosevelt. It seemed that at least once a week, there was mention of him in the newspaper. Teddy won the Nobel Peace Prize for his help in ending the Russo-Japanese War. He also sailed on the battleship *USS Louisiana* to Panama. Teddy read *The Jungle* by Upton Sinclair. He then ordered an investigation of the conditions of the meat-packing industry. As a result of the investigation, Congress passed the Meat Inspection Act and the Food and Drugs Act. Gigi wondered if HJ ever regretted that he had not become a politician.

The year was filled with glittering social events. They went to jolly little dinners, society balls, banquets, receptions, and theater outings. The parties seemed to follow one another in an endless succession. Most of them were not brief events, more like never-ending rituals. One part Gigi did enjoy was wearing a variety of elaborate gowns. On HJ's arm, she would parade into the dining area. They were usually seated at a long table that could accommodate a multitude of forks, knives, and spoons. Each course was served on a different type of china. HJ made sure that Gigi followed the strict protocol of the day, which required her to alternate speaking with the person on the right and left with the change of each course.

As Gigi matured, she learned to use her intellectual ability to gain knowledge from other people and to use their knowledge as her own. A dinner companion or a casual acquaintance provided her with information that she could use in conversation with HJ. He was not aware how little she actually knew, but he was impressed with the variety of subjects that she talked about with apparent ease. Gigi enjoyed the large parties they gave that enabled her to learn the latest happenings in Hollywood. The new friends helped fill the empty spots left by HJ's absences.

HJ's social code demanded a great deal of self-discipline. Social obligations were sacred to him; no matter how Gigi felt, party attendance should be given first priority. He refused to let anything interfere with his business endeavors. When HJ was just a young man, he set this pace and tone for his life. To him, the burning issues were wealth and power.

The Whitleys hosted one of the largest, most elaborate receptions ever given in Hollywood. Their home, one of the most beautiful in the entire valley, lent itself admirably to such events. About eight hundred invitations were sent, and it seemed as though everyone responded yes. Gigi's invitation list became so extensive that she sometimes felt it impossible to include everyone she knew. Among the many up-and-coming newly rich, it was somewhat difficult to make a fair choice. They invited Hollywood's elite in all its dazzling glory. For her, it was a great expenditure of time, energy, and vast amounts of money.

The reception was one of the most enjoyable ever given in Southern California, and it was a farewell party for Gigi. She designed the party to allow guests to wander among flowers, feasting their eyes on the beautiful garden until the pathway brought them to an open-air dining room. There, the guests dined alfresco amid the perfumes of flowers. Of course, no party would be complete without music. The party was lively and crowded. After finishing their dinner, they watched the musicians and talked amongst themselves. Voices drifted across the yard, laced now and then with laughter that rang like chimes waltzing in the breeze.

The family planned another extensive trip to Europe. Gigi hoped that HJ would close the house and travel with her and Grace for seven months. As HJ thought it over, he realized there was no possible way for him to be away from business for that long. He could see enough in three months. The trip would carry them to Holland, Denmark, Germany, Switzerland, England, Scotland, France, Italy, and Belgium. Gigi was at her best when accompanied by HJ; but when he returned to the States, it took her several weeks to adjust.

Even as Gigi wandered about the world over the years, seeing amazing sights, there was always one kind of occasion remembered and yearned for above the rest. Her favorite time was when she had HJ all to herself, away from business.

Grace's favorite part of the trip had been when HJ acted as a gondolier, taking her out on the Venice canals. He sung along with the other boatmen. She loved being the center of his attention. He called her "little angel," and she never doubted that she stood first in his heart. While in London, Grace became quite an expert in the game Diablo. When she returned to Hollywood she taught the game to her friends.

In Paris, they dined in strange places, ordering the specialties of the house. Gigi and HJ kept a leisurely pace as they made their way along the Seine, looking at many secondhand stores. HJ bought books, books, and more books everywhere they went. HJ was well versed in French, so he did all the bargaining in Paris.

Picasso was in his blue and pink period, and the Wright brothers were making aviation history. Paris was the hub of the fashion world. By now, tailored suits were firmly established in the fashion world. HJ despised them. He loudly objected to Gigi's tailor-made clothing. They lacked femininity and challenged male authority. Women seemed to be making a clear statement that they deserved and wanted more independence. HJ saw the new styles as a threat.

Tailor-made clothes were ideal for traveling by all "in the know." Gigi ordered several tailored skirts of wool and serge. Their elongated trumpet bell shape fit her perfectly. She would wear them with shirtwaist blouses. Gigi needed traveling suits for their weekend trips traveling about the countryside. Her major purchases were skirts, blouses, hats, and handbags. They bought several additional steamer trunks to handle them all. After touring Paris, HJ returned home with the trunk filled with books and clothes to his ever-pressing business.

It was a blistery afternoon when Grace and Gigi arrived in Edinburgh, Scotland. Gigi was greeted by a short, old man with thick, gray hair and horn-rimmed glasses who introduced himself as Graham. After giving her a brief tour of the house and showing her the rooms, he vanished. She was instantly homesick. Later that night, Gigi continued to be depressed in a way she could not define. Gigi felt lonely without HJ and could not stand the boredom.

Grace became very ill, so much so that Gigi could not even go for her strolls along the roads or up to the desolate graveyards to search for distant relatives. Cemeteries were intriguing to her. They brought her perspective and helped her realize the delicacy of life. There was an unusual calmness about them. Since walks were out of the question, Gigi took out a pen and began to compose a love song to HJ. In a few days, Grace was well and the cloud over her lifted. They continued their travels up north.

Gigi awoke as the day was breaking. Outside, all was still except the splashing waves along the shore. The window of Gigi's room overlooked Stonehaven. It was a few miles from Dunnator

Castle. She sat gazing at the scene as the misty, black sky began to be touched by red and gold. Gradually, the red paled to a diminishing peach and the gold to lightening shades of yellow. Not far away, Gigi could hear men joking as they walked down the seashore. As the day grew light enough to start casting shadows, the streets began to show some life. Nature inspired her in a special way. Gigi drew great strength from the environment.

Instead of heading to another country, Gigi decided to go back to Edinburgh and spend time with Grace in tea rooms, libraries, and local shops. She wanted to learn more about their family's Scottish heritage. Gigi even decided to buy HJ a kilt and bagpipes. She bought Grace a dancing skirt and found a young lassie that would come to the hotel each day to teach her country dancing. Before they left Scotland, Gigi promised Grace that she could continue dancing lessons when she returned to the States.

Fashion was extremely important to Gigi. She enjoyed wearing the latest trends. She felt compelled to wear the norms of fashion to appeal to the public. Whether consciously or subconsciously, Gigi put a lot of effort into selecting her outfits for herself or possibly to impress her friends. Whether it is fair or not, a person's first judgment of another is based on clothing. People she knew who wore things that were out of season had been rudely stared at, whispered about, or worse—they had been cited as examples of fashion faux pas. When Gigi returned from her trip to Paris, she remarked to her friends about the many extravagant gowns that HJ purchased for her.

Gigi was glad she received a bounty of invitations that year. The parties gave her a chance to display her new wardrobe. Gigi loved parties. It seemed to her that entertaining to promote business was on HJ's list of socially acceptable activities.

That year, Gigi aspired to give the finest parties of the season. To start the year off, HJ and Gigi hosted a masquerade party at the Hollywood Hotel. There were about three hundred guests present—all dressed as famous characters of history. The hotel's reception room was beautifully decorated in red, white, and blue. At nine o'clock, a great march was lead by EW Elliott, who was dressed as Simple Simon, accompanied by his wife, who was dressed as Martha Washington. HJ dressed as Uncle Sam, and Gigi was Betsy Ross. Gigi permitted Grace to pick her own costume. She came as Cleopatra. The party was an enormous success, which gave rise to the problem of making the next party even more spectacular.

By now, Gigi was a natural hostess, with a flair and friendliness toward all whom she knew. Every party Gigi gave proceeded with ease and grace. The dinner was perfect. The service was perfect. Even the background music was perfect.

The objective of the parties was always the same: to forge business relationships with clients that translated into business and, ultimately, profits. HJ viewed these special events just like any other service he was selling. The presentation of the party determined if it was a success or failure. His goal was not to have fun. It was an opportunity to make personal connections, to learn more about his colleagues, his clients, and his employees. He would use this information to his advantage during the coming years.

HJ was way ahead of his time. He was into networking even before the concept was developed. He understood how to influence his existing contact base of family, friends, professional colleagues, and other acquaintances to generate other contacts.

These expanding set of contacts were gradually built into genuine, mutually beneficial relationships. His goal was to advance his business interest while simultaneously assisting others in advancing theirs.

The next party Gigi and HJ gave was held at their residence on September 15, 1906. A large staff was hired to make the residence picturesque. Each room was decorated with flowers whose colors harmonized with the walls. The dining room was a perfect marvel with its wealth of tropical fruits. The produce grew in the nearby valley. HJ enjoyed feasting on pineapples, oranges, and figs. He was keen on the fact that the party advertised the many luscious fruits the region offered and left a lasting impression on his guests. HJ hired two special cars to bring guests from Los Angeles to Hollywood. He considered it a pint-sized party since only 150 guests had been invited.

The sight of the tropical fruits and flowers was not the only treat in store for the guests. The entertainment opened with a rendition of Mendelssohn's "Song without Words" on the piano. Then Floy Galpin read a paper that gave a sketch of upcoming events in Hollywood and the marvelous growth that had taken place. The guests enjoyed hearing stories of HJ's business triumphs.

Seven hundred invitations were sent by HJ and Gigi for an evening reception to be held at their home located on Hollywood Boulevard and Wilcox Avenue. They hosted an evening that was of one of the largest and most elaborate social functions of the season. The grounds surrounding the Whitley mansion presented a beautiful picture. Incandescent lights were strung about the grounds from tree to tree and in the shrubbery and vines. Beneath the tropical trees and among the flowers, seats had been constructed for the guests. On the veranda, Arends's orchestra played Broadway songs from *Florodora*, *A Chinese Honeymoon*, *The Wizard of Oz*, and many other of her favorite tunes. HJ hired men to move Gigi's piano to the veranda. Beautifully decorated tables were placed on the drives and walks. HJ and Gigi received the guests on the large porch at the south wing of the house. They were assisted by forty of their close friends.

Gigi received many compliments on her French gown. It was fashioned of cream *crepe de Chine*. The skirt was elaborately trimmed with rose point lace. It fell in graceful folds. Gigi wore a necklace of rare amethysts. Several smaller stones were pinned among the folds of her gown.

To add a little pizzazz to the party, HJ hired vaudeville dancers to perform the Cakewalk. Couples with their arms linked above the elbow promenaded in a dignified manner, alternating a series of short, hopping steps with a series of very high, kicking steps. They would bow low, waving canes and hats. The name Cakewalk originated in the South when plantation owners, for entertainment, would hold dance contests for their slaves. The winning dance couple would receive a cake. At the end of the dance, the waiters brought little cakes to each table for the guests to enjoy. At HJ's parties, everyone had fun. On the top of each cake was written, "That Takes the Cake!" After the Cakewalk, the guests were invited to enjoy the ballroom music that followed.

HJ occasionally let his eyes rest on Gigi. He often told her that she was a woman he was proud of. Prosperity became her. HJ and Gigi spoke very little at the party. He whispered to her that he could hardly wait until they were once again alone to enjoy her completely. He hoped that Gigi longed for him too. Later that evening, he caught her eyes and smiled at her sheepishly.

HJ planned a special treat for Gigi that evening. Once the last guest departed, Gigi heard the band strike up her favorite song. HJ turned and softly said, "May I have this dance, my love? You were the most beautiful woman at the ball."

They walked to the porch, holding hands as HJ sang, "I Love You Truly," which caused her eyes to glisten and one small tear to roll down her cheek. HJ revealed his love to her in the most amazing ways. After two chorus lines of the tune, they politely said good night and retreated to the bedroom upstairs.

HJ enjoyed attending parties with Gigi on his arm. He realized that he missed many things that were going on during the party. When they returned to their room, they laid awake in bed while Gigi gossiped to HJ about who said what, the goings-on in the community, and undercurrents that seemed to be the privilege of the female conversations. He learned from the past that her information was remarkably accurate, and he would miss it when Gigi was gone with the children. If Gigi heard from one of the ladies that her husband was about to set out on a business venture, she was inevitably right. He looked forward to her latest nuggets, and they would talk into the wee hours of the morning.

Their friends gave them a farewell party. Gigi was moving to Berkeley for several months. Ross, a favorite member of the young social set, was attending Stanford University.

Grace attended Miss Head's Fashionable School for Girls. At the school, she received a progressive education and was taught to be independent and politically aware. Grace was absolutely taken by an elegant and brilliant senior girl who took interest in her and what she had to say. Grace blossomed in a way that HJ and Gigi began to regret, rebelling against the strict norms of society. It was the beginnings of the woman that she would later become.

When Ross was sixteen, he was ready to go to Stanford; but HJ was opposed. He said that if Ross went to Berkeley he would give his consent, but he did not want Ross to live in a fraternity house. He was still very young, and HJ felt that he should live with his mother. Gigi moved the furniture and fixed up a place near Berkeley to live, but Ross would not go to that university. He said that his credits would be higher in Stanford. If he could not go there, he did not want to go at all. Six months passed. Neither father nor son came to an agreement, so Gigi made plans while HJ was away on business to enroll Ross at Stanford.

They returned home for the summer. One afternoon, HJ unexpectedly returned from work. When entering through the door, a strong odor of smoke drifted down the stairs as he uttered, "I smell smoke!"

In the dim light from the window, he saw a figure sitting in the overstuffed chair. "Ross has a few friends in his room. Perhaps they are smoking," Gigi replied.

Without another word, HJ rushed up the stairs and gave the door a decided knock. Before anyone opened it, he pushed it with a bang; and there sat two young men, leaning back in their chairs, with their feet on the table. Cigarette smoke drifted casually over their heads, losing itself in the rafters. One of the young men coughed.

Sensing the tension, the young man dropped the butt into his almost-empty cup of coffee, it sharply sizzling in its death throes.

"Ross, are you smoking?"

"No, but I am going to."

"Well, if you do, I will disinherit you!"

With that, HJ slammed the door and stomped down the staircase, exiting the house with an attitude on his face. He walked down the lane to a sharp jog that led him to an open field. Alone, he looked off into the distance and thought in silence. HJ was a puritan at heart and felt that smoking spoiled the fresh air he was entitled to have. Plus, he hated anything burning in the house that might be left unattended.

As he looked into the field to calm himself, HJ could not help but think that Ross did not seem to take his education seriously. He would not tolerate such obstinance. HJ was the head of the family, expecting to be obeyed. If Ross did not want to become a real man on his own, HJ would have to increase the pressure to ensure that he did. When his friends were gone, HJ had a long talk with Ross, advising him, "Man is the maker of his own fortune...He is either self-made or never made. By industry, diligence, and good use of leisure time, Ross, you can become almost anything you please...Idleness is a curse."

Ross should not only work hard but have character. He wanted to be sure that Ross would cultivate good manners, for manners made the man. He would encourage him to improve himself by studying the lives of men who had become great— learn how they succeeded and why others failed. It was important that Ross always be a gentleman. He was born to be a gentleman—educated and brought up as such. HJ wanted him to know that it was now up to him to remain so. Still, he had a nagging thought. Would he ever be able to teach Ross that the pain of self-discipline was only momentary and the payoff of good habits was long-lasting?

When would Ross realize that the actions he was now embracing would soon become bundles of bad habits? HJ wished that Ross would give more heed to his conduct since he was still young and shapeable. Ross was rolling the dice, and HJ was concerned that evil would win rather than good. He felt that even the smallest vice would leave a scar on Ross's character. If Ross would faithfully keep busy each hour of the working day, he would definitely become a success. Why did young people not know this truth in advance, when it counted the most?

With HJ gone, Gigi let the events of the last few minutes sift through her mind. Gigi had high standards of what a wife and mother should be but not the faintest notion how to obtain them. She realized how trying she must have been to HJ. Gigi really was never taught how to raise her children. She saw how funny some of the early tragedies of their married life had been. Gigi realized that HJ did not just want his son to be a successful businessman but also a gentleman. The tension this created was dividing him from his family.

There is a big difference between how boys and girls view their identities and the expectations they each have concerning their life. Gigi needed to persevere if she was going to understand Ross. She did not want to have a "What can I do?" attitude. There was a meeting point. It was up to her. It might take time and a number of attempts, but Gigi would never give up. She was sure that the struggles between HJ and Ross were not a sign of failure but of something new being born. Gigi would look for the good in Ross and find it. She was instrumental in helping Ross by supporting his relationship with his father. HJ did not foresee and plan as Gigi did, but he did love his son. Maybe all the commotion was just a sign that Ross was becoming a man and wanted to stand on his own two feet.

Ross sat in his room after the talk with his father. He was not sure why he put off doing many of the things HJ demanded of him. Avoiding the temporary unpleasantness of the demands only left him feeling guilty. He understood that he was not doing what was right. He regretted not being more disciplined like his father. The fun activities of life always called so loudly. With HJ off at work most of the time and Gigi a pushover, Ross found it simple to put things off until tomorrow, or the next day, or the next. Then, if he was lucky, Gigi would get one of the staff to do it for him to keep peace in the house. Ross never did learn to complete his work, and Gigi was partially to blame for that bad habit.

With all the changes taking place in society, there was still much to be learned. Growth was slow. Livery stables were still outnumbering garages. More wagons were hitched in front of stores than parked cars. The Toluca Stage was still running from the bank at the corner of Hollywood Boulevard into the San Fernando Valley. And Hollywood was still very much fruit orchards and flower gardens.

Photo Gallery

Hobart Johnstone Whitley at the beginning of his career in 1875.

Hobart Johnstone Whitley in 1888, age forty.

HJ, Gigi, Ross, and the nanny are standing outside a tepee in Guthrie, Oklahoma, shortly after the opening of the Oklahoma Territory.

In 1894 HJ purchased a magnificent three-story imposing Queen Anne-
style home. It was located at 839 Flower Street, between Eighth and
Ninth Street in the heart of Los Angeles. Grace, Ross, and Gigi are
standing on the massive front porch, and Gigi's sister, Mary, is standing
at the left side of the home near the lawn.

A rare family photo of HJ, Gigi, Ross, and Grace.

Grace, age five, is pictured standing in
the lobby of HJ Whitley Company.

A striking panoramic picture of the valley the way it appeared in the
early 1900s. Hollywood was mainly farming land, a narrow belt of
fertile soil and dazzling weather that ran along the foothills of the
Cahuenga valley. Isolated by bad roads and lack of communication,
Hollywood had remained simply a territory of fine orchards and unsurpassed winter vegetable gardens.

HJ finalized the deal with Mina Hurd to purchase the estate in Hollywood on April 11, 1899, for the price of $22,500 gold coin. The new property ran along Prospect Boulevard (now Hollywood Blvd.). The Whitleys' Hollywood holdings now amounted to 480 acres.

Pictured standing, fifth from left. Grace sits in front with the driver.
Gigi took her friends for a Tally-ho ride in the early
days of Hollywood (1901).

Los Angeles-Pacific Boulevard and Development Company

H.J. Whitley, President

M.H. Sherman, Vice President

F.H. Rindge, Vice President

Clem. S. Glass, Secretary

Thos. Keith, Asst. Secretary

This is a map of HJ Whitley's land holdings as of 1900. The Los
Angeles-Pacific Boulevard Company purchased three hundred acres
from HJ Whitley to develop as the Hollywood Ocean View Tract. HJ
Whitley became president of the newly formed privately held corpora-
tion. Many years later he would develop Whitley Heights, Whitley
Hill, and the Whitley Family Estate.

Pictured here is a sketch of the Hollywood Hotel, which was designed and built by HJ Whitley in 1902 on the corner of Hollywood Boulevard and Highland Avenues as an emblem of glamour and elegance for travelers and businessmen alike. It was a large and quiet country resort nestled amid the lemon groves covering more than four acres of ground. It was located in the center of the civic and social life and would be the home of many of the stars over the years.

Los Angeles Times Building after a terrorist bomb levels the building.

This is the opening day of Van Nuys, February 22, 1911.
HJ was the guiding genius who foresaw and developed Hollywood.
He was now the force developing the San Fernando Valley. He divided
the land into three cities, Van Nuys, Marion (now Reseda),
and Owensmouth (now Canoga Park).

General Otis and HJ Whitley just got off the Pacific Electric Car in Van Nuys at the opening day celebrations.

WM. HORSLEY FILM LABORATORIES

DEVELOPING AND PRINTING
IN ALL ITS BRANCHES

WM. HORSLEY, Pres.
ARTHUR T. HORSLEY, Bus. Mgr.
WM. C. HORSLEY, Lab Supt.

TELEPHONE
HOLLYWOOD 3693

6060 SUNSET BOULEVARD
HOLLYWOOD, CALIFORNIA

NOVEMBER 22, 1921

MR. H.J. WHITLEY

638 VAN NUYS BLDG.,

LOS ANGELES, CALIF.

DEAR SIR:

HEREWITH I AM PLACING IN YOUR HANDS MY CHECK FOR $500.00
TO BE USED AS FIRST PAYMENT ON LOT FIVE AND SIX (5 & 6) WHITLEY
HEIGHTS PARK, A PORTION OF LOT FIFTEEN TO TWENTY FOUR (15 TO 24)
HOLLYWOOD GRAND VIEW TRACT, COMMONLY KNOWN AS WHITLEY HEIGHTS
PARK.

I WILL PLACE IN EXCROW $2500.00 ON SIGNING OF AGREEMENT
AND AS SOON AS ESCROW IS COMPLETE AND TITLE READY FOR DELIVERY
I WILL GIVE MY NOTE AND TRUST DEED FOR $2600.00, ALSO NOTE FOR
$800.00 WITHOUT INTEREST, TO BE PAID IN THE EVENT THAT I DO NOT
BUILD ON ABOVE STATED LOT AS PER YOUR RULE. I AGREE TO START
A BUILDING ON SAID LOT THIRTY (30) DAYS AFTER COMPLETION AND
ACCEPTANCE OF PLANS, AND FURTHER AGREE TO CONTINUE WORK DILIGENTLY
ON SAID BUILDING TO COMPLETION WITHIN SIX (6) MONTHS FROM SAID
DATE, PROVIDING HOWEVER, FOR UNAVOIDABLE DELAYS SUCH AS STRIKES,
CLIMATRICAL CONDITIONS, SHORTAGE OF MATERIALS, ETC.

YOURS TRULY,

Wm Horsley

QUOTATIONS SUBJECT TO CHANGE WITHOUT NOTICE AND BASED ON NET CASH SETTLEMENT AT END OF EACH WEEK UNLESS OTHERWISE AGREED UPON
ALL AGREEMENTS ARE CONTINGENT ON STRIKES, ACCIDENTS, AND ALL OTHER DELAYS BEYOND OUR CONTROL.

This a contract with William Horsley to purchase land in
Whitley Heights. In a few years William Horsley would
become a leading executive at Universal Studios.

Gigi is pictured as she traveled by rickshaw while traveling in Japan.
Her tales of her trips to the Orient inspired Sid Grauman to
build the Grauman's Chinese Theatre.

Gigi in 1912 at age forty-five. This is the year the
movie producers first began moving to Hollywood.

On October 26, 1911, the Whitley Estate was used as the set of the first movie ever to be filmed in Hollywood. The movie was filmed in the orange groves by William Horsley, who later became a major player at Universal Studios. In this picture HJ is looking at the camera with Ross and Grace sitting nearby.

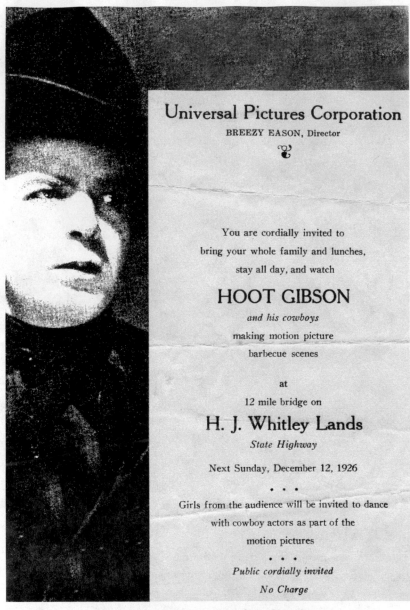

Universal Pictures Corporation

BREEZY EASON, Director

You are cordially invited to
bring your whole family and lunches,
stay all day, and watch

HOOT GIBSON

and his cowboys
making motion picture
barbecue scenes

at

12 mile bridge on

H. J. Whitley Lands

State Highway

Next Sunday, December 12, 1926

• • •

Girls from the audience will be invited to dance
with cowboy actors as part of the
motion pictures

• • •

Public cordially invited

No Charge

This is an advertisement for a film that
was to be produced on Whitley land.

The Whitley Heights sign was the first sign to light the Hollywood hills. If you look closely at the upper left of the picture, you can see an H, the first letter of the Hollywood sign being constructed. In 1923, HJ (along with some other men in a syndicate he had belonged to) discussed the idea of adding an additional sign to the Hollywood hills. In addition to the Whitley Heights sign, a new sign honoring the new town would be placed for all to see. HJ felt that movie publicists had nothing on land developers when it came to marketing and bright lights. The original plan was to have the sign there for a year or so. The sign would read "Hollywoodland" (later becoming "Hollywood"). Electricity was still a rather new commodity; the public was fascinated by it.

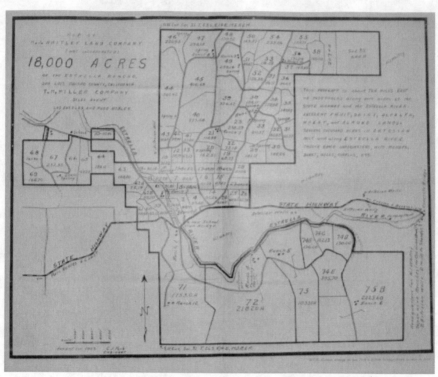

Whitley Valley was the last development of HJ Whitley.

Chapter Fifteen

No story of the growth of Hollywood would be complete without a story of the growth of the San Fernando Valley. Just across the hills from Hollywood lay the fertile acres whose development amazed the world just as Hollywood's development attracted attention. But not only the location and its natural relation to Hollywood entitled the San Fernando Valley to gain notoriety. A personal relation connected the two places. HJ was the guiding genius who foresaw and developed Hollywood. He was now the force developing the Valley. He recognized the immense advantage that would accrue to Hollywood through the development of these lands. Late at night, when the house was quiet, he smiled from time to time as he nestled back in his luxurious chair. Indeed, he had a right to feel well pleased, for against the odds, he convinced four of the most powerful businessmen in the area to join in this enterprise. The results had been brilliant beyond all he expected. No other man in California had such a daring plan or the skill with which to execute such a vast development.

From the moment HJ saw the San Fernando Valley, he began to discuss it with his business colleague, General Otis, and his son-in-law, Harry Chandler, owners of the *Los Angeles Times;* MH Sherman, electric railroad tycoon; and OT Brant, a leading land-title man. Most of the Valley was a farm frontier, but HJ could see that the area was ripe for change. The Southern Pacific Railroad was just completing two additional lines across the Valley, giving people easy access to it. By 1909, HJ pulled together a group of the most powerful men in the area. HJ negotiated the purchase of the 47,500-acre ranch of Isaac Van Nuys at a cost of $2,500,000—around $53 an acre. The partners would then own nearly the entire south half of the Valley. These five men headed the board of control for their new syndicate, the Los Angeles Suburban Home Company. They were straightforward, thoughtful, highly respected men.

HJ quickly attracted an additional thirty participants to help finance the rest of the project. When the transaction was announced in the *Los Angeles Times,* the lengthy account read, "The largest single body of fertile, level land in this part of the State, and said to be the largest single body of land lying so near a big city in the United States." The board projected that there was room in it for at least twenty thousand people.

No major land developer had ever conceived an empire with more sweeping imagination than HJ. As was his custom, he paid attention to every detail. He divided the land into three cities: Van Nuys, Marion (now Reseda), and Owensmouth (now Canoga Park). The lots would be priced from $150 to $600 an acre. The parcels ran from five to twenty acres.

To make all this possible, HJ designed a road over the Cahuenga Pass—which became the first decent road that automobiles could use to access the Valley. HJ got Pacific Electric to build an interurban railway over the pass by offering them $150,000 and a free right-of-way across the company's land.

HJ stood at the edge of the Valley, surveying the acres of fields with his broad hat shading his eyes from the afternoon sun.

Finally, HJ could envision the entire subdivision linked together as one endless sea of homes and farms. "Now let us build a boulevard that is a Boulevard," he advised the board. Against the objection of one colleague who could not visualize a boulevard running through barley fields, HJ's compelling speech persuaded the others that, by the next year, the lands would be the beginnings of a small empire. It was a bewitching moment when five of history's greatest town builders all scanned the horizon, chatting, joking, and planning. HJ used the opportunity to discuss in detail the future of the Valley and the trials of dealing with the many layers of town building. At the moment, the major issue was water. The others respected HJ for his candor, his directness, and the air of leadership he exuded; and they told him so. It was not surprising that he spent a good deal of time asserting his own vision for the towns and their locations.

The board returned from their tour greatly encouraged. They reconvened several nights later for dinner. Clearly, the dinner was a weapon meant to ignite enthusiasm and show the other thirty participators that the board fully intended to go ahead on its grand boasts about the San Fernando Valley. It was the first of a sequence of impossibly rich and bountiful banquets.

HJ spoke first. He offered a rousing ovation on the brilliance of the future towns and the need for the great men of the syndicate to think first of the towns and last of themselves. Only through their self-sacrificing efforts would the towns succeed. The applause was ardent and warmhearted. Chandler spoke next. He described his own vision of the towns and his resolve to make that vision real. He too urged teamwork. He asked each of them to serve as united soldiers on a campaign. This time, the room erupted in cheers. They were optimistic and full of confidence.

The board ruled everything. In his private business, HJ was accustomed to having complete control over expenditures needed to build his towns. Now he needed to seek approval from the board at every step—even the locations of the towns. It was all immensely frustrating. There was progress but at a slower pace than HJ was used to. Soon, the struggle for control progressed into a personal conflict between HJ and Harry Chandler. The battlefield centered on a disagreement over who should control the sales of the land. HJ thought it obvious that the territory belonged to him. Chandler believed otherwise. Chandler even went so far as to sell land without the board's approval. The conflict simmered. To resolve the issue, HJ invited Chandler to dinner. They argued quietly until one o'clock in the morning. HJ felt that the time was well spent and that he and Chandler paved a path that would be much smoother from that time forward.

HJ spent little time with his family. Only a small train ride separated him from seeing Gigi, but the mounting demands of the towns made that distance as difficult to span as the Atlantic Ocean. HJ wrote letters and wrote them often. "You must not think this busy pace will last forever," he wrote in one letter.

HJ employed surveyors, teams, and concrete mixers. Even with his busy schedule, he took time to remember and recall all his employees' names, including the basic laborers. When he was asked questions by his employees, he was always extremely pleasant and cheerful. HJ was vitally interested in the things they told him. He had the gift of putting people at ease. HJ said, "Teamwork is what counts with good management." Across the entire valley, over twenty-two miles, he would build Sherman Way (today it is Van Nuys Boulevard) and name it for his business associate MH Sherman. He divided the road in half—one side for the horse-drawn traffic and the other for automobiles. HJ's boulevard became a prize showpiece of California.

The town's progress had become like a tempest, and he wanted to be done with its fury. Every dawn, he inspected the improvements the crews made. Hundreds of men with shovels, wheelbarrows, and horse-drawn graders slowly scraped the landscape. Despite the presence of so many workers, there was a maddening lack of noise and bustle. The new highway was too big, the men too spread out, to deliver any immediate sense of work being done. The work advanced slowly, impeded by the worsening relationship between the members of the board of control.

Moreover, the town entered that precarious early phase common to every great construction project when unexpected obstacles suddenly emerged. The civil engineers were late on completing their drawings. HJ advertised for bids. Recognizing that the delays put everything behind schedule, he inserted into the construction contracts clauses for penalties. Each contract contained a deadline for completion, with a financial penalty for every day beyond.

As construction at last got underway, anticipation about the opening of the towns began to increase. On the drafting board, the new towns looked spectacular. Publicly, HJ struck a pose of confidence and optimism. Although there were still a few questions of design and plans that were still undetermined, HJ saw no reason why they would not be able to complete the work in time for the opening ceremonies on February 22, 1911. To celebrate the opening of the Red Car, a gala event was planned. HJ arranged to have special gasoline-driven coaches of the Southern Pacific to transport people to the Valley to survey the land. The sales motto was "Back to the Land," which was influenced by HJ's readings of Horace Greeley. People were encouraged to establish roots by buying land. The slogan's phenomenal success persuaded many people to relocate to the valley over the next few years.

Planning to attract several thousand visitors to opening day, HJ hired caterers. The barbeque would be given in the old-time Spanish style. When the bills started to come in for the necessary equipment and supplies to feed ten thousand people, HJ began to realize what a party it would be.

He hired the telephone company to call every subscriber in southern California, inviting them personally to the opening. The telephone company ran a school for operators. These students were hired to make calls to solicit attendance to the opening of the subdivision. This established the first telemarketing enterprise in California. The company was charged five cents a call. HJ created the written dialog that was used on these calls.

The auctioneer's stage was erected as workmen finished the railway depot and a few homes. From Los Angeles, trains loaded to capacity brought people to the Valley. The crowds were so dense that the police had been called to close the train's doors and disperse those unable to get transportation over the Southern Pacific. Hundreds more came in automobiles, leaving a trail of dust in the open fields. The opening was held at the Patton Ranch, which was the headquarters of the American Sugar Beet Company. It was the single largest field in the world. It was ten miles long. Automobiles were provided to allow the guests to view the orchards, vineyards, and gardens. Men and women helped themselves to produce and marveled at the prolific vegetation and abundant crops grown without irrigation.

Standing on a platform, HJ gave the opening address. His forceful personality won the people's confidence. He was an expert showman and understood human nature. Everything he did, every gesture, every intonation of his voice, every smile was carefully rehearsed in advance. His actions were timed to split seconds. In addition to that, HJ had a genuine concern for people. He was grateful when large crowds attended his sales events. They made it easy for him to make a living in a most enjoyable way. He promised himself that he would always give the very best he could. HJ never stepped before the crowds without saying to himself over and over, "I love these people."

After his speech, he then turned the proceedings over to the auctioneers. The auctioneers sold lots at a rate of thirty per hour. At four o'clock, the auctioneers planned to stop; but customers pleaded with them to continue and put one more lot up for sale. HJ said, "I have never seen anything like this in California. People are in such a frenzy to participate." The success of the auction was due largely to the foresight of HJ. It was he who insisted that buyers would not respond unless ample evidence that building of the city was actually underway.

With a band concert in the afternoon, the celebration began. The people came to inspect the fertile valley and its improvements. As the sun stood high over the valley, the pits were opened and an old-time barbeque was served. It brought back the days of gallant caballeros and fair senoritas that HJ and Gigi saw on their honeymoon. Dinner was served to several thousand hungry visitors shortly after one o'clock and continued until almost five o'clock. As the sun began to set, HJ threw on the electric switch to light up the Valley in a most spectacular way. No one had ever seen anything quite like it.

This was followed by an automobile parade to usher in the evening party, where Van Nuys was the scene of a moonlit Mardi Gras. Each guest was given an inexpensive mask to add to the festivities. The masked ball took on added glamour with the first official appearance of the king and his court, who arrived by a royal automobile. They were paraded through the crowds, and the king was presented the keys to the new city. The dance area was decorated in purple, green, and gold, designed to capture the public's imagination. Symbolically the colors signified justice, faith, and power. But, of course, the big attraction was the dancing. The band kept the tunes coming.

At the event, whether he was talking to two people or twenty, whether the people were friendly or indifferent, HJ tried his best to keep his mouth shut and hear what they had to say. He listened to people talk about their jobs, their dogs, their back pain, and things they remembered from childhood. No blinding insights emerged from these conversations. If anything, HJ was struck with just how modest people's hopes were. They wanted a home for their families and a place to retire with some dignity and respect. He felt that a common set of values bound mankind. Each human being had a thread of hope that a good life was just around the corner.

HJ, to Gigi's delight, began construction on their new country mansion at 5849 Van Nuys Boulevard. The three-story country house overlooked a parklike landscape of manicured gardens. The gardens were well kept, butterflies bustled in the flower beds, and not a sound from the outside world was heard. In the afternoons, under the gazebo with HJ and a book, Gigi felt like the luckiest person in the world. Although Gigi loved the glamour of Hollywood, her heart still yearned for love and serenity.

With such an exciting beginning, HJ understood that he needed to move quickly to give the town a solid infrastructure.

Through bonus payments, HJ secured the telephone and electric service. Within a short time, he was able to encourage forty businesses to open up. Over two hundred new homes were built. HJ did not just aspire to sell the land; he sought to put together a stable town.

Since HJ's passion was developing land, Gigi was expected to push land sales at every opportunity. She was always by his side and in the background, supporting him, giving him inner strength. He would receive credit for the extensive event, but Gigi was just as instrumental in seeing that each detail was preformed flawlessly. That was just how it was. Gigi had her own individual identity, her own friends, her own life, her own reputation; but what her husband did was paramount in Gigi's life.

With one town almost completed, HJ vigorously pushed plans for a second town. It was named Owensmouth (Canoga Park) because it was situated at the mouth of the Owens River. HJ planned to use even greater marketing skills to attract people to this opening. He advertised master free barbeque, band music, aerial stunts, and a race between an automobile and an airplane. The crowds that these promotions drew were phenomenal. Owensmouth originally consisted of a real estate office and a water tower. A year later, there was a suburban railway station, a department store, and a power plant. Since HJ and Gigi felt that education was the keystone of society, they were instrumental in getting a school bond passed that funded construction for a two-story brick school building.

Finally, on July 20, 1912, HJ launched his third big subdivision, Marion (Reseda). He was encouraged, as the sales staff had already sold 18,700 acres for $5,750,000. The farm frontier that reached across the Valley was quickly disappearing. Now, North Hollywood seemed to stretch across the Valley.

The one remaining issue HJ faced was a permanent source of water. By 1905, sparse rainfall resulted in a rapid drop in the San Fernando underground storage basin's level. Except for the water that is brought to it from two rivers, the Owens and Colorado, Los Angeles would still be a part of the great desert which surrounds it. Originally, in the days of the padres and for sometime after, wells were sufficient for the needs of the ranches.

The Suburban Home Company and HJ agreed to put down a well in the town site of Van Nuys. He got Layne and Bowler to drill. This water was piped along Sherman Way to keep shrubbery growing and to take care of rose bushes on bordering streets. All realized that if a great community was to be built in the San Fernando Valley, there must be additional water.

Los Angeles, which also received much of its water supply from the basin, decided to build a 250-mile aqueduct that would bring water to the Owens River. Across the Mojave Desert, an army of workman completed the task. At the opening ceremony, the San Fernando Valley saw that they were able to secure a permanent position and realized that a bright future was on its way. No one anticipated the federal restriction that only gave water rights to the city of Los Angeles. The simple solution was easily reached in 1915 when the residents voted to be annexed into the city of Los Angeles. The river was then used to irrigate acres of sugar beets, beans, and potatoes that were grown in the valley. As time passed, other crops were added, such as walnuts, oranges, and alfalfa. HJ marveled that all these things sprang from the earth as never before. As part of his total plan to make the Valley area a balanced economy, HJ introduced the poultry and dairy industries to the area. Being adjacent to Los Angeles made it easy to supply local markets with eggs, milk, and meat.

On Wednesday afternoon just after Easter in 1915, the phone rang. It was HJ with a shaky voice. "Gigi," he said, "you need to start packing. We need to take a short trip to our country home. I want to leave for Van Nuys as soon as you are packed."

He told Gigi he needed to visit the organ factory. He was concerned at the way people had been complaining about the foreman. "He was acting high and mighty. Why do you put up with his shenanigans?" the employees had asked.

Gigi could see the house from a great distance and was delighted to return to what she considered her beautiful paradise of flowers, fruits, and vegetables. The garden had four levels connected by steps and bordered by veneered brick walls and paths. Recessed stone benches accented the edges of the garden and provided a place for her to sit and enjoy the surrounding fragrant roses.

That night, HJ was at the factory until nearly morning. He knew that there was a great deal of skill and ability represented by the workers but very little harmonious leadership. Everyone was a prima donna. Gigi heard him come in; and as he went to the parlor, he groaned pitifully. Gigi rose from their bed to hurry and see what was wrong. Realizing it was just exhaustion, she offered him some tea and hot, buttered toast. She found it difficult to see HJ suffering untold agony.

As they sat sipping tea, he told her that two big business deals were faltering. How could he have miscalculated business conditions? In the beginning, the organ business had thrived with the movie industry; but he had never anticipated talking movies. HJ revered the past, but tradition may have hampered his ability to see the changes that were coming. Maybe he should have considered that it is not always business as usual. New trends had affected many traditional businesses: stables, horseshoeing, vaudeville, kerosene lamps, outhouses...

Gigi lay silently by him in bed until he finally dozed off for the night. While stretching her hands and feet to the posts of the bed, her eyes opened after several watery blinks. Gigi crawled out from under the comforter, edging awkwardly like a butterfly from a cocoon. Swinging her legs over the side of the bed, she became aware that HJ was gone. Gigi realized he must have quietly crawled out of bed bright and early, off to survey the work for the day.

Never had a territory been born in such a short time. For HJ, it had been a backbreaking adventure. There was a constant cloud of anxiety and agitating pressure over the syndicate. HJ injured his health and made money for ungrateful people. Tension grew so high that he bought out the balance of the Suburban Home Company tracks and formed another syndicate to market them. By this time, he was sixty-seven years old; and his enormous energy was beginning to wane. HJ recognized that he himself would have to take over direct supervision of the work, but he felt less up to the duty than ever. He was deeply sad. The task of sorting through accumulated paperwork and taking over the syndicate's work now seemed beyond him. Gigi began to worry as she saw ill health descend in upon him.

He said to her late at night, "It is certainly a very unpleasant losing transaction for me and the regret of my life that I had anything to do with it."

HJ kept the letter from MH Sherman to encourage him when he had a rough day. The letter read:

When I was in the railroad work and had so many discouragements and had so much fault found with me by so many people (people who did not understand what struggles and hardship my partner, Mr. Clark, and myself were going through), I often had the heartache and felt that I was not appreciated. (I think we all feel that way sometimes.) Well, I want you to know that we all do appreciate you, and I want a rousing banquet given to you (in your honor) the day we finally close the San Fernando Valley matters. Hoping to be in Los Angeles before long and to see you there.

I beg to remain most sincerely,
MH Sherman

Although the banquet was never given, it was only fitting, after many years of endless work, that the first child born on October 18, 1911, in the new town of Van Nuys was named Whitley Huffaker. HJ believed that respect was the best way to begin a relationship with others. But couldn't others realize that he too was human? All he truly desired was to be respected. He was sure that others had been taught the golden rule that if you wanted to be respected then you should respect others in the same way. Although some people may deserve special consideration, he still felt that treating every person with respect lifted humanity to a higher level.

Despite his feelings about it, HJ's valley promotion was not a failure. He and his associates put a huge number of farmers on the finest land in the world. All the towns were beautiful settlements that paved the way for a million future homemakers. Once again, HJ's vast empire of new towns grew, a process that had several more chapters before it was to be complete.

As Ross matured, HJ attempted to make up for lost time and tried to connect with him. Ross hoped that, in the new business arrangement, he would finally obtain his father's approval. From 1909 until 1919, he assisted HJ as general manager of the Los Angeles Suburban Homes Company. Together, they built stores, banks, schools, and residences as they developed over 47,000 acres in the San Fernando Valley. They purchased large quantities of trees and shrubs for planting the parkways and orchards. Several industries were promoted, but the major one was sugar beets. This required HJ and Ross to meet in Washington, DC, with the Food Administration.

Initially, HJ and Ross seemed to have come to terms with each other, but the problems began when Ross and his father disagreed over disagreeing. HJ did not believe that family members should openly disagree with others—especially not one's family. But how was Ross to grow if this rule was always followed? Ross, in entering the business to be near his father, was preparing for that time when he could disagree with him and still have his approval. Time passed, but Ross felt that he could never meet his father's expectations. He became president of the First National Bank of Van Nuys, vice president of the State Bank of Owensmouth, and director in the Homes Savings Bank of Los Angeles, one of the largest institutions in the city. HJ just seemed to want to push him further. Although HJ greatly loved his son, it was impossible for him to relinquish the power that drove his life.

Ross realized that he did not enjoy the rigors of competitive business as HJ did. He eventually decided to step out on his own and returned to one of his passions: golf. He owned and developed the Whitley Park Country Club, three hundred and twelve acres, on Ventura Boulevard. The property included a nine-hole golf course, a one hundred-foot tiled pool, tennis courts, stables, and a $75,000 clubhouse with large recreation rooms and a seating capacity of four hundred. The club operated with a membership of 1500 families. Ross arranged all the entertainment and food services. For a time, Ross was at peace with himself.

Chapter Sixteen

Built in 1910, Hollywood High School opened just as the formerly peaceful village of Hollywood was being flooded by movie producers. It was located at the corner of Sunset Boulevard and Highland Avenue, just east of a lemon grove. Students tethered their horses on the athletic field. Hollywood High School did not have the twenty-seven students in attendance, as required by law, so HJ advertised in the city papers that anyone who would move to Hollywood and have children attending the high school could have free rent for a year. He built new homes at the west end of Hollywood that he would use for that purpose. By the 20s, Hollywood High School became the school of choice for the children of movie stars. As the offspring of wealthy and prominent businessmen, they received a superb education.

After returning from high school one day, all Grace talked about was the arrival of Halley's Comet as it passed over the sun. Its arrival had been a top-rated story for several weeks prior to its arrival. A story was widespread that when this comet approached the earth, it would swing around and the tail would touch the earth and set it on fire. It would be the end of the world. Grace and her friends discussed the pros and cons of this theory until the appointed hour of the comet's arrival drew near. Her best friends' younger sisters were spellbound as they listened to the tale—afraid to hear it but too curious to run away and hide. Grace and her friend were merciless in frightening them. There were nights of troubled sleep for the wee ones, who talked in whispers about what it would be like if all the world was afire. Would the river be a safe place to hide, or would it be better to find a deep cave to hide in while the fire burned?

Even many adults were frightened by the comet's approach. News reports rumored that the comet would give off a poisonous gas. Taking advantage of the potential hysteria, one clever businessman made a fortune selling comet pills, an antidote to the poisonous gases that might penetrate the earth's atmosphere. May 19, 1910, the night the comet was visible, passed without incident. There was a conscious sighing of great relief when the population awoke as usual and found themselves still alive and everything normal. Halley's Comet proved that no matter how much scientific knowledge is put forth, when a comet appeared, it still had a magical and wondrous effect on people.

Besides tormenting her friends' younger siblings in her teenage years, Grace entered her rebellious phase, which lasted the rest of her life. HJ truly loved Grace; but in his eagerness to have her become a proper lady, he badgered her constantly with lectures on good behavior and the obligations of wealth. She refused to obey and did the opposite of what was expected. The rebellion was not a happy one for either of them. HJ was distressed by her behavior and hurt by her animosity toward him. For Grace, life was just more and more difficult.

Grace's skirts gradually rose scandalously to her ankles, but the final outrage for HJ was when he saw her shamelessly kissing in public. She defied the rigid social mores that HJ placed upon her. It was times like these that made HJ wonder where his little girl had gone. He was her idol at one point; now he was simply a figure to be defied. Had his work, making him absent for most of her life, really been the fuel for such rebellion? He heard Gigi tell him how important it was for Grace to be with her father. Business blinded him not only with his beloved daughter but with Ross too. Gigi learned to accept it, but she did not think that Grace could understand it at her tender age.

Early in the morning, right as the sun rose over the eastern horizon, HJ sat munching on a piece of bacon while appraising his morning paper. The news reported that Theodore Roosevelt delivered his New Nationalism speech stating his Square Deal Policy. HJ felt that it was a good plan. He took personal satisfaction in knowing that the government was fighting the criminal rich and soulless corporations. HJ regarded them not only as lawbreakers and malefactors of great wealth but as despicable men since they used their power to oppress the poor and helpless classes. Stronger than HJ's sympathy for any individual was his love of justice. He was raised to be the perfect gentleman, expecting no less from others.

The automobile was also in the news. There were only a half dozen in Hollywood when HJ's interest began to stir. He was amazed that many people who just arrived in Hollywood had never seen one. The prices were high in the beginning, and HJ found it hard to justify buying one when the streetcars were so handy. In 1905, HJ and Gigi visited the Los Angeles Auto Show. They were attracted to the show more by the novelty of the cars than the notion of buying one. The Model T Towncar finally enticed HJ to purchase his first car. He was impressed at how fast it could travel, and he loved to give Gigi and the children a thrill by going twenty-five miles an hour. He felt that, at $900, the car was a steal. HJ loved the striking look of his black car. By 1910, HJ's company purchased one of the most powerful passenger automobiles ever built, an Oldsmobile passenger bus that had been converted into one of the first limousines in Hollywood. It could accommodate up to twenty people and averaged speeds up to thirty-five miles per hour.

As time passed, HJ learned to occasionally include Gigi in his business affairs. Many times, Gigi felt that she kept him from making mistakes because she considered herself a child of divine prophecy. It was, without a doubt, time for her to make a very important life decision. The question: Should Gigi share her concerns with everyone, revealing her last perplexing dream? In the final analysis, it was her strong religious beliefs and the realizations that her gift was God-given that led her to reveal the dream.

As was his usual pattern, HJ spent many nights at work with his business partners, returning home after midnight. He and Gigi argued once again. The look he gave her convinced her that he did not intend to skip even one meeting. HJ stomped out and left Gigi uneasy and unhappy. Her fits of violent anger disturbed him, yet he knew he deserved them.

Gigi prayed for peace of mind and eventually fell asleep. At about two o'clock, she was awakened by a nightmare in which Gigi saw a tall building explode and catch fire. The next day, she told no one of the dream; however, Gigi insisted that HJ go to no more meetings at the *Times* building. Finally realizing how upset Gigi was, HJ called Harry Chandler and postponed the evening meeting. Surprisingly, Harry did not object and commented that his wife complained that he never spent enough time with the family.

At dinner that night, HJ tried to explain to Gigi that he did not like neglecting her but he had more responsibilities than she could ever realize. "Home means everything to me. It is just that business takes so much time," he solemnly stated.

As a special treat, he decided to take her to a play; and, as many tired men do, he slept through most of it. On the way home, Gigi told HJ about the dream. He was quite disturbed by the news and went for a late-night walk to clear his head.

In the morning, he received a called from Harry Chandler's office. The nightmare came true! On October 1, 1910, a bomb exploded by the side of the *Los Angeles Times* building. The blast weakened the second floor, and it came down on the office workers below. Fire erupted and spread quickly through the three-story building. By the time the fire department put out the fire, twenty-one people working for the newspaper died. A nightmarish scene awaited Harry when he arrived at work the next morning. When HJ and Gigi arrived at the *Times* building they found Harry sitting in ruins, crying like a child and saying, "Gigi saved our lives. We would have died too. All the night force was killed. I usually work until 2:00 a.m., but last night I went home early to be with my wife. Gigi will always have a special place in our hearts."

Later, HJ and Gigi discussed the events of that fateful evening. The blast had been felt for many miles. One of their friends said, "The force of the blast was incredible. People were jumping from the windows to escape the fire. Many people died. Flames and timbers flew in all directions. It was painful to see that nothing remained of that beautiful building except smoldering debris."

It was later learned that two brothers, John J. and James B. McNamara, set off the bomb. They were skilled in dynamite and engaged in violence for many years. The labor union rallied around the brothers and claimed that they had been framed. Attorney Clarence Darrow was hired for their defense. Pleading guilty, the McNamaras avoided the death penalty. HJ thought that it was a wise decision. If the brothers had been executed, he was sure they would have been considered martyrs. Everyone gradually lost interest in the case, and the brothers were left to live with the consequence of their actions.

The Christmas open house that year was held on December 18. The evening was filled with unsurpassed food, delightful music, and charming friends. The house was decked out in its finest holiday décor. Red poinsettias lined the steps up to the front door. Once inside the house, guests were ushered to the dining room to fill their plates with an array of holiday treats. Throughout the evening, guests listened to holiday music played by a string quartet.

HJ's favorite time of the year was Christmas. He loved when the house smelled of the freshly cut Christmas trees and baking cookies, the wonderfully delicious aroma of Christmas. Christmas was the perfect opportunity for gift giving. It was a glorious day for the entire family, one of the only days the family was sure that business would be put on hold.

The buffet table was draped with a garland of holly and a candelabrum filled with myriad red tapers that softly lit the room. The spacious dining hall presented a picture of rare beauty. The polished maple dining table was draped through the center with a plush scarf embroidered with golden angels. Arranged about the table were several dainty tête-à-tête tables covered with embroidered linen and set with fragile china and silver. Here and there, massive silver baskets overflowed with luscious fruits. The smell of prime rib with Yorkshire pudding danced into the room from the kitchen.

This year, Gigi invited her sister Elizabeth's family to the celebration. After dinner, Gigi enjoyed playing Christmas carols as the family sang along. Elizabeth commented that she fondly remembered their mother saying that the first Christmas carol was the sacred one, sang by angels over the fields of Bethlehem.

The family tradition included HJ reading Charles Dickens's *A Christmas Carol*. Dickens wrote with the intention of being read out loud. It was a precious gem of a book; and as HJ spoke the words to them, it was difficult to forget their many blessings. The sheer power of HJ's voice inspired each of them to be a little kinder.

With the candles lit, cups filled with eggnog, and cookies on the table, all was peaceful at the Whitley residence. HJ lit the candles on the tree, to the delight of the children, keeping a watchful eye that nothing caught on fire. It would take them nearly two hours to open all the presents around the massive Christmas tree. No one in the family wanted the day to end. As Gigi looked toward the new year, she realized that there were many challenges facing them that, once accomplished and finalized, would change the face of Hollywood forever.

Chapter Seventeen

HJ continued to complete things when no one noticed. He was an invisible man. He made personal sacrifices for no credit. Why did he spend so much time working on a task that would take so many years to complete? He somehow knew that God was watching him, and that was enough. He personally resolved that it was okay that they didn't see and didn't know. All he really wanted was to have people visit Hollywood and say that they loved it. There was no place in the world like it. That was the motivating factor that enabled him to collect the majority of directors, producers, and movie stars and talk them into living in one town: Hollywood.

In 1911, a new, exciting era of Hollywood was ushered in. The motion picture industry already operated several studios in the heart of Los Angeles. The movie *In the Sultan's Power* was produced in 1908 by Colonel Selig. It was the first full-length motion picture shot in an old mansion he rented at Eighth and Olive. As time passed, many others were drawn to Los Angeles, including the marvelous director DW Griffith.

The motion picture industry did not come to Hollywood until HJ spent over fifteen years and millions of dollars developing and beautifying the area. Considering how strenuously others urged producers and directors to settle in a number of other excellent sites, it is amazing that one man could convince the majority of them to settle in Hollywood. The first Hollywood motion picture was taken on October 26, 1911. Although the movie never really had a name, Gigi felt that it was a true piece of Hollywood's history. The Whitley home was used as its set. The movie was filmed in the middle of their groves. The motion picture was directed by David and William Horsley and Al Christe. HJ was fortunate to meet the Horsley brothers as they were touring Hollywood and suggested that they might be able to lease the Blondeau Tavern on Sunset and Gower. He felt sure that it could easily be converted into a movie studio.

HJ knew at once that he had found a rare, untapped jewel that would make his town stand out from others. The rules of the game he now played were simple, much like the game of marbles Ross played when he was a child. The games would last several minutes, and the best player would leave with all the jewels. In this new game, the jewels were movie producers and directors. Others would try; but HJ possessed a decisive edge, a mystical power that drew people to him. HJ's charm disarmed strangers and made them instant friends. He was a friend to everyone, one who would cheer you on when you were successful and who would support you when the going got rough. It was difficult to explain just how HJ created these bonds. After knowing HJ for just a few hours, it was like you knew him all your life; and you knew you would be friends forever. HJ stood out from others because of the levels of concern and service he offered.

David Horsley was walking down Hollywood Boulevard near the Hollywood Hotel and looking a little lost and confused when a pleasant, well-dressed gentleman appeared and asked if he could help. David told HJ what he was looking for. HJ not only pointed him in the right direction; he escorted him all the way down the street to his destination. David asked him his name and occupation. To David's surprise, he introduced himself as the developer of Hollywood.

"I built the bank and hotel at the corner of Highland and Hollywood Boulevard."

When HJ spoke, his face lit up with an inward fire. He was transfigured. As the conversation wore on, an instant friendship developed. HJ even offered David the use of his elaborate gardens for filming. HJ was thrilled with the idea that this young, budding filmmaker would soon be opening a studio that would enhance the face of Hollywood.

Horsley's studio achieved great success; and soon, many other studios were drawn to the area. HJ convinced David to purchase three lots: 3639 Whitley Heights, 3737 North Heights, and 4546 Whitley Heights Park Tract. He never lost a chance to make a sale. Hollywood began to grow by leaps and bounds, attracting many others to its famous hills.

The Hollywood Hotel played an enormous role in placing Hollywood on the world map. Industry giants, such as Jesse Lasky, Carl Laemmle, Louis B. Mayer, Harry Warner, and Irving Thalberg would stay at the hotel. Producers, directors, and writers held conferences on its broad verandahs. There was a continuous flow of silver screen stars arriving daily.

Many of the famous silent screen movie idols made it their home. They were a lively bunch who attended dances held every Thursday night in the ballroom. Rudolph Valentino taught tango lessons to an influential studio executive, June Mathis, who later offered him the lead in Metro's *The Four Horsemen of the Apocalypse*. The movie was a commercial and critical success and the beginning of Valentino's career as a star. The Hollywood Hotel gained celebrity status when Valentino impulsively married actress Jean Aker in the lobby days after meeting her there. Rudolph Valentino lived in room 264.

Where there were stars, there was gossip about their adventures. It was considered the place to be seen, and many business deals were transacted in its rooms. HJ made a suggestion to movie mogul Joe Schenck to put his entire company, including his movie star wife, Norma Talmadge, at the hotel while moving his studio from New York to Hollywood. Many years later, Norma would be their neighbor in Whitley Heights. HJ and Gigi became friends with other notable stars that stayed at the hotel. The hotel register listed Charlie Chaplin, Norma Shearer, Douglas Fairbanks, Fatty Arbuckle, Lillian and Dorothy Gish, King Vidor, Lon Chaney, Carrie Jacobs Bond, Blanche Sweet, Mary Pickford, Lionel Barrymore, Buster Keaton, and countless others. As a thank-you to their faithful patrons, the hotel painted stars on the ceiling of the dining room with the actors' names inside them. That way it was easy to identify which table belonged to which star.

Silent film stars danced and romanced in the hotel's Dining Room of the Stars. As Hollywood grew, the hotel had a continuous flow of silent screen movie stars making it their home. Many ordinary citizens would stay at the Hollywood, hoping to get a glimpse or an autograph of their favorite star.

The Cahuenga Pass also played its part by offering a route through the hills to the Valley. It had originally been a simple, winding trail over which cattle had been driven. In 1911, the tracks to the Red Car were laid. When the San Fernando Valley became a center for the movie studios, the pass was the main link between it and Hollywood. For the biggest stars in Hollywood, there were mansions. The hills of Hollywood were filled with directors, producers, writers, stars, HJ and Gigi's close friends.

But the crews and struggling extras that stood in line daily, hoping to get picked for parts, needed less expensive places to live. HJ saw that the Valley offered such a spot. Soon, thousands of hopeful young men and women came to California seeking fame and fortune in the motion picture industry.

On February 10, 1912, Gigi entertained a large company of guests at the Hotel Alexandria, now considered one of the swankiest hotels in town. Gigi wore a pastel pink and green chiffon dress. It was covered with delicate gold and crystal embroideries.

The lobby and entrance to the dining room was a masterpiece of decorative art in marble, bronze, white, and green. Gigi loved its grand rococo style, crystal chandeliers, and marble columns. It became the stomping grounds for big movie deals and the talk of the town.

The guests were received in the large French music salon. Hand-painted sketches of George Washington framed in a cherry wreath marked places for each guest. The room was decorated with red flowers in crystal baskets. Miss Mary L. O'Donaghue, who recently returned from abroad, entertained them with a piano recital. She played patriotic tunes in honor of Washington's birthday.

After the performance, awaiting the guests at the tables was a meal of sirloin of beef, chateau potatoes, creamed carrots, chocolate and vanilla éclairs, and French vanilla ice cream. The tables were fragrant with American Beauty roses, violets, and lilies of the valley.

The dinner not only offered entertainment for the guests but gave HJ the opportunity to meet men in the smoking lounge to discuss the astronomical figures of upcoming business. Heated discussions of the movie industry ensued. The demand for films had increased; and audiences expected more complex plots, multi-reel films, and gossip about the stars. David and William Horsley pointed out that the development of more sophisticated and organized methods of production were needed. Film studios with assembly line production could film more movies and keep up with the high demand. David Horsley suddenly realized that he needed a new business plan. Eventually, David would unite with others to form the Universal Film Company. He was elected treasurer of the new company, the perfect contact to enable HJ the opportunity to have his land used in many upcoming movies. HJ thought that this was the best and least expensive way to advertise his property.

With time, HJ was acquainted with all the important movie men—William Fox, Cecil B. DeMille, Mack Sennett, and Jesse Lasky. These men would help the American Dream leap out larger than life, ultimately touching everyone everywhere. The movies were made in sites other than Hollywood, some quite nearby and some far away. But nowhere liberated our fantasies and stirred our hopes and fears, our tears, and our eternal romances like that single unrivaled word: Hollywood. Audiences were mesmerized by the new invention that made moving pictures.

HJ established the necessary infrastructure in Hollywood. There was a ready labor marketplace, the best climate in the area, and plenty of sunshine, which opened the way to outdoor shooting. But best of all, HJ chose Hollywood's location for his most triumphant town because it was endowed with an unrivaled variety of settings: mountains and canyons for westerns, beaches and cliffs for high sea adventures, villages for romantic comedies, urban Los Angeles for gangsters, and deserts for pioneer days.

They referred to the stars as "The Sun Worshipers" because sunny days were necessary for them to complete their work. Work stopped on the open stage as soon as the sun went behind a cloud. Gigi heard that it was a habit with actors to go to the window to assess the weather as soon as they woke up. On a cloudy day, they would not even bother to show up at work.

Filmmakers were drawn by the year-round sunshine, the variety of landscapes, and the endless hours of daylight. They made one and two-reel movies. HJ and Gigi's favorites were the westerns, comedies, and dramas. The films were short and often took a little more than a week to shoot. Studios were producing from two to three films a week. Hundreds of silent films were produced. HJ realized that the need for pianos and organs had greatly increased as the silent movie industry grew. To offset their need for pianos and organs, HJ built a plant named the Johnstone Organ and Piano Manufacturing Company to produce the much-needed instrument. They were manufacturers of the celebrated Murray M. Harris pipe organ. These organs were capable of sounding like horns, harps, drums, thunder, train whistles, and much more. In 1904, the company produced an organ for the St. Louis World's Fair.

Over twenty thousand motion picture houses began establishing a movie-going habit that was almost as strong as eating and sleeping. The larger theaters were competing with each other to be given the title of the most luxurious theater in town. Theater owners made film far greater than before by accompanying the movies with the music from $25,000 organs, hundred-piece orchestras, a uniformed corps of ushers, and elaborate stage presentations. HJ was always looking for ways to promote revenue-making venture in his newly developing towns, and the movie industry offered many new jobs to the area. The organ factory in Van Nuys employed very skilled, high-class people.

It would be another five years before Hollywood became the capital of filmdom. DW Griffith's *The Birth of a Nation*, the story of the lives of a Northern and Southern family during the Civil War and post-Civil War Reconstruction period, gave Hollywood a worldwide spot on the map. The film made its debut at Clune's Auditorium in Los Angeles. It was a controversial but landmark film. It was technically and artistically the first epic movie. Every movie that has been made since then owes something to this film. It was an ambitious effort at complex storytelling. HJ particularly enjoyed the Civil War battle scenes, which were expertly done and extremely moving.

Originally, the filmmakers had been attracted to Hollywood by her choicest of gifts, sunshine; however, HJ was able to offer much more. HJ made sure that when the picture companies first saw Hollywood, they realized the opportunities for progress it offered.

On Cecil B Demille's advice, Jesse Lasky headed to Hollywood. Seeing all the wonderful improvements that HJ accomplished, he decided to make it his home. HJ met Jesse Lasky at the Hollywood Hotel. There was something stirring in Jesse's blood. It was a mixture of self-confidence, ambition, zeal, artistry, and fortitude. HJ said several times, "Personally, I found him rather likable. He impresses me as being a man of vision and sincerity."

The first film Lasky sold was the *Squaw Man*, and it was filmed without a studio. HJ and Gigi were amazed when they heard that Jesse sold the rights to the film for $40,000. HJ appreciated the substantial profit Jesse made. He was pleased that this would draw more people to Hollywood. In time, the

Jesse L. Lasky Feature Play Company would merge several times. Finally, it partnered with Zukor and evolved into Paramount Studios.

As DW Griffith told them, movies would change the world. "The human race will think more rapidly, more intelligently, more comprehensively than it ever had. We do not 'talk' about things happening, we actually show it—vividly, completely, convincingly. It is ever-present, realistic, and nothing ever devised by the mind of man can show it like moving pictures."

By the 1920s, millions of Americans were going to the movies each week. The studios worked nonstop to produce films for their unquenchable appetites. The first film studio was built on Sunset Boulevard. Small film companies would churn out short silent films as quickly as they could. Many studios suffered from bad business management, resulting in a rapid secession of turnovers. Parts of Sunset Boulevard became nicknamed "Poverty Row." The most popular films for the small studios were the one and two-reel westerns that were cheap to produce. HJ often saw a cowboy and his horse standing on the southwest corner of Gower Street, hoping to get a job as an extra in an upcoming film.

With the unprecedented growth at the movie studios, many social concerns began to appear. HJ and Gigi realized that they played a pivotal role in maintaining the moral character of the city. The desire for instant fame drew many beautiful, single women to Hollywood. Together with the help of the Young Woman's Christian Association and the Hollywood Businessmen's Club, they started the Studio Club for Women. Its purpose was to keep the girls off the streets and offer them a safe home environment while they answered the call of the camera. Gigi felt that the purity of Hollywood's women would be the cornerstone of Hollywood's growth. Young women free for the first time in history were unsure what that freedom meant and what risks it entailed. Things were different here, less rigid and formal. Everywhere Gigi went, she found young women, unescorted, holding jobs, living their own lives. Therefore, the rules of the Studio Club were strict while the atmosphere was home-like. A newspaper article in 1919 described the club this way:

> The club is more of a sorority, with delightful picture 'atmosphere,' than anything else, and the same happy atmosphere will pervade the new home. A dominant note is the refining touch of home life and sense of protection, with assurance of assistance, not only in material way when need arises, but in one's work, as well. Financially, many desperate cases among young women have been tided over by the Hollywood Studio Club.

What made it so desirable to the new arrivals was its low rent and free meals. Over the years, such notable stars as ZaSu Pitts, Myrna Loy, Dorothy Malone, and Marilyn Monroe stayed at the Studio Club. Studios continued to spring up like wildflowers; yet the leading studios were William Fox, Lasky, Universal, Fine Arts, Mabel Norman, RKO (Radio-Keith-Orpheum), Chaplin, Rowan, Vogue, and Yorks. HJ and Gigi felt that before the dawn of 1918, every company in the movie industry would be represented in Hollywood. That year, the first full-length feature cartoon, *The Sinking of the Lusitania,* was created by Winsor McCay. It took twenty-two months to produce.

The great growth of the studios brought many complaints from those who had already found the serenity of the Hollywood hills. Many store owners along the busy boulevards put signs in the windows saying, "No dogs or actors allowed." They worried that the cinema invasion corrupted their town. HJ made a great effort to let everyone know that it was merely the artistic end of the work that would be done in Hollywood. There was no danger of Hollywood ever becoming a factory center. All the motion picture production work connected with issuing of film prints and the manufacturing end of the business was done in the East.

HJ personally knew of over a hundred people during 1919 that had moved to Hollywood. All of them needed homes to live in, and many were now paying rents as high as $150 or more a month. Because of the phenomenal growth, five additional automobile agencies entered the city. All these people were connected with the motion picture industry and came out West to find golden opportunities.

By 1921, it became apparent to even HJ that a problem was developing. He approached the Chamber of Commerce to address it. Hollywood became a magnet for those seeking fame and fortune. Too many hopefuls were converging on Hollywood. It was decided that the chamber should publish a warning. The warning stated, "Do not try to break into the movies in Hollywood until you have obtained the full, frank, and dependable information. It may save you disappointments. Out of a hundred thousand people who started at the bottom only five reached the top."

The image of the pretty young girl being a victim of exploitation became a public relations problem for Hollywood. One industry observer wondered if extra work would ever be anything other than "an alibi for prostitution." To stop the exploitation of extras, the Central Casting Company was created to regulate the film industry. Producers went to Central Casting for extras. The service was offered for free to the struggling newcomers.

As Hollywood's influence grew, Gigi became fascinated with the film stars. As her looks began to fade, Gigi longed for the attention she received when she was young. Stars lived such colorful lives. The attention they received was all that Gigi secretly dreamed of. Gigi saw glamorous Hollywood stars at premieres, the best parties, restaurants, and charity functions. At times, they seemed mysterious and inaccessible. Gigi realized that many of the stories she heard about them were invented by the studios as publicity. Yet the images they painted became true in her mind. The thought of being a vamp was almost inconceivable to her. It was utterly wrong, against her principles. Why was Gigi so spellbound by them? After all, she was a good, Christian woman.

Additionally, Gigi loved that Hollywood was becoming a world style center in and of itself, rivaling Paris and New York. Hairstyles, clothing, gloves, hats, and gestures that originated for screen purposes were now copied all over the world. Fabrics became lighter, colors were brighter, and styles were looser. Lowered necklines became popular. Hemlines inched up. Gigi's friends began to ask stores for the things they saw on the big screen. Often, these were things that staff artists treated as symbols of gracious living to indicate the social strata of fictional characters. Everyone seemed to be oblivious of that fact. They all wanted to be like the actresses they saw on the screen. Theda Bara, Billie Burke, Norma Talmadge, Gloria Swanson, Mabel Norman, Lillian Gish, and Mary Pickford became household names that shaped their new society. It was the decade that began Hollywood's transformation and which ultimately resulted in changing the world.

HJ would never stand for such flamboyance. He wondered how Theda Bara, queen of the silent screen, was able to make dressing with feminine allure and glamour popular. A proper lady needed to earn her position in society. It was not obtained by the purchases she made. The only reason HJ tolerated the stars' sometimes seedy promotions was the phenomenal growth it brought to Hollywood. At times, he would ponder what effect this would have on future generations. Gigi said that it was only harmless fun. No one believed the stories the studios made up. Movie stars' standards were not likely to influence the world. Christian standards were too ingrained in the United States.

Between 1910 and 1920, the population of Hollywood increased from five thousand to thirty-five thousand. As hopeful actors, directors, and writers flocked to Hollywood, HJ saw the demand for his hillside property in Whitley Heights soar. It was the most sought-after location for the wealthy.

After a while, other places began to put in a bid to try to take the movies away from Hollywood. They did not seem to realize that it took other things besides money to accomplish what was being done in the Hollywood foothills. Gigi was the first one to enlighten one would-be rival to Hollywood.

Gigi was given an opportunity to set a movie industry competitor straight when she took an automobile trip to New York. Rain made the roads around New York City very uncertain, compelling her to stop overnight at the Waldorf Astoria to wait for better weather. Gigi was with her attendant, Victoria. They decided that, rather than fight the elements, they would dine at the hotel.

They just received their dinner when a young woman approached their table and asked, "Are you Mrs. Whitley from California?" Gigi assured her that she was, when, to her surprise, the stranger began informing her, in a rather rude manner, that her company in Hollywood, Florida, would soon outshine the Whitley's work in California. They would just show the Whitleys how to build the motion picture capital of the world. As the woman became breathless, the entire dining area watched to hear Gigi's response. Then, to everyone's surprise, Gigi began to laugh as she said, "Now, that just brings the sunshine back! You plan on taking the motion picture industry by storm, but you cannot even come up with an original name for your town."

For a moment, the woman looked at them dumfounded; then she stomped out of the room with a scowl on her face. With that, Gigi returned to eating her dinner. Few people know what happened to that part of Hollywood, Florida. On September 18, 1926, *The Big Blow* struck. A vicious hurricane slammed into South Florida, and Hollywood was among its victims. The city was devastated by the hurricane's high winds and swelling floodwaters. It claimed thirty-seven lives, uprooted trees, tore down electrical wires, ripped off roofs, and flattened houses. They never heard any more about the motion picture industry moving there; and the seemingly unlimited growth of Hollywood, Florida, stopped overnight without warning. No storm in previous history did as much property damage. It passed through not only Florida but Alabama and Mississippi too. The hurricane killed 372 people and injured over six thousand others.

With Florida and many would-be contenders out of the way, Hollywood made enormous progress. One of the world's largest production companies opened studios in Hollywood's sunshine: William Fox Studios. In 1926 every business endeavor in Hollywood accomplished great success. The progress made by the motion picture industry brought a new dimension to the beautiful city. The homes began to take on the character of its new residents, and its architecture became so varied that nowhere on Earth could one find such an exciting city. Hollywood, California, became synonymous with the movie industry.

Chapter Eighteen

More exciting to HJ than all the movie stars was his meeting with President William Howard Taft, the twenty-seventh president of the United States. On October 11, 1911, President Taft was invited by prominent Los Angeles businessmen to speak at a banquet. Taft and Roosevelt seemed to be disagreeing on many political issues, and HJ wanted to find out firsthand from Taft how the problems had arisen. He told HJ that, unlike Roosevelt, he did not believe in stretching presidential powers. He preferred to use the court system to make such decisions. With time, this disagreement would lead to the division of the Republican Party.

As the president's train pulled into Los Angeles, some hundred thousand people gathered to see him. People from the region streamed into the city by horseback, buggy, and the occasional automobile. Whether Democrat, Republican, Socialist, or Progressive, no one wanted to miss the chance to see President Theodore Roosevelt's successor—a man expected to stand for a second term in 1912.

In organizing the general committee for the Taft reception, HJ was assigned to the auditorium reception committee. He was given a seat on the stage. At the banquet held later that evening, he was seated at the table with President Taft.

You could feel the anticipation in the air as the doors opened to the banquet. Guests poured in to celebrate President Taft's visit. The sound of music lured people inside the banquet hall, and the ceremony began with a special tribute to the president. The room was decorated with red, white, and blue banners and flags. The tables were laden with silver and fine linen tablecloths. Shortly after the opening of the banquet, the guests listened to many speakers praise the work of President Taft. The attendees of the banquet were treated to the divine flavor of one hundred turkeys, eight hundred pounds of mashed potatoes, fifty gallons of coffee, thirty gallons of milk, one hundred loaves of bread, six gallons of cranberry sauce, fifty bunches of celery, six gallons of green peas, six gallons of gravy, three hundred pounds of dressing, twenty-five pounds of butter, one hundred mince pies, and one thousand oranges.

Many old-time members complained to HJ about the evils of the movie industry. One crotchety old man said, "I feel movie-going is a ploy used by the devil. Alcohol may be the worst, but movies are right up there with it. Immodesty has spread shamelessly, and they even attack the church and its ministers. What is the world coming to?"

HJ replied, "If cinema art wants to continue drawing the public to its movies, they will soon realize that people have high ideals. The public will eventually demand higher morals and greater truth in story lines."

From talking with friends in the movie industry, he realized that the producers were mortally afraid of federal censorship. In 1911, Pennsylvania became the first state to pass a film censorship law. Most people agreed that not all movies were suitable for all audiences. There needed to be some limitations placed on the type and content of films that young children were exposed to. Film producers were anxious for the flow of money to continue, so they adopted an industry code. This would be the first of several efforts to convince the public that the industry could censor itself. HJ wondered if they really would. If not, he was sure that measures would be taken to ensure they did.

Photoplay, the first true movie fan magazine, debuted in 1911 and gave rise to the idea of a celebrity culture. Catering chiefly to the public's passions for information about their favorite stars and the plots and characters of upcoming films, its format would set a precedent for almost all the celebrity magazines that followed. To make the magazine's cover unique, an artist was hired to specifically draw colored pictures of the stars. The key to the layout was a proper balance between pictures and stories. There were brief editorials and extensive stories on celebrities such as DW Griffith and the Gish sisters, Lillian and Dorothy. *Photoplay* was an escape outlet, giving many people a chance to spend a few minutes away from the everyday realities of life. Just like a box of chocolates tasted good and was easy to eat, so was the gossip in celebrity magazines. Gigi loved to read about Hollywood romances and hear news on upcoming society weddings.

It was a whirlwind courtship that began with a casual meeting. Ross, who was now twenty-four years old, was enthralled with Mary. He first saw her while she performed in a vaudeville act. Mary appeared to be easygoing and had a good sense of humor. Ross was captivated by her good looks and seemingly sweet nature. They had so much fun together. As they drove to a scenic spot overlooking the Pacific Ocean, Ross was secretly praying that all would go well. As the sun melted into the ocean, he held Mary gently in his arms and proposed. To bolster the proposal, he handed her a beautifully cut Whitley diamond ring. How could she refuse?

Although Mary seemed like a nice girl, there was something about her that Gigi did not like. HJ told her that he would not attend the wedding, disapproving of the relationship from the beginning. Why would Ross want to marry a showgirl who had little education and social graces? Why did Ross throw all sense to the wind? He had been brought up with high standards and sent to the best schools. It took much begging and tears from Gigi to convince HJ to attend the wedding.

There was nothing more to do other than congratulate Ross on his impending marriage and reflect on the truth that most people did not want advice they had not asked for. They would go ahead and do what they wanted to do anyway, no matter how hard you tried to convince them to do otherwise. HJ knew that that applied in every area of life. It was a human truth of universal relationships—but one that most people, he felt, knew little to nothing about. He just hoped that his business associates did not learn much about his future daughter-in-law.

The wedding was to be a magical affair. The Whitleys' home offered a sophisticated atmosphere. Ross and Mary knew the mood they wanted to create for the wedding reception. It was important that their guests be comfortable and that they experienced the incredible beauty of the estate. The wedding had a glamorous new Hollywood feel. Everything was perfect, from the invitations to the décor. The bridesmaids were dressed in a soft shade of pink taffeta with three roses in their hair and tulle veils floating down their backs. Mary wore a stunning dress made entirely of Brussels lace and carried a bouquet of white roses.

The wedding was small considering how many people HJ and Gigi normally invited to their parties. The majority of the guests were young people—Ross and Mary's friends. Their effervescing spirits made the wedding blissful. The bride came down the broad staircase to where her father was waiting. On his arm, Mary went across the hall to the parlor, where the ceremony was performed. They left amidst the shower of fragrant rose petals. In 1913, Ross married Mary Safrona Joyner. For the first year of their marriage, they were a happy and popular couple who lived a busy social life.

Mary hoped that her marriage to Ross would catapult her into the arena of the stars. Mary Pickford delighted her, with her beautiful blonde curls and engaging face. She hoped that they would share the silver screen someday. Silent movies were simple. All you needed to do was follow the director's cues. Now that she was part of high society, she knew she had a chance; she just needed to get to know the right people.

To help her new daughter-in-law establish her presence in the society she had now entered, Gigi hosted one of the most delightful social events that season. The reception was held in honor of Mrs. Ross Emmett Whitley. The guests all left Los Angeles at about 10:30 in a private trolley car arranged by HJ. The women enjoyed a chance to get together and discuss the ever-so-interesting film stars. As usual, the major topic for the men was business. An old-fashioned chicken dinner was served at noon at the Whitley Estate. Mary was now part of the posh Hollywood society.

A few weeks after the wedding, Lasky studios threw a party for two hundred guests at the Hollywood Hotel to welcome their new star, Geraldine Farrar. Farrar was the reigning diva of American opera. *At last,* Gigi thought, *real class is coming to the motion picture industry.* When Farrar detrained, she was escorted by the mayor down a red carpet while five thousand fans waved and cheered. Schoolchildren tossed flowers on the path. Elegant and beautiful, she captivated the crowd. Gigi was glad that Farrar came to establish the prestige of the grand opera in Hollywood. HJ was right; movies had an artistic overtone when the right actors and actresses were hired.

The Farrar expedition in the wilds of Hollywood was heralded in banner headlines across the continent. The mayor and other dignitaries formed a welcoming committee. Geraldine Farrar and John Drew led an old-fashioned grand march into the ballroom at the Hollywood Hotel. HJ and Gigi attended the white tie and tails affair. Some fabulous parties were thrown by the movie colony, and this was the first social icebreaker that Gigi remembered. To her recollection, Geraldine Farrar was the first movie star to receive the full treatment of what henceforth would have been given only to someone as important as the president of the United States.

HJ realized that, for the first time in history, mere entertainers possessed power over the masses that were now surpassing the strongest political identification. He was concerned that the new stars might lead the public down the wrong path. On screen and off, the stars were influencing the public by tapping into the deepest aspirations of their audiences. This force seemed to have energy of its own. HJ was not sure the right people were at the helm. Many stars had little education. How could they possibly be qualified to direct public policy? Many people did not realize that the stories generated from Hollywood were myth rather than truth. This disturbed HJ immensely. Even Grace seemed overly mesmerized by them.

The stars were just ordinary people who were able to transcend their personal identities through the magic of movies. They would touch their audiences with glamour and possibilities of obtaining extraordinary things. It offered the viewer a respite from their daily routine, allowing them to dream of a future that might await them in a week, a month, or a year. HJ hoped that, as new more educated and decidedly artistic performers were hired, the standards of Hollywood would rise.

For a treat, HJ and Gigi were fond of walking down the Boulevard, window shopping, and talking with friends. Gigi enjoyed HJ's company, even if she had to share it with others. Over the years, HJ and Gigi made many friends in Hollywood. HJ met Charlie Chaplin at a social event and was glad to see him again as they walked down the Boulevard one day. Charlie reminded HJ of Ross. He was a remarkable person with this vibrant and vital presence. Charlie had an aura of vitality that was hard to put in any other way—a zest for people. He had a pair of brilliant sapphire blue eyes and always looked at you when you spoke with him.

HJ loved giving advice, so he listened intently as Charlie told of the troubles he was having with his director. He complained that the director ignored almost all of his suggestions, sabotaging his best bits of comedy. "How am I supposed to work at such a frantic pace? It is so different from the polished routines I am used to doing. I believe I have been ridiculed for some of my actions, but I always try to do my best. The whole desire of my life is to amuse people in a way that meets the public's favor. I sure hope I can make it in the movies. Many people see a subject on the screen and say that such-and-such a thing should be done this way or that. They do not realize that I do things on the spur of the moment and that my mind is under a constant strain. I feel like I work night and day," Charlie said.

"Maybe you should start your own studio. You seem very intelligent. I think you could make a go of it. I sympathize with you. It is so hard to make everyone happy," HJ replied.

Before they knew it, it was growing dark. A quick good-bye, and HJ and Gigi were on their separate way. As they continued walking down the street, a gentleman approached HJ and wanted to discuss a business proposition with him. It was late and HJ wanted to get home, so he invited the man to call on him the next day at his office.

When they were alone again, he said to Gigi, "I wish people would realize that I do not want to do business every waking hour. It is so difficult to relax when I am never left alone."

"You know, all important men have that challenge. Let us just forget it for now and enjoy the rest of our evening together."

HJ gave a tremendous amount of time to people. It was difficult to help everyone when he was already concerned about other urgent business. How sad that they would feel slighted when he did not have time. Some even went so far as to curse his name. If they only understood…

It was a lovely day, although it was quite windy. Grace and Gigi headed to Tally's Theatre for a relaxing afternoon. Poor communication between them caused conflicts, misunderstandings, and resentment. The big problem was that even when they refused to talk, they still communicated something in the silences, with their observable behavior. They did not make regular time to be together. Life had been too busy for Gigi and too painful for Grace. Perhaps it was underlying jealousy. Grace seemed to steal Gigi's precious time with HJ. She was either severely depressed or out of control. She often shouted and banged doors in a destructive behavior.

They saw *A Florida Enchantment* (1914), directed by Sidney Drew. Edith Storey was a very fine actress, and she offered a magnificent performance. As they passed the Griffith lot on their way home, they saw them filming a mob scene. There was no dialogue, so the actors told the story by their looks, their eyes, and their hands. It seemed to Gigi that all the actors played their roles to great excess, seemingly overemphasizing their expressions to help make up for the lack of actual dialogue. Most of the time, the lead actress held her hands near her eyes and opened her mouth into an O. She used this expression to suggest everything from mild surprise to horror, making her one expression serve many purposes.

Gigi was hoping that a letter HJ received from their old friend Harry Chandler might convince HJ to slow down and spend time with her attending the many movies Hollywood produced. Harry wrote:

> Your work in Hollywood, Whitley Heights, and the San Fernando Valley was so protracted and so strenuous that one would have thought you with your large fortune might have settled down like the normal man to enjoy leisure and luxury in your declining years ... However, we who were associated with you here in your phenomenal activities and tireless energy never would expect you to violate all your natural tendencies and so are not surprised that you are still going forward under a full head of steam.

HJ was way up in years when he decided to start working on what he said would be his last project. He was the supervisor of the dangerous mountain road, the Ridge Route. (In later years, the Grapevine would replace it.) There had been a lot of talk about dividing California into two states. The division would have been north of Los Angeles. It was extremely time consuming to travel from Los Angeles to San Francisco. Detours had to be made way out to the East. Southern and northern California were essentially two worlds. Because of the swift rise of the numbers of cars and trucks, HJ decided that a shorter vehicle route between the north and south should be built.

Technology would not allow blasting and tunneling. Roads had to be built to accommodate horses and wagons. They followed the contour of the land in order to avoid extreme gradients. This helped minimize washout damage. Additionally, they needed to minimize the road's twists and turns. They had narrow ridges atop steep cliffs. There were 697 curves built—each one going around a hill. It was an enormous task taking out those treacherous curves.

As the funding became tight, HJ and Gigi went to Sacramento so he could speak to the Senate to get approval of additional funding. Governor Richardson was pleased to see him. HJ feared that the Senate would think it was just an old man's hobby when what he was attempting to do was save lives. He pointed out the necessity of making safe roads and the number of causalities the roads had already caused. Gigi remained in her room at the hotel, praying for the bill's passage. When the vote was taken, HJ had his funding.

HJ wanted to catch an early train the next morning, for there was much work to be done. When they woke up, the sun had just come up over the horizon. The hotel did not serve breakfast until eight, so they decided to dine on the train. Gigi was concerned when she heard HJ say, "I am so tired. It has been such a long struggle. I will just have to persevere and work hard. Everyone is counting on me."

The years took their toll on HJ. Some of it was just a function of getting older, yet part of it was due to personality flaws. His reoccurring habits worsened with time. One of his flaws was a chronic restlessness, an inability to appreciate—no matter how well things were going—those blessings that were right in front of him. It is a flaw that is endemic to big business. In any event, it was as a consequence of that restlessness that HJ decided to take on one more project.

Gigi did not learn until after his death that HJ paid $10,000 to get the work completed. HJ was always doing constructive things because he loved the feeling that helping others gave him—an ingrained habit of many years standing. Gigi remembered the grin on his face and the gleam in his shining blue eyes when he saw the road completed. What finally resulted was a wild, low-speed ride as thrilling as any roller coaster of the day. The road was oiled and graded in 1915 and later surfaced with reinforced concrete in 1919. It was a narrow strip of concrete twisting across the mountaintops. And, mostly because of the existence of this new road, California remained as one state— from Oregon to Mexico. When it was completed, it saved travelers a fifty-mile trip through the Mojave Desert. The Ridge Route was considered a miracle of modern engineering.

HJ was invited to address the commercial club about the benefits of a city uniting its residents to promote its general improvements. HJ, once again, needed a break from his strenuous business commitments and felt that a trip to Hawaii might do the trick. The trip to Honolulu was very trying in many respects. January was seasonally a very bad time to cross that part of the Pacific. Their voyage in 1916 hit one of the worst storms. Severe tidal waves tossed the ship as though it was a tiny twig. Everything that was not solidly fastened moved—including the dishes, which were dashed to the floor. With a crash, their existence ended. It was humorous to Gigi that the cruise line sent an inspector on that particular trip to see why so many dishes had been broken on previous trips. He had little problem in issuing an informative report. The voyage was so rough that a sign was posted on the deck: "Anyone going on deck is risking their safety—the ship will not be responsible."

Gigi was ever so happy to step onto solid ground, but HJ was barely fazed by the storm. In his address to the commercial club, HJ emphasized many aspects of developing and beautifying the island. Teeth gleaming, eyes flashing, and arms pumping, HJ was performing a task that delighted him: encouraging others. He told of the importance of churches and schools to developing communities. He felt that it was equally important to have up-to-date lighting systems and roads.

Gigi was somewhat saddened when she realized the many improvements that would soon be part of the Hawaiian scenery. As much as Gigi enjoyed modern conveniences, she was also appalled at the destruction of the environment. She wondered if the improvements merited the sacrifices. Gigi remembered the beauty of the islands from her previous trip to China.

Equally alarming to Gigi was the talk of impending war. It was unclear what profound evil lurked on the horizon. She hated to see either: man versus nature or man versus man. Either way, it seemed that something magnificent and unique would be lost forever.

Chapter Nineteen

Worrisome news arrived from Europe, the first hint of forces gathering that could pull the United States into the war. In a rather hushed tone, HJ read Gigi the morning newspaper. Germany utilized poisonous gas to attack the Russians. Using chemicals on humans seemed so barbaric. Her prayers that night would include the young troops, who Gigi was sure would be suffering from fear of dying a painful death. She hoped that the United States would not be required to make a stand against this evil force.

War was declared April 6, 1917, and the climate in Hollywood was tense. The start of the war interrupted European film-making and eventually brought it to a halt. Europe had sizeable shortages of power and supplies. European films never recovered their dominance in movie production. Fortunately, Hollywood thrived in the European marketplace, using its profits to produce even bigger and better motion pictures.

For Gigi, the war was a crucial time of self-discovery. Over the years, she lost a good deal of her crusading spirit for those who were less fortunate. The shock of the war awakened her to the plight of others.

Groups were organized at once to meet the usual demands of wartime. Many of Gigi's friends joined the Navy Red Cross.

The Red Cross distributed free wool for knitting. Gigi did little war work beyond the inevitable knitting that every woman undertook and which became a constant habit. Women did not go anywhere without their knitting.

It was quite accidental how Gigi first discovered knitting as a companion for a rainy afternoon. She found that one of the best ways to put herself in a meditative mood was to take a walk outside. However, there were certain days when it was just not very pleasant to be outside. Gigi needed an alternative practice for those days.

One day, it occurred to her to try knitting. It worked. The repetitive motions of her hands were a perfect substitute for the repetitive motions of her body while walking. The knitting kept her busy but freed her mind and heart to ponder the problems that were currently bothering her. With the needles in her hands, Gigi found that knitting put a certain distance between her and the problems of war, even those problems that seemed so all-encompassing.

Gigi learned that knitting was a great diversion from worry. As she sat quietly and knitted, her mind would slowly calm. Soon, ideas and worries would start to bubble up to the surface one by one. Gigi found that if she simply acknowledged them and then let them simmer rather than try to actively concentrate on them, amazing things would happen. Vague hints of solutions would begin to appear in her subconscious. By refusing to think too hard, Gigi could open her mind to all sorts of answers that she would never have considered otherwise.

Most importantly, Gigi gradually came to a feeling of peace. Her mood, after a knitting session with friends, was always drastically improved. Even when the problems that worried her were essentially out of her control, after knitting for a while, it would seem less horrible, less terrifying. Quite simply, knitting made Gigi feel better.

Never one to leave well enough alone, Gigi decided that she needed to know why this was. She asked her friends how knitting affected them. Why had she felt so much better after knitting? After talking with her friends, the fact seemed so obvious. On the most basic level, knitting was doing something; and Gigi almost always felt better when she was accomplishing something, anything. Knitting also provided an escape from the thoughts of war. By losing herself in a particularly challenging pattern or stitch, Gigi shut out her worries for a time. But perhaps the best part of all was that the beautiful sweaters that Gigi knitted were sent to the servicemen who were heroically defending the nation.

Gigi was sure that everyone would agree with her when she said that there never had been a time in the history of the world when so much was expected of women. A woman must work, she must plan, she must think, and she must build up while men tore down. Gigi hoped that, someday soon, men would give a toast to women for their noble part—for she was now doing many things that had been thought impossible of her.

All through history, women inspired the world with their heroic deeds. At last women had every opportunity to show what they are capable of doing—in science, in politics, in professions ... In fact, education in all directions was open to them. Since the war began, women were called upon to do men's work in shops, factories, offices, tilling the soil, and even in the war work. For the first time, women were not treated as inferiors but as equals. The crowning touch, in her opinion, was that women had their own proper representation before the public in the weekly newspaper, the *Woman's Press*. At last, there were articles and pictures in a newspaper that were of interest to women.

Before the United States entry into the war, foolish people said that only financial resources would be needed and that the only branch of the service that would be called upon to fight would be the navy. On entry into war, however, both services were in action. There were many arguments about sending troops to France. HJ argued that the Allies were tired and that the United State's help would boost their morale.

Since HJ was one of the outstanding pioneers in developing good roads and boulevards in the nation, he was asked to speak at a conference before the Senate and Congress. For several days, he sought their approval of a plan to build three national highways across the country. HJ conceived and completed more roads and boulevards than any other man in California—operating in both the northern and southern parts of the state. He believed that work should be started at once to provide employment for thousands of returning soldiers and to make use of the motor transport release by the returning army. He wanted the roads built under federal control and according to federal specification.

His goal was to have the roads last as the Roman roads did in France. Having been one of the men that created Sunset Boulevard and Sherman Way, HJ used his time and influence to secure the legislation necessary for the construction of a road from the Atlantic Ocean to the Pacific Ocean. He suggested that one highway go via St. Paul and the northern tier of states to Seattle and Tacoma, a second through Omaha and Denver to San Francisco, and a third by way of the southern route through El Paso to Los Angeles. HJ favored the plan of Senator Townsend to create a national highway commission with five members. During the next five years, these roads would be completed.

As new roads crossed the country, equally amazing changes seemed to traverse Grace's personality. Grace's uncontrolled impulses, lack of social consciousness, and her quest for popularity played important parts in the next phases of her life.

Chapter Twenty

Gigi decided to throw an extravagant reception at which she could present their debutante daughter. Miss Grace Whitley, who was to make her initial bow to society, was one of the prettiest girls to be presented in many years. She had an appealingly interesting face, eyes the color of a deep lake, and lips that glistened while she innocently smiled. Her violet velvet dress was very seductive and continental. The edge of shyness had worn off, and she blossomed into a glamorous young woman. HJ felt that she was too young, but Gigi promised her several years before, "You can have your choice of a coming out party when you are eighteen or nineteen or travel abroad for two years." Grace found men irresistible, loving the attention they paid her. Her decision was quite simple: "Let's have a party."

The reception and dance party were given December 14, 1913, at the Hollywood Hotel. Grace was now nineteen years old and felt that she was more than ready to enter the adult world. The hotel was elaborately decorated in pink roses. Only the elite were invited. At this party, Grace was introduced to the debonair William Widenham.

Grace belonged to Hollywood society that thought itself as self-important. Mr. Widenham gave choice parties. He was charming, good-looking, and loved by those who encountered him. He loved life and was a natural sportsman, a good golfer, and a good rider. William was the first man in her life to give her the attention she longed for.

Grace had a great curiosity about life, desiring to participate in every experience that would give her the attention she desired. She seemed to have a need to hurry, without rhyme or reason. Although the courtship had been incredibly stormy, when William proposed, she accepted. She never thought that she was young and inexperienced. Gigi asked her if she was really in love. Grace solemnly replied, "Yes." HJ demanded that the wedding be postponed so that Grace could go back East to complete her education. As fate or conniving would have, William wired Grace that she needed to return home, as he was seriously ill. He was experiencing abdominal pain, nausea, and vomiting and was sure that it was appendicitis. There was no effective medical therapy, so appendicitis was considered a medical emergency. Miraculously, William recovered without needing surgery, and a new wedding date was set.

The marriage was held at the Whitleys' country home in Van Nuys. The countryside, with its intense blue skies and fresh, clear air had an atmosphere of Southern charm. The house was decorated beautifully with pink and white roses, rare ferns, and lilies from the garden. Grace's gown was French crepe trimmed in white appliqué lace. Her bridal bouquet was orchids. On June 22, 1914, Reverend WE Edwards pronounced Grace and William man and wife as the clock struck noon. It was many years later that she realized that she never understood what being in love really meant.

William had sweet words for women—maidens to widows. His pursuit of women did not end on the dance floor. Whatever Grace expected of marriage, this could not have been it.

She experienced passion but no kindness, and it showed in her countenance. She found it impossible to talk about her marital problems. Her only way of coping was not to see what she did not want to see, not to feel what she did not want to feel. Grace became an expert of denial. She not only disavowed her emotional needs; she slowly, as survival required, began to live in a dream world. Grace did not expect much from men, and her husband greatly filled that bill.

Gigi cried when she heard that Grace was pregnant. There was little hope of a stable marriage. The labor was long, leaving Grace exhausted. Her husband was nowhere to be seen. One could only guess where he was. On a cloudy spring day, Sunday, April 13, 1915, Margaret Virginia Widenham was born.

Chapter Twenty-one

The explosive growth in the entertainment industry forced the opening of innovative and luxurious restaurants on the Boulevard. Musso and Frank's Grill was an instant hit when it opened. HJ and Gigi would often meet his business acquaintances at Musso's. It was in a convenient location at the corner of Hollywood Boulevard and Cherokee Avenue. HJ knew the maitre d' and he enjoyed being seated at the best table. It was an easy way to impress his colleagues. Gigi particularly liked this spot, as they would run into Charlie Chaplin there. His regular table was in the front. HJ liked the excellent service that the male waiters offered. His favorite meal was a big, juicy steak. HJ was fond of the dark wood décor, the leather booths, and the fine feel of a gentlemen's club.

The concept of hillside development in Hollywood was new. No two lots would be quite alike. The terrain constantly changed, with curving streets and steep gentle slopes. The zigzagging flights of stairs that dotted the hillside were driverless, slow, and serene, put there to contrast the aggressive, winding streets. This project would require HJ's professional engineering expertise for planning, design, construction, inspection, administration, and maintenance of the city's new infrastructure. HJ also realized that the development would move slowly and would probably take a decade to complete.

HJ was the first developer to take advantage of Hollywood's Mediterranean climate and scenery. He sent his architect, Arthur Barnes, to study the hillside architecture of Spain and Italy. Arriving home, Barnes used this information as a motivation for the blueprints of many of the residences on the hill. Barnes supported HJ's idea to pattern the streets after those he had seen in Italy. The countless villas of Hollywood would weave themselves, spiraling around terraces shaded by palms, lemon trees, flower-filled gardens, and cascading, multicolored bougainvillea. Together, they subdivided the land into irregularly shaped lots, thereby creating long, winding, narrow roads. The popularity of this architectural style would mushroom throughout the Los Angeles area. The traditional Victorian home was a thing of the past.

For nearly a year, HJ worked on Whitley Heights before the area was opened for public sales. The roads were graded, retaining walls were built, and building sites were leveled. Each lot was designed to take advantage of the magnificent panoramic views of the hills, city, and ocean. The property was located four blocks from the Hollywood Hotel.

Whitley Heights was the ritzy, closed society of the mushrooming film capital. Charlie Chaplin had been attracted to the area because no two homes were alike. Whitley Heights was the most desirable address for the first film idols. The parties the stars gave were legendary and would include such notables as Harold Lloyd, WC Fields, Marie Dressler, Jean Harlow, Rudolph Valentino, and William Powell.

HJ understood that powerful new forces were acting upon Hollywood, causing a nearly miraculous expansion. The city was growing in all available directions—especially the lots that had views of the Pacific Ocean. Everywhere he looked, he saw evidence of the city's prosperity. The city's newspaper, *Hollywood Citizen,* loved to crow about the startling increase in the number of workers employed by the movie studios. As the movie industry soared, the demand for workers remained high; and workers and their supervisors needed places to live.

To attract more people to Hollywood, HJ hosted a party for one thousand important businessmen in the area. After dinner, the assembled guests drove to the commanding summit of the Whitley Heights tract. The final touch to the evening occurred when a monstrous electric sign, the first of this type in Hollywood, was turned on, reading "Whitley Heights." It was so large that it could be plainly seen from as far away as Wilshire Boulevard.

At the closing speech, HJ said, "Whitley Heights will be my last subdivision. I look upon it as the culmination of a lifetime of development and, frankly, the most beautiful piece of property ever developed. I have owned and held it with the idea that it should be my last piece of development work, and I even promised Gigi that it would be."

The earliest visitors to Hollywood saw immediately that the city's greatest power lay in the homes themselves. They produced an effect of majesty and beauty that was far greater than HJ imagined. No single element accounted for this phenomenon. Each building was impressive, unlike anything the majority of visitors had seen in their hometowns. The shared color produced an especially alluring range of effects as the sun traveled the sky. In the early morning, when HJ conducted his inspections, the buildings were a pale blue hue. Each evening, the sun colored the buildings golden ginger and lit the swirls of dust triggered by the breeze until the air itself became a soft, yellowish brown veil.

Real estate advertisements were full of testimonials to Hollywood's location and appreciating values. One resident recalled how immediately after the stars started to live in Hollywood, "there was such a rush for homes in Hollywood and the population increased so rapidly that it was impossible to keep up with it."

The homes in Whitley Heights were creamy stucco with red tile roofs, balconies, terraced yards, arched doorways, and astonishing views. The two- and three-leveled houses were built on upward or downward sloped lots, depending where the home was positioned. It was important to take advantage of the breathtaking scenery below. He gave buyers a discount if they agreed to develop quickly and use a Mediterranean architectural design.

During HJ's first few months working on Whitley Heights, everything seemed to come at him at once. He had to hire staff and set up the office. He had to negotiate work assignments and get up to speed on the issues of architectural design. There was a backload of correspondence and many speaking invitations. He was shuttled from one meeting to another.

He was glad that he had bothered to learn the rules of business when he was young—not just the rules but the precedents as well. It seemed that not many people bothered to learn them these days. Everything was so rushed, so many demands on one's time. But rules unlocked the power of business. HJ thought that they were the keys to the kingdom. Ambition alone was not enough to win in business. Whatever the tangle of motives that pushed HJ toward his goals, he found that to succeed, he must have a fanatical single-mindedness, often disregarding his health, relationships, and mental balance. After looking at his calendar, he realized that over the span of a year, he had only had seven days off. The rest of the time, he typically worked twelve to sixteen hours a day. Most of his sins of business came from one large sin: the need to win—but also the need to not lose. Certainly that was what the money chase was all about.

Gigi wanted their home at 6643 Whitley Terrace to stand out from the others on the hill, so she convinced HJ to build a European villa. When designing their new home this time, they completed the project together. To Gigi, it was essential that HJ incorporate her creative ideas. HJ could be in charge of quality control, as it was crucial in a project that demanded so much detailing. But Gigi would be in charge of its design. Passionate about the visual images found in the sun-drenched landscape of Hollywood, Gigi wanted a home whose design would radiate noteworthy splendor and tranquility—a home embracing eloquent balconies, lush gardens, rustling palms, and glittering views of the Pacific Ocean. Both indoors and out, the estate would be a thoughtful mix of formal and informal spaces—all detailed with the interests of each family member in mind. Their new home embraced a unique brand of classicism with balance, symmetry, and harmony—a perfect blend of universal design. Gigi wanted a calm, peaceful home where HJ could escape the rigors of his work.

Nestled atop a stretch of gorgeous land with breathtaking views, the property commanded a 280-degree vista reaching from Los Angeles to the Pacific Ocean to the mountains. "It is a wonderful site," said HJ, whose enthusiasm was shared by Gigi. They had chosen this spot for their home over thirty years ago while on their honeymoon. A lot of people build their home as an investment, but Gigi only wanted to build something she would love.

The interior conjured up the feeling of heaven. It was handsomely adorned with a rich mixture of pastel silks, taffetas, and embroideries. As Gigi entered the home, to her left was the living room, which was connected to the library. With comfort considered in the design of their home, the living room was very spacious, light, and airy. In the center of the room was a beautiful oriental rug that HJ and Gigi purchased on one of their many trips abroad. The house brimmed with their ever-present collection of art objects and contemporary furniture. In the center were paintings of Gigi's parents, Margaret and William Ross. Throughout the house, the walls were plastered with rich finishes that complimented the textures of their furniture.

Above the main level were bedrooms, including an especially comfortable master suite. It opened up to an outside balcony. Gigi had it designed with comfort and privacy in mind. The upstairs porch next to her bedroom was used as an aviary for her beloved canaries. The house included a small staff quarters and a generous housekeeping area on the lower level.

Beautiful manicured gardens with a park-like appearance surrounded the west of the home, including sweeping lawns, splendid trees, and colorful flowers. The formal gardens Gigi planted there departed from the standards set for the other residents. Gigi may not have been a star, but there were other ways to be notable in society.

The ample grounds offered a small cottage and a play area. In the afternoon, their grandchildren rode a miniature train around the yard, shaded by a canopy of trees. Ever creative, Gigi instructed their nanny to plan story times, poetic recitations, and dramatic productions for them to perform.

One of Gigi's favorite parties in Whitley Heights was a lavish affair given by William Powell and Carole Lombard. Carole's beauty was matched by a good heart and a bubbly attitude. William was debonair, a classic picture of confidence and elegance. They had purchased a home on Iris Circle. Supper was served on the terrace overlooking the valley. An orchestra of about five pieces furnished the music. The decorations upon both lawns and through the many gardens were beautiful. Just after dark, the electric lights were turned on, simultaneously illuminating the gardens' natural beauty. The guests danced and laughed into the wee hours of the morning.

If evenings at the Heights were seductive, the nights were ravishing. The lamps that laced every home and walkway produced the most elaborate demonstration of electric illumination. The electric wires had been placed underground, an important engineering milestone. What residents liked most was the sheer beauty of seeing so many lights switched on in one place at one time. For many visitors, these nightly illuminations were their first encounter with electricity. Having seen nothing but kerosene lamps for lighting, this was like getting an unexpected vision of heaven.

Gigi loved the glamour and pizzazz that the stars brought to the Heights. Reflected in much of the architecture was not only the richly decorative Mediterranean style but also the richly ornamented lifestyles of the stars who lived there. They liked the warm feeling of community it held, even though it was in the heart of the city. It was a wealthy, private community with winding streets. Gigi could stand on the terrace and watch Valentino driving up the hill in his Roadster. As he passed, he would wave to her. When he rumbled up and down Whitley Avenue in his convertible, people's heads spun to follow him. Valentino was a star who acted the part, and people enjoyed seeing him drive by. Sometimes, when HJ and Gigi were on an early morning walk, they would see him with his two faithful dogs. Valentino would stop to talk with HJ about events in the news.

Over the years, Whitley Heights housed an array of Hollywood stars. HJ had been the city's best advisor and constant mentor. In the highest sense, he was the planner of the city. An artist, he painted with wooded slopes, with lawns, mountain sides, and ocean views. One of Gigi's favorite homes, besides her own, was a honeymoon house built for Valentino's new wife on 6770 Wedgwood Place. The two-story, eight-room house included two master bedrooms with baths. It was beautifully landscaped with terraced gardens and enhanced by Italian cypress trees and interesting shrubs. They were a flamboyant couple who added spice to the little hamlet on the hill.

As HJ and Gigi walked the neighborhood in the evening, they enjoyed seeing their neighbors. Just down the street from them, they would pass 6672 Whitley Terrace, the home of Barbara La Mar, a brown, stucco house with a red tiled roof. At times, they would see her on the little sun porch, spending some leisure time with her baby, kept cool by the breezes blowing through the Cahuenga Pass. She was always so happy holding the baby, a beautiful smile gracing her face. HJ liked to talk with her when they occasionally met. She possessed a razor-sharp intelligence and a keen sense of humor.

Continuing on to 6691 Whitley Terrace was the Barthemess house, where they saw Norma Talmadge, a friend of Sid Grauman. Gigi considered it interesting that her home had finials shaped as pineapples. Perhaps it represented the current craze for tropical fruit. Norma played the courageous, brave, tragic heroine. Gigi felt that no one could suffer on the silver screen better than Norma. All her neighbors loved her warm and thoughtful disposition. Sadly, like so many others, Norma's shine would not glitter strongly enough to see her through cinema's transition to sound. Gigi wondered how this would affect her, as she was someone who had virtually grown up onscreen. It was equally difficult for Gigi to imagine that there was ever a time before the talkies.

Next door, at 6697 Whitley Terrace, was a large villa that was owned by director Robert Vignola. He directed many of the movies in which Marion Davis, William Randolph Heart's mistress, starred in. Rumors in the neighborhood suggested that Marion and William used the home as a romantic hideaway. Marion was one of the funniest comedians around. She was a big-hearted girl who always waved hello when Gigi saw her. Unfortunately, when talkies replaced silent film, Marion suffered the same fate as Norma Talmadge. Her career ended due to a childhood stutter that became stronger when she was under pressure.

Up the street, a mansion called "Topside" housed the illustrious star Blanche Sweet. William Powell and Carole Lombard lived in a Spanish-style home on Iris Circle between Charlie Chaplin and Harold Lloyd. Marie Dressler lived at 6809 Iris Circle.

Wealthy stars were attracted to Whitley Heights by its amazing views and modern architectural design. From the hillside, they could witness acres of green California grass that had been accented by brilliant, multihued flowers. The avenues were lined by royal palms that brought a magnificent contrast to the white roads. Carman Miranda lived in a bungalow on Padre Terrace. Leo G. Carroll, who stared as Topper, had a home on Grace Avenue. Among those who later had homes were Gloria Swanson, Bette Davis, Jean Harlow, and Tyrone Powers.

It seemed that the tiny village was a magnet to a wide array of stars. It was in close proximity to the Electric Theatre, which presented the first performance of a moving picture. Additionally, the nearby Hollywood Hotel, by this time, was doing exceptional business. Those who had invested with HJ in Hollywood would accumulate a 72 percent return upon their investment in an amazingly short time. The project proved to be one of the most notable and successful legitimate real estate ventures of record anywhere.

Yes, undeniably, the Heights possessed a mystifying allure to wealthy actors and producers. In fact, the first map of the stars' homes printed in 1918 showed that most of them lived in Hollywood homes. The Heights' allure came on the ocean breeze in the whisper of distant laughter, a delightful melody, and a whiff of alluring fragrances as the hill lay gentle and tranquil beneath the soft, moonlit sky. Fascinated with the rhythm of the town, they were drawn to it with stars in their eyes and great expectations. There was a rustle in the trees and then all was silence, but it seemed that the hill was smiling for those who lived and loved and laughed on her lovely expanse.

Not only did HJ promote and change the name of Prospect Boulevard to Hollywood Boulevard; he was also instrumental to its design. HJ designed the Boulevard to have one side for autos and the lower grades for streetcars. How did he know the value of rapid transit way before others? Electric trolley cars crisscrossed the entire county, connecting people to their schools, jobs, and choices of entertainment for only a nickel a ride. HJ did not want the wide streets where the buildings were small and set back to lose their definition, so he lined the streets with trees. That way, the Boulevard did not feel primarily like a transportation corridor but rather like a place where people lived and socialized. In addition, curbs and trees provided a physical and psychological buffer between sidewalk and car traffic that increased a feeling of safety. Hollywood might have developed in the traditional manner of the past, but HJ had a nose for a new type of development.

Among HJ's holdings in Hollywood was the magnificent hill on which he built their beautiful home. The home was constructed at the entrance to the pass and overlooked the city and the sea. Additionally, he had a splendid, ten-thousand-square-foot county villa at Van Nuys. There, he bred fine, fancy stock, registered breeds of turkeys, geese, ducks, chickens, and pigs and landscaped the grounds with beautiful flowers, trees, shrubs, and fruit orchards. Everything was on a large scale in the white-glazed brick mansion with its patio, conservatory, roof garden, spacious living rooms, den, billiard parlor, and library. The grounds were enhanced by the most expert landscape gardener. With such a country house and the hill home in Hollywood, Gigi longed to hear that HJ was, at last, satisfied.

By now, Hollywood Boulevard had developed a skyline of new office buildings, apartment houses, and hotels—each with its personal architectural temperament. Many of the new buildings were four stories tall, the legal height limit. These new buildings made Hollywood a more desirable location for doctors, lawyers, and other business professionals. The demand for high-quality housing continued to increase.

HJ was saddened when he read in the newspaper of the death of his longtime friend Theodore Roosevelt. It was a cold January morning in 1919 when he read the news as he sipped his coffee. The only good news was that he had died doing what he loved most: working. Although their friendship had become distant over the years, HJ could still remember the many nights around the campfire when they had made plans for their future. Each had a healing effect on the other. He and Teddy had made a promise to one another that they were to wear out, not to rust out. Equally important to both of them was their drive to improve the life of those less fortunate. They pledged to work for the good of mankind.

HJ considered himself blessed by the spirit, friendship, and vision that Teddy had shared with him. With an unshakable faith in the values of his country and the character of its people, Teddy rallied Americans in confidence and pride. His optimism, strength, and humility symbolized the American spirit. Roosevelt believed that God took the side of justice and America had a special calling to oppose tyranny and defend freedom. HJ felt that, through his courage and determination, Teddy had enhanced America's security and advanced the spread of peace, liberty, and democracy. He only hoped that, in his own way, he had changed the face of the world as significantly. HJ deemed himself stronger and better for having Teddy as a friend.

Chapter Twenty-two

Gigi was of the opinion that only a few women, more advanced than all others in the days gone by, knew enough to make an effort to demand their own rights. She found this odd because she could not think of a day that her rights were not imperative to her. Fortunately, many women knew enough to make an effort to demand their rights. It had been difficult, as men had held power for so long. Women were trodden down for centuries, having no opportunity to mingle in the daily affairs of life. They spent many years reaching the goals set forth by the Woman's Movement. Gigi felt fortunate that some women were wiser and cleverer than others. These women found the key to some men's hearts, which were nobler than other men. Through them, they won their freedom. As in all great events, God had always used some women to work out his plans. All great and good things in life were won.

Gigi appreciated that America was founded on justice. No nation on earth had ever given women such freedom as America. That was because women had helped form the Republic. The patriotic society of the Daughters of the American Revolution, of whom she was a member, had dedicated their first building in honor of the glorious patriotic women who fought for our nation's freedom. It stood as the first building in the whole world erected by women to honor their ancestors.

In all good works, women had to band together to help enlighten other women and men to understand the needs of the day. So, after groping in the darkness for ages for the password to those things for which women were searching, women had found the key to sisterhood. Women were free. No longer would it be necessary for them to plead their own cause. The government would do that for them now that they could vote.

Roses filled the chamber of the House of Representatives on August 18, 1920. Yellow roses represented those supporting women's right to vote while red roses represented those who were opposed. The suffragist needed one more vote as the roll call began. Congressman Harry Burn, who had just turned twenty-four, entered the chamber with a red rose on his lapel, but he also had a letter from his mother folded in his pocket:

> Dear Son,
>   Vote for suffrage and do not keep them in doubt. I notice some of the speeches against. They were very bitter. I have been watching to see how you stood, but have not seen anything yet. Do not forget to be a good boy...
>   With lots of love,
>   Mama

When the roll call reached Harry, he voted for ratification. Suffragists in the balcony erupted in cheers. His response to his vote was simple: "I know that a mother's advice is always the safest for a boy to follow."

Now that women had the vote, Gigi believed that they needed to work for peace, children's rights, the right to use birth control, and women's economic empowerment.

Gigi clearly realized that each of her rights was fought for long and hard by many generations of women that came before her. Their victories were her victories. Gigi found it difficult to imagine the future dimensions of women's liberation, but she knew that it would require vision combined with a depth of devotion.

For HJ and Gigi, the 1920s were an odd time. As Gigi had often said to HJ, Columbus may have discovered America, but it was a woman, Queen Isabella of Spain, who financed the trip. It was now the time in history for women to take their proper position in society. Gigi was overjoyed that she lived in Hollywood and had experienced a time of great wealth and new modern ideas. The role of women changed. Sports and entertainment stars were celebrated, and modern technology changed Hollywood's landscape. By 1921, Alice Robertson of Oklahoma became the first woman to preside over the House of Representatives. By 1922, the Episcopal Church voted to delete *obey* from the marriage vow.

Gigi felt that today's women were strong, confident, and moving toward self-sufficiency. As the movie industry evolved, society's opinion of a woman's ability had transformed enormously. Gigi was glad that women would no longer simply be seen as just pretty faces. Men were beginning to realize that women wanted to be respected for being intelligent, independent, and self-confident. Somehow, Gigi felt that being a woman in this era would be more complicated. While Gigi wanted to be seen as independent, she also wanted to embrace her femininity and be treated special. At times, Gigi had to think about what she really wanted.

These changes matched her personality perfectly. Gigi was more prone to voice her opinion, probably, than most women.

And with her, there was no such thing as compromise. Still, Gigi knew that she had found something in HJ that she had never seen in another man. He talked to her and listened to her opinions. When he told her of his day, it always seemed like a marvelous adventure.

"I wish you were there, Gigi," he told her as they sat on the couch, their heads close together within the light of the fire.

On the other hand, HJ clung to the past, where the generational wealthy remained fiercely conservative and religious. Grace loved the fashions that the new freedom brought and quickly embraced them. As part of the popular crowd, she was one of the first girls to cut her hair short into a bob. HJ thought it was scandalous—women looking like men. He detested flappers. The reality was that Hollywood was a divided city. Gigi's inner turmoil was much the same.

For some, as the roaring twenties evolved, it was as simple as tossing out the old way of doing things and bringing in the new. HJ found this almost impossible to do. He watched, amazed, as men shaved off their mustaches, emulating the look of college chaps, full of coy self-awareness and never-ending possibility. Sometimes, with their cocked straw hats and feet on the running board, they looked a little suspect to him, like salesmen who were not ashamed of themselves anymore.

He could not understand why women closed their eyes to their mothers' lessons on how a lady should appear in public. These women slowly jettisoned corsets, shed chaperons, and hiked their hemlines over their ankles. They faced the camera with amused, smart-aleck caginess. Sometimes, for mischief, they posed with cigarettes. The face of intrigue became the face of sexuality.

For all the changes in status during the twenties, HJ still firmly believed that a "woman's place is in the home." Men definitely should learn more than women because they supported wives and children; they did the more taxing work. In reflecting on the change in society, HJ wondered whether, rather than criticizing men for expecting women to stay at home, women should try walking in a man's shoes. Perhaps he would respect them if they were willing to do unpleasant but necessary work. He found few women willing to do work as roofers, road pavers, or prison guards—work that often put one in an early grave. Talk needed to be extremely fair and balanced when addressing the rights one deserved.

Besides women's position in society changing, it appeared that the world's social value system was being tested. Nothing seemed sacred anymore; nothing was personal if it had publicity possibilities. Everywhere one looked, the boundary between the moral and wicked seemed to be degrading. Elizabeth Cady Stanton argued in favor of divorce. Clarence Darrow advocated free love. A young woman named Borden killed her parents. Scandals rocked the Hollywood newspapers in the early 1920s: the death of Virginia Rappe in the Fatty Arbuckle case, the murder of director William Desmond Taylor, and the drug-related death of matinee idol Wallace Reid. Gigi loved the newspaper. She read and reread it. It brought the whole world to their breakfast table. However, those stories had a dark side; and she was appalled that such things could happen. What was becoming of their beloved town? HJ had been supportive of the movie industry and wondered if he had made a mistake allowing them such an esteemed position in his elite community. Fortunately, they were able to keep their family scandal quiet and out of the newspapers.

Local churches, the Hollywood Women's Club, and reformers had blood in their eyes. Hollywood's sinfulness and moral laxness was seen in the films they produced. Many of Gigi and HJ's friends were demanding censorship. Over a hundred censorship bills had already been introduced in thirty-seven states that year.

There were ominous rumblings of disapproving public opinion even before the Arbuckle and Taylor cases. Some opportunists wrote a rash of vulgar books, plays, and songs; and they were making movies that violated good taste and decency. Some towns retaliated by banning all motion pictures. More and more, pressure groups demanded federal censorship and regulation of films. The nation's box offices began to reflect the movie industry's loss of goodwill. Gigi prayed that something would soon be done before things got too out of hand.

In 1922, Ross and Mary Whitley moved to the five-hundred-acre Tu-Tock-A-Nula Ranch in the newly developing San Fernando Valley. It was located on Ventura Boulevard, about seven miles from Hollywood. This peaceful spot would be a great spot to raise children. The ranch was highly developed, with livestock, fruit, and other diversified industries. It was considered one of California's model ranches. The beautiful home was in a canyon about half a mile from the main highway. As one approached the Spanish ranchette, they were greeted by an artistic swimming pool surrounded with beautiful rare plants. Ross employed twenty-five men to maintain the ranch.

The impulse to reverse directions haunted Ross as he returned to the ranch early one afternoon. He feared what he would find as he had known for quite some time that things were not right between Mary and him. Ross just had to know the truth. He had come this far, facing his worst fears. He would see this situation through to the end, he told himself determinedly. Ross also reminded himself that, if not for this one intriguing woman and the intense attraction he had for her, he would not be in this predicament. Why had he gone against better judgment and married her? Could the rumor he overheard the other day have been a lie?

As he stood in the shadows of the barn's walls, he watched in horror. Mary was having an affair with the ranch foreman.

Ross leaped from the shadows, his face flushed. His grip tightened forcefully around Mary's arm. "How could you?" he shouted. Releasing his grip, he walked away. Over his shoulder, he said, "I will be home tomorrow evening, and I expect you to be gone."

Ross never spoke to Mary again. By the end of the year, the divorce was complete.

Luckily for the Whitleys, the citizens of Hollywood seemed to gorge themselves on the daily scandals of movie stars. The public quickly moved from one serving of gossip to the next. Each tidbit seemed juicier than the one before. HJ managed to keep their family secret hidden, even if it was a tasty morsel.

After the stressful divorce, Gigi was happy to have her attention diverted to more pleasant endeavors. Cultured society flocked to Hollywood with the opening of the Hollywood Bowl. In 1910, a group of civic-minded men and women who were their friends gave birth to the idea of creating an outdoor park and art center. They hoped that it would spark community spirit in their small town, which had a population of five thousand. Finally, the Theatre Arts Alliance had set out and found a suitable location for the presentation of outdoor theatrical performances. Nestled in between sagebrush, rolling hills, and pine trees, the Bowl was perfectly tucked into a canyon behind Whitley Heights. After a trial performance, it was found that the site's acoustics were perfect. As Gigi heard the beautiful music played by the Philharmonic Orchestra on Easter morning, she drew inspiration from God to carry on.

Deciding what cultural events to produce at the Bowl seemed no easy task for the Alliance. Funding for the Bowl's first concert season in 1922 was difficult. The local community and students from Hollywood High School donated funds; but it was the gathering of celebrities, both onstage and in the audience, that ensured the growth of the Bowl. The first season, which HJ and Gigi attended, was the *Symphonies Under the Stars,* which consisted of forty concerts in ten weeks. They were seated on simple wooden benches. The crowd was exhilarated with Tchaikovsky and Strauss waltzes. We all have our guilty pleasures, and Gigi's was symphony music. As Gigi listened, her foot began to gently twitch longingly to the beat of the music. The Hollywood Bowl changed her experience of listening to orchestral music by presenting it outdoors. Gigi felt that these programs had done more to spread the gospel of good music during the last ten weeks than had been done since she arrived in Hollywood.

Under Gigi's guidance, the Hollywood Women's Club members organized a Hollywood community sing. They started with thirty-five singers and grew to over nine hundred participants. They took part in the first Easter sunrise service at Whitley Heights in 1919. They also participated in raising funds for the pilgrimage plays, the new Hollywood hospital, and the famous Hollywood Bowl.

Whatever alienation may have come during the scandals, Hollywood had emerged in the national imagination as one of the most powerfully symbolic towns in America. The myth of Hollywood had been born: a place where American dreams were created, dreams that offered romance, a better home, more creative occupations, upward mobility, and never-ending excitement. Americans loved the stories and the imagery movies gave. Filmmakers were more than willing to cash in on their dreams and give the public what they wanted.

To counteract the scandals, their friend Cecil B. DeMille decided that, rather than fight public outcry, he would get on the religious bandwagon to re-establish favor with the American people. DeMille's grandfather was an Episcopal clergyman and raised him to treasure the Bible. Likewise, Cecil's earliest childhood memories had been sitting at the feet of his father, hearing the Bible being read. HJ and Gigi heard that *The Ten Commandments* was going to be released in 1923. It was a great method to teach the general public. One could entertain while teaching values. Gigi liked the idea that DeMille was using men of God as his advisers on this production. A church service was held on the set every morning before shooting began. DeMille said, "Give me any two pages of the Bible, and I will give you a picture."

Just like HJ, DeMille was a natural-born showman. He had the uncanny talent to know just what the public liked, and he gave it to them. He was careful not to overdo it. Too much glamour could easily turn into something implausible, and DeMille knew just where that line was. He was an expert at getting his name in front of the public—and the names of his pictures too.

Hollywood once again seemed to be emphasizing American decency over glamour. HJ had wanted Hollywood to be a place that blessed the people who lived in it. Hollywood had opportunities for upward mobility; but people would need talent, education, moral character, and a willingness to work hard. There was a new religious fervor in Hollywood, and the community relied on the churches to alleviate many of the social problems that the movie industry brought. The church generally took on a certain amount of personal responsibility for those less fortunate.

In 1922, the Motion Picture Producers and Distributors of America were formed, despite Hollywood's attempt to avoid it. Under the auspices of the Catholic Church, general principles were established. Prior to setting up the code, filmmakers often crossed the bounds of what the church would accept. Such movies as *A Daughter of the Gods* (1916), in which Annette Kellermann bares it all for director Herbert Brennon as she sits among the waterfalls, and *A Fool There Was* (1915), in which Theda Bara plays a seductive femme fatale that led men astray, were too risqué for most viewers. No picture should be produced that would lower the moral standards of those who saw it. They hoped to ensure that the sympathy of the audience would never be thrown to the side of crime, wrongdoing, or sin. The code did not have any legal authority and very little power. Religious reformers were upset by the public's lack of concern and their inability to produce change.

The American public developed an unquenchable craving for what happened in Hollywood, especially the private aspects of star's lives. Movie studios were more than happy to foster this interest. Everyone across America noticed when movie stars' lives became questionable. Norma Talmadge fell in love with her costar, Gilbert Roland. They saw her drive down Hollywood Boulevard in a convertible with her arms around Gilbert. Mary Pickford tried to avoid reporters when she went to Nevada for her divorce. Rumors of her affair with Fairbanks tarnished their reputations. HJ sensed that society was losing a moral battle and that, possibly, the reputation of Hollywood itself was being marked. A love-hate relationship was started between Hollywood and the press.

Carolyn and Gigi had seen each other over the years at club meetings, but their friendship never took off until they began going to the movies. They would meet at noon for lunch and then go to a matinee. Movie-going became ingrained in them. When they went to the movies, they wanted to be cheered up. If only for an afternoon, they needed to feel part of the fantasy they saw on the screen.

It was the coming of sound that provided a dramatic climax to their movie-going adventures. Their love of seeing movies seemed to grow exponentially over the years, and neither of them tired of spending time together. Their friendship brought an uncanny sanity to Gigi, and HJ encouraged her to spend time with Carolyn.

Gigi's longtime pastime now became a full-time passion. On any excuse, they ran off to the movies, as the theaters in Hollywood were excellent places to see a show. Gigi no longer went just to have a distraction. She felt she had become a movie critic, perhaps better than the ones in the newspaper. Her insightfulness made analyzing the plots and judging music and lyric quality a simple task. They saw a wide variety of movies: dramas, classics, comedies, and her favorite, musicals.

After a delicious lunch at the Hollywood Hotel, Carolyn and Gigi walked to the Egyptian Theater located on Hollywood Boulevard. One of their favorite movies was *Robin Hood*, with Douglas Fairbanks as the leading man. Over lunch, Carolyn and Gigi discussed the many rumors that they heard about the film's production. HJ told Gigi that hundreds of carpenters had worked on the set, creating a dramatic castle and a medieval town.

Over the years, they would meet as often as their busy schedules allowed. That year, they both enjoyed Buster Keaton in *Cops*. For Gigi, Buster Keaton was the best of the silent clowns. Keaton had one of the most expressive faces in silent film. His reactions to the peculiar events around him left no doubt about his point of view. Keaton did not need to smile or laugh; that was the audience's job. The running chase was the high point of the film.

Gigi especially enjoyed seeing her friends and neighbors up on the big screen. They had rich voices, and their facial expressions brought characters to life. On her list of favorites over the years were Lon Chaney in the *Phantom of the Opera*, Rudolph Valentino in the *Son of the Sheik*, Charlie Chaplin in *The Kid*, Douglas Fairbanks and Mary Pickford in *The Taming of the Shrew*, and Gloria Swanson in *Sadie Thompson*.

The radio was the movies' only rival. Hollywood acquired its first three stations in 1922. HJ felt honored that his friend Harry Chandler had founded a station with the call letters KHJ. The station specialized in public affairs and children's programming. The station's identification theme was provided by canaries, which Gigi raised at her home. HJ and Gigi held a special spot in Harry's heart since the bombing of the *Times* building.

HJ and Gigi were still working on the construction of their home at 6643 Whitley Terrace. On the second floor of the home, HJ had the architects design a bird aviary for Gigi's beloved canaries. Every morning, Gigi was happily greeted by their wonderful songs. Gigi even trained some of them to do tricks. Sound produced by these little birds made every day sound like springtime. While at her Aunt Sarah's farm nestled in the foothills of Alabama, she was first introduced to canaries.

The skyline of Hollywood Boulevard dramatically changed as skyscraper mile arrived on June 3, 1922, when Security Trust and Savings opened the tallest building in Hollywood. The six-story building was located on Hollywood and Cahuenga Boulevards. Thousands of guests and many movie stars toured the bank on opening day. The bank boasted that it had one of the largest lobbies on the Pacific Coast.

Chapter Twenty-three

A quarter of a century after the sign lit the Hollywood hillside, Gigi would brag to the family that HJ was the genius who came up with the idea. Her stories were a jumble of remembrances. The decades ran together like a box of chocolates filled with a variety of candy. She would start out talking about the naming of Hollywood and in mid-sentence cross over to the time she saw her first motion picture. She crowed about the naming of Hollywood for over forty years. Her stories were always consistent; and the facts never changed, even when they were told in a variety of ways. Perhaps the reason it was hard to relate a tale without switching to another was the fact that many events happened during the same time period. HJ was busy starting new projects while he was still completing twenty others.

In 1923, HJ (along with some other men in a syndicate he belonged to) discussed the idea of adding an additional sign to the Hollywood hills. In addition to the Whitley Heights sign, a new sign honoring the new town should be placed for all to see. HJ hoped that this additional sign might help him finalize the sales in Whitley Heights. HJ felt that movie publicists had nothing on land developers when it came to marketing and bright lights. He realized how successful the Whitley Heights sign had been in promoting the sale of homes in his prestigious subdivision.

The original plan was to have the sign there for a year or so. The sign would read "Hollywoodland" (later becoming "Hollywood"). The giant electric sign would add another exclusive touch to the area. Electricity was still a rather new commodity; the public was fascinated by it. Harry Chandler, one of HJ's long-term business partners, took this advice, convincing the syndicate to place the sign on the hill to advertise the new five-hundred-acre subdivision. The letters would be thirty feet wide and nearly fifty feet high. The thirteen-letter sign was studded with more light bulbs than Gigi could imagine. At night, even if they were some distance from Hollywood, they could see the sign lighting their way home.

People would ask HJ why he thought Hollywood had grown so rapidly. HJ would answer, "A greater factor in Hollywood's growth than climate, scenery, or location is Hollywood's citizenship. I feel Hollywood has gathered a class of broad-minded, forward-looking, clean-living citizens that make the highest advancement possible."

New arrivals, of course, were impressed initially by the scenery. As they stayed a while, the pleasures of life with people of refinement grew. The spirit of advancement and bigness in thought were contagious. Hollywood had splendid schools, thanks in part to HJ and Gigi's generosity. It also had splendid churches with able leaders. HJ felt that if you would place these same people in a desert, they would make an oasis. "The hills they could not duplicate; the location they could not parallel; climate they could not equal; but, still, it would not have been the wonderful place it is without the people." That is why HJ always said, "Hollywood's greatest asset is its people."

Gigi asked residents of Hollywood why they chose to live there. Otho Houston told her that he had come from Texas. He said, "I have been over in Paris, and the beautiful street known as Avenue des Champs-Elysées is no prettier than a look down Vine Street in Hollywood. In Hollywood, you can make sure fast friends, and you can see them whenever you want. I feel as if there will be no more moving for me. I have found the spot where I want to live and make the acquaintance of all the good people that I can."

Another resident of Hollywood, L. Frank Baum, the author of the *Wizard of Oz*, said, "It is the greatest place on Earth. I have visited all the show places of Europe, judged them from a residential standpoint, and found Hollywood the most desirable city of all. It is the city of enchantment, and I thank Mr. Whitley for having such insight to develop it in such a manner. We can be glad, you and I, and praise God in our hearts. We live in Hollywood."

Gigi thought Hollywood was as close to Oz as any town could get. She marveled that HJ developed a city with such high character and public spirit. The people came in increasing numbers every year until, at last, Hollywood was becoming the art capital of the world.

Hollywood's greatest impact was how it changed the way Americans perceived themselves. It primed the whole of America to think of cities in a way that they never had before. Hollywood led people out of the wilderness of the commonplace to new ideas of beauty and nobility. Overall, HJ was pleased with the progress made in Hollywood. He thought that it was a most satisfactory and encouraging endeavor. He found it hard to believe that so many men of technical education and ability had been recruited and suitably organized to work together so well. He thought it a notable circumstance that there was so little friction, so little display of jealousy, envy, and combativeness as had appeared in the progress of other enterprises.

Chapter Twenty-four

HJ was once again summoned by an unrelenting urge to conquer a new frontier. How could he resist owning the three thousand acres of the Sacramento Ranch and the eighteen thousand acres of the Estrella Ranch when they offered such a challenging adventure? HJ invested over $1,250,000 of his personal money on these projects, constructing over twenty miles of roads, planting five orchards, and erecting various groups of ranch buildings. The Associated Almond Growers then purchased ten thousand acres of the Estrella lands, planting over seven hundred acres of almond trees.

HJ and Gigi arrived in Paso Robles to look over his properties. He took a much-needed rest at the baths at the Hot Springs. Gigi had just returned from a summer trip through France and Switzerland. She was not surprised to find that HJ had already acquired several businesses in the area, along with banking interests. Gigi had hoped that he would retire and enjoy his final years with her. Why did he always have to be so busy and not take it easy like other people his age? He was similar to an anxious horse—chafing at his bit, impatient to be doing something all the time. Gigi reminded HJ that he promised to retire. His response was like the repetitive squawking of a parrot: "I will make it up to you later. There is plenty of time. I will build my career now so that when we are older we will have plenty of money to spend on activities we all enjoy."

Gigi reminded him that his time might run out. "You are not getting any younger. Your busy lifestyle has not changed. It has just become more deeply ingrained. Each day has twenty-four hours. What you do with those hours speaks volumes about what is important to you. I know you say I am important to you. Please show me."

One can block a river and even divert a river, but eventually the force of the current will overcome any impediment set in its path and the river will find its way right back to where it started. And so it was with HJ. He promised to try; but the new, tiny pathway he started to follow was quickly swept away by business concerns. Once again, exhausted from overworking, HJ took another trip to Paso Robles Hot Springs to refresh. He wired Gigi her monthly allowance of $1000. He dropped a quick note to Ross:

> Sorry I did not have more time with you to explain matters before I left, but I hope to be back in Hollywood in a week or so and back to work. I can go over things with you then. I am glad you are getting started on your subdivision of your canyon tract and hope that you will do well with it. Major Pickerell and wife and Mayer and his wife are taking baths here as well. With best wishes to all.
>
> I am affectionately your Father,
> HJ Whitley

With HJ gone to Paso Robles, Gigi decided to play matchmaker. She arranged for one of her close friends, Murnie Hubbard, to throw a small dinner party. Gigi would not allow things to happen by chance this time. Ross was seated next to Irene Preston, an ordinary beginning in which to meet. He glanced at Irene and took in every aspect of her. He wanted to speak to her, but he choked on his words. As he shook her hand and gazed into her striking blue eyes, he knew before he had taken his next breath that he would like to ask her out to dinner. She was perfect. What made her remarkable, unlike anyone Ross had ever meant before, was her silent charm.

From there, it was like a whirlwind. Ross's heart spun out of control. A clever woman, Irene perceived how to win HJ's approval from the start. Irene was a highly intelligent woman and a considerable scholar. She carried it all with conscientiousness and reserve. Memories of his past marriage had faded, becoming fragments that evoked little feeling.

Ross Whitley and Irene Preston were married April 17, 1923. HJ did not want to draw attention of his business associates to the fact that Ross was marrying for a second time, so the wedding was simple and held at the Whitley home in Hollywood. There were no maids of honor; instead, Irene's four sisters—Ina, Stella, Antoinette, and Dorothy—acted as informal attendants, holding her bouquet of rose buds. It was a perfect California day with sunshine and brilliant flowers. The couple stood in the garden under a flower canopy as the minister began the ceremony. Two pink satin pillows were placed on the ground in front of the bride and groom. When the reverend pronounced the blessing, the couple knelt before him.

After the ceremony, the guests walked to the terrace for the catered brunch. In the house, the guests could view the wedding gifts. At three in the afternoon, the bride and groom departed for a honeymoon in Europe.

Eight months later, when Irene told Ross she was pregnant, they felt every joyous emotion humanly possible. Ross told HJ and Gigi that a baby was on the way, and they were delighted.

Gigi's long devotion to her son would now extend to her grandchild. Gigi's attitude was straightforward; she focused on her son, his family, and their happiness. As long as Ross was content, Gigi was satisfied. Irene showed no sign of resenting her central role in their lives. Ross never recognized Irene's frustration, as he remained very self-centered. Thankfully, Irene, the ever-optimist, learned to handle Gigi in ways no one else could.

The idea of fatherhood unleashed a basket full of emotions in Ross. He found it refreshing, intimidating, exciting, and terrifying all at the same time. He wondered what sort of father he would be. He wanted to be just like HJ, and he wanted to be nothing like him.

On Sunday morning, September 28, 1924, Johnstone Whitley was born at home in the small cottage on the country club where Ross and Irene lived. Gigi just loved his blonde fuzz and blue eyes. There were many milestones Irene would record. Johnstone's first steps came at eleven months. He was quite proud of his new accomplishment. Irene took great delight in caring for Johnstone.

The things Johnstone remembers about his grandfather were not always spoken things but things he did. To his grandchildren, HJ was a big man with a wrinkled face and laughing eyes. He smelled of peppermint, keeping his pockets full of candy, which he offered them on a regular basis. Experience had taught him that the quickest way to train the young man to open a door for him was to offer him a dime. As he came to visit, his grandson could see him from a distance, appearing out of nowhere like an angel. Johnstone would rush to open the door for him. Smiling, he would slip the shiny coin in his opened hand, saying, "What a good boy you are to open a door for me. I am sure you will be a fine gentleman when you are grown."

By the time he was a grandfather, HJ had softened in his demands on children. He understood that they would become restless at times, especially when required to sit for long periods. Invariably, he brought along peppermints or other goodies that he doled out at the appropriate moments along the way. He used them as a means of teaching the children to behave properly. Good behavior had its rewards.

When Johnstone was a child, a variety of sweet-smelling roses welcomed him into his grandmother's home. Single long-stemmed roses and bouquets of a dozen velvety red roses were stationed throughout the house, presented as symbols of love to Gigi's family. She was certain to place a couple of roses in a small vase on the bedside table of the room where he stayed on weekends and summer visits. Johnstone knew that those fragrant red roses would be there for him, Gigi's subtle greeting of love.

When the older grandchildren stayed with them, they loved to see all the filming that was done around Hollywood. It was quite exciting that filming was not limited to the inside of the movie studios. Much of what they saw on the silver screen was shot outside, right on the streets of Hollywood and the surrounding communities. In fact, it was hard for them to travel about town without bumping into a site where a well-known movie was being shot. Producers used virtually all of Hollywood as one giant movie set. They often stood gawking at the stars.

Chapter Twenty-five

Business was flourishing on the Boulevard, but it was decided that merchants should leave their lights on after 9:00 p.m. to draw more business to the area. Hollywood's thriving business boom occurred only in the daytime; by 9:00 p.m., the streets were deserted. With the lights glowing, life on Hollywood Boulevard ended later. Merchants watched their business sky-rocket. Large department stores and specialty shops began to take up residence on the Boulevard. Shoppers from Los Angeles turned up at the new shops in hopes of seeing one of their favorite stars. Hollywood achieved a reputation of being one of the most exclusive shopping districts in the world.

Their once quiet suburb of stately residences that had long ago replaced acres of lemon groves underwent an astonishing change. Gigi saw great hangarlike studios erupt overnight among the beautiful residences, causing quite a commotion.

Scenes were shot all over Hollywood. Gigi was stopped on the street and asked to participate in filming to enhance a scene but declined because she was afraid of what HJ might think. Private homes were used for family dramas. Banks were used on Saturday and Sunday for hold-up scenes. Stores were robbed regularly before the cameras. Streets were roped off for automobile accidents. She often saw actors dining in costume at local restaurants. The continuous public vaudeville show lured the tourists to fill hotels and restaurants. Gigi even said that she tried to locate the dining spot of her favorite star.

HJ decided that it would be great publicity for a motion picture company to film on his lands. Western films were uniquely American, becoming increasingly popular in movie theaters. HJ approached Breezy Eason with the proposition of filming a movie on his land. It was arranged that Universal Pictures would film *The Denver Dude,* staring Hoot Gibson as Rodeo Randall. An ad was placed, stating, "You are cordially invited to bring your whole family and lunches, stay all day, and watch Hoot Gibson and his cowboys making motion picture scenes at 12-mile bridge on HJ Whitley lands next Sunday December 12, 1926. Girls from the audience will be invited to dance with cowboy actors as part of the motion picture."

The classic B movie was released February 13, 1927. HJ and Gigi attended its opening. The movie begins with Rodeo Randall, a broncobuster, returning home after some years' absence. Rodeo Randall falls in love with Colonel La Mar's daughter, Patricia. He is then framed by the ranch foreman for a robbery he did not commit. Rodeo Randall escapes, pursues the bandits to their hideout, and returns La Mar's money. He then wins Patricia's hand in marriage. The film, with all its remarkable shootouts and action sequences, had a captivating quality.

Almost every shot offered vistas of vast lands and clear skies. Gibson's acting appeared so authentic that the audience even cried out as the shootout took place. Gibson wore a gun shoved in his belt. He was not what Gigi would call handsome, yet he had a contagious smile and angular nose. She thought that his character, a certain cowboy spirit, appealed to his fans. Hoot told them that he always felt comfortable in westerns because the minute he got on the horse and had a pair of boots on, he did not feel like an actor anymore. He felt like a real cowboy.

HJ was pleased with the movie; but more than that, he was pleased with the free publicity. Good marketing was like a good conversation; it revealed an idea in a way that made people want to be part of it. It was not magic. It was recognizing the buyer, knowing people, and knowing the words that worked. The movie industry was a valuable lure.

As its power and popularity grew, the film industry became more influential. Founded on May 11, 1927, the Academy of Motion Pictures Arts and Sciences was a professional honorary organization dedicated to the advancement of the arts and sciences of motion pictures. It all started in Hollywood, planned as an elite club. Gigi heard that, while dining with friends, Louis Mayer thought up the idea to improve the standards of films and promote the filming industry. Membership was by invitation only and based on distinctive achievements in one of the branches of film production recognized by the academy. Its original thirty-six members included both production executives and film celebrities. Douglas Fairbanks was the first president.

The first feature-length Hollywood talking film, *The Jazz Singer*, opened October 6, 1927. The movie was, however, only about 25 percent sound synchronized, and the rest was silent. It was an enormous accomplishment, responsible for transforming Warner Brothers into Hollywood's most up-to-date film factory. The commercialization of sound-on-film and the transformation of the industry from silent films to talkies became a reality with the success of this film.

HJ was confident that Hollywood represented the spirit of prosperity. The property he had purchased for $53 an acre was now worth over $10,000 an acre. The town he had named so many years ago was now known around the world. Even more amazing to him was, for once in his life, he was getting the recognition that he deserved; various newspapers and magazines were calling him "The Father of Hollywood."

It was not long before they heard more exciting news about upcoming developments in Hollywood. Sid Grauman was a personal friend of theirs. Actually, Gigi was good friends with his mother, Rosa. They often dined out together at the Hollywood Hotel. It was a custom to sit at their usual table. On one special occasion, Gigi remembered discussing her trip to the Orient with Sid and Rosa. Gigi told him of the wonderful temples and bells she saw. She saw a number of people in monks' clothes performing various functions around the temple. There were courtyards linked by large halls; esthetic, dark red pillars; intricate, imperial gold tiling on all the roofs; and bright, symmetrical painted designs on the crossbeams. Sid found her stories fascinating. Gigi liked to credit her influence on Sid as being the catalyst for his Grauman's Chinese Theatre. After her trip to China, Gigi shared its wonders with her friends.

Sid appreciated Californians' fascination with the mystifying aspects of the Orient. In 1926, he decided to build a theater resembling a giant red Chinese pagoda, which had a huge dragon across the front. He planned to make it an authentic museum of Chinese arts, architecture, and culture.

He obtained official government authorization to import authentic temple bells and pagodas. Gigi remembered seeing the beautiful bells on her trip. They had been used since the earliest times for signaling purposes. The bells were used in every aspect of life: to call the family to dinner, to announce the time, for weddings and funerals...

As Gigi walked into the lobby of the new theater, she noticed its elaborate wall murals depicting life in the Orient and a large, elaborate Chinese chandelier. It was one of the largest theaters she had ever been to. HJ liked the bright red seats. The grandeur of the theater was far beyond what Gigi thought most people could imagine. It was by far one of the most magnificent theaters in the world.

What really made the theater famous was the quirk accident that happened to Sid. Sid accidentally slid off a plank into the wet cement. After seeing his footprint, he had an epiphany, giving him the idea to decorate the entrance of his theatre with stars' immortal footprints. Sid, with the help of Norma Talmadge, concocted a story about her accidentally stepping in the cement. Talmadge had become one of the top box office attractions. Sid wanted to use her popularity to draw the crowds. He felt that no one would be able to resist comparing their hand or shoe size to that of the stars they loved. Gigi had gone to the theater many times to see the celebrities' handprints, footprints, and signatures, which were enshrined in the famous courtyard.

On May 18, 1927, HJ and Gigi were invited to the grand opening of Grauman's Chinese Theatre in Hollywood. It was the most spectacular theater opening HJ and Gigi attended. Thousands of people lined Hollywood Boulevard. A hullabaloo occurred as fans tried to sneak a quick look at their favorite stars, aggressively attempting to obtain autographs from them. Mary Pickford appeared, swimming in mink and diamonds in the best Hollywood tradition, with Douglas Fairbanks at her side, handsome as ever. Opening night was attended by a large array of stars, producers, writers, and technicians. The premiere was the most glamorous and exciting exhibition in the city's history.

The show started with the "Glories of the Scriptures," a live vaudeville opening presentation concocted by mastermind Sid Grauman. Sid Grauman was a master showman, with a quick wit—a jokester at times—and the warm acceptance of any who met him. He gave audiences what they craved, and he understood the importance of making the theater experience something more than just finding an empty seat and watching the big screen.

Gigi especially enjoyed the opening act, which was accompanied by a Wurlitzer organ and a sixty-five-piece orchestra. This lively opening was followed by Cecil B. DeMille's *The King of Kings*. The general public was not allowed into the theater until its public opening the next day. Gigi looked forward to reading the big write-up about the opening in the morning paper.

One day, many years later, as Johnstone and Gigi were walking down Hollywood Boulevard, the window of a chauffeur-driven limousine rolled down. Rosa Grauman stuck her head out the window and invited them inside the car for a chat. Then she gave Johnstone and Gigi tickets to *King Kong*. Johnstone still remembers the wonderful vaudeville show that preceded the movie. The girls were dressed in jungle attire. As the movie began, he was haunted by the incredible images of dinosaurs and the great apes as they dashed across the screen.

While all this was going on, the Hollywood Chamber of Commerce was nearing completion of its new site. It had become quite a civic event; the spirit of cooperation made such a venture possible. The committee had selected the corner of Sunset and Hudson Avenue to be the site of the new chamber building. Every member of the chamber was invited to its grand opening on July 14. HJ suspected that the civic-mindedness of the community assisted its citizens in making Hollywood the dazzling diamond of California. Funds were raised by the two hundred lifelong members of the chamber; HJ was one of them. The honor roll list adorned one of the interior walls of the new building.

The new chamber building made it possible to welcome visitors to a glimpse of the wonderful commercial and residential properties of Hollywood. Gatherings were held in a large room at the rear of the building. At social functions, they presented motion pictures showing the development of Hollywood. The chamber completed a questionnaire that asked, "What is the spirit in back of the growth of Hollywood?" HJ's favorite answer was, "The pioneer spirit, the play spirit, the spirit of romance, cultural background, ideal home, living conditions, and contentment." HJ took this answer as a pat on the back, a job well done. Many businessmen recognized that he was instrumental in the contentment others found in Hollywood; he was the Father of Hollywood.

Gigi had run into Norma Talmadge, and she told her about the magnificent party that was being held at the Roosevelt Hotel on Hollywood Boulevard on May 16. Gigi enjoyed events that would allow her to dress up. But first, Gigi would have to convince HJ that he wanted to go. Perhaps Gigi could even get him to think it was his idea. Over the years, she had learned to use the same approach HJ used on others. Things always seemed to work better that way.

Gigi got up early that morning, making sure that HJ's breakfast consisted of his favorite things: bacon, fried crispy; eggs over easy; biscuits; and piping hot coffee. It was bright and sunny when Gigi went downstairs for breakfast. The cook pulled the pan from the oven, which revealed the golden top and pale, yellow-sided biscuits. HJ could smell the biscuits from their bedroom before they came out of the oven. He hurried to the kitchen. HJ spotted the bacon sizzling in the pan. The cook was buttering half the biscuits and would leave some plain. The coffee brewed, the smell mixing with everything else.

As HJ sat down at the table, he twisted open the jar of orange marmalade that was sitting at his end of the table. Gigi mentioned hearing that Charlie Chaplin was receiving an award at the Roosevelt Hotel. "It would be great fun to see all our old friends again. We have not done that much entertaining this year. Do you think it is easier to go to someone else's party?" Gigi asked.

The morning paper was full of news, and by this time HJ was reading and only half listened to what Gigi said. He agreed, saying, "Great idea. You handle all the arrangements."

That morning, Gigi called a few of her friends; and they all decided to go together. HJ wore his tails and white-wing collars. Gigi wore her striking new lemon yellow, chiffon, embroidered dress. The tickets were ten dollars.

As they entered the lobby, a mere snippet of a song from the past echoed from the pianist playing the baby grand. It triggered memories of her childhood. The cheerful thoughts instantly placed a smile upon her face. Gigi noted how beautiful the Spanish lobby appeared, surrounded by potted palms, a bubbling fountain, and a giant, wrought-iron chandelier.

The event was held on a lovely spring evening. Gigi was amazed that she did not even hear a whisper of the sagging economy. She figured that many people wanted to keep the festivities light and cheerful. After a dinner of filet of sole and broiled chicken on toast, the master of ceremonies, Douglas Fairbanks, began to hand out the awards. They presented fourteen awards that night. Two honorary awards were given. One went to Charles Chaplin for versatility and genius in acting, writing, directing, and producing his movie *The Circus*. The other went to Warner Brothers for producing the movie that revolutionized the industry by bringing the world sound: *The Jazz Singer*. *The Jazz Singer* was ruled ineligible in the best picture category because it was considered unfair for a sound film to compete with silent movies. However, Darryl Zanuck was awarded a special Oscar for producing the pioneering talking picture.

HJ was pleased that the World War I air combat epic *Wings* won best picture. He had an intense interest in historical events and the lessons they taught. Gigi was thankful that only about five minutes were taken to present the academy of merit awards.

As he left the banquet, HJ realized that the movie industry in Hollywood had rapidly become much too magnificent to be contained within its city's limits. George Eastman had just demonstrated the first color motion picture. He saw Hollywood's influence swiftly sweep across the nation and around the world. Hollywood taught the world, from children to old folks, how to walk, talk, and dress. It rescued the world from the harshness of the Depression, promising everyone that they could overcome any crisis. In a world that had become hard to live in, it gave the public music and dancing, love, sex, laughing, and crying. It trained them how to live and how to die. It seemed to be shaping the future.

Chapter Twenty-six

Every love story does seem to be unique; but when sharing it with others, one suddenly realizes that there is nothing new. It is as old as the world itself, as natural as gusts of the wind playing with young green leaves in the trees, like birds singing early in the morning, like rain generously watering the ground. Love is as simple as life itself.

As their forty-third anniversary approached, Gigi wondered how so much love could have grown between them. She decided that it grew a speck at a time with each smile, each kind word, each hug, each flower, each laugh, and even each box of candy. HJ often brought her flowers, pretty pictures, and gifts; but mostly, he loved her, even if work sometimes got in the way. That night, after eating his favorite dinner, they held hands and watched the sunset. He found it difficult to use his own words, so he began to sing "Little by Little." When he finished, he kissed her gently on the lips; and the passion quickly came, as it always had. HJ flashed her a smile; and then they made their way toward the bedroom, turning off any unnecessary lights along their way.

HJ hated that it was so difficult for him to shape his emotions into words so that they would precisely reflect his feelings. After shutting down his emotions after experiencing so much grief in his early life, he found it difficult to risk opening up again. To HJ's mind, it was very important to live in every moment, not to put off love until tomorrow. Tomorrow never seemed to come to him on terms he knew how to handle. Inside his heart, he would say, "Let's celebrate the love and life we have." But somehow, the unconscious fear of previous losses prevented him from doing so.

Gigi knew deep inside that HJ felt that the objective of life was to try to live each day with honor and love. She realized that no one was perfect. HJ had struggled with this issue for years.

Fortunately, HJ and Gigi did see genuine goodness in each other. Over the years, they experienced intense, passionate love if only for a month, week, or day here and there. If the manner that HJ and Gigi chose to love perplexed and intrigued one, perhaps it was because it very graphically symbolized a basic truth most preferred to overlook: love was as much a matter of releasing as it was of joining. People can neither own nor forever hold the ones they love exactly as they want. Love was the gift shared when the opportunity arose.

After a small bit of sunshine with HJ, tragic, gray clouds seem to engulf the family. In 1929, Grace gradually lost her mind. Mr. William Widenham had begun to drink, and drink, and drink almost as soon as the marriage vows were complete. Though he rarely drank when working, it was common for him to finish off more than a quart of gin a day. As his consumption of alcohol increased, Grace began to nag him about his drinking. Though he did go though long dry periods, if he even had one or two drinks, they would change his personality profoundly. Not only did his personality change, but a physical change transpired before one's eyes. Though he could hold his liquor better than most men could, alcoholism was a progressive disease; and he eventually succumbed to its long-term effects.

The more Grace nagged, the more his disgust for her grew. At first, Grace believed that the beating was her fault; perhaps she had pushed a little too hard. Grace had a passionate nature that, more often than not, overruled her reason. Again and again, in matters of love, she had expected too much; and each time, she felt the pain of disappointment. But as the beatings intensified, her spirit began to crumble. She tried to hide her bruises from everyone, even Gigi. She lived in constant fear of the next beating; the waiting was the worst part. HJ confronted him about his drinking, but he was unable or unwilling to take any blame for his actions. He told HJ to talk to Grace; she needed to be put in her place. A flourishing alcoholic, wife beater, and womanizer, he considered his problem Grace's fault. Their separation came shortly after the birth of their second child, William Widenham. The last beating Grace received from William was so severe that she was hospitalized.

Grace finally understood the meaning of her father's long-forgotten warning to her on her wedding day. HJ sensed that, now and then, William would find that he must escape from himself—and find it turning to alcohol and anonymous, welcoming women. HJ never liked William, but he knew that he would have to put up with him if Grace insisted on marrying him. He had tried to prepare her to forgive him too, forgive without ever letting him know that she knew. She had promised, but she was not equal to that. HJ had never anticipated that William was violent.

Unable to endure the beatings, Grace fled to the safety of her parents. William finally admitted that, at times, he had become so frustrated with Grace that he would hit and shake her. With time, his anger had grown, only increasing the abuse. She grew indolent and became indifferent to her once proud possessions.

The only way Gigi knew to deal with her pain was to write in her diary:

> For many days, she wept like an abandoned child, her mind blank, her heart swollen with grief. A divorce followed, but the mental damage remained with Grace for her entire life. Even after the marriage ended, Grace continued to live in a very destructive manner. The most destructive emotional abuse she endured was the one she learned to inflict upon herself. Grace could no longer endure the trauma to her heart and spirit from being betrayed by the people that she loved and trusted. Grace's heart laid in broken pieces upon the ground. She suffered agony over the loss of her family. Yet, ever so slowly, hate bubbled up deep from within. A strange mist engulfed her, chilling the tears on her cheeks as she lost her mind. As the stock market lurched and skidded, recovered, and then crashed in sickening drops—so did Grace.

Hollywood seemed, for a time, to mirror the events in Grace's life. It was having a wonderful time and doing terrific business when the stock market crashed on October 24, 1929, Black Tuesday. It floated through the economy like a slow-working, infectious disease. Hollywood, where enormous sums of capital were on the line in subdivisions and movie studios, was hit especially hard by the collapse of the big money superstructure. Banks failed. The president of one bank confessed to embezzling six million dollars in bank assets. Foreclosures were common, and many of their neighbors and associates lost homes and businesses. There were breadlines, men holding signs that begged for food, and children going door to door asking for scraps.

That same year, HJ had his first stroke. He was not dead, though Gigi had a moment of dreadful fright when she saw him lying crumpled on the floor. His eyes were closed, and his face was like wrinkled wax. Gigi leaned over to look into his pale features, noting the dominant nose and narrowed black eyes with their faint lines that fanned the corners. His face was soft with a hint of aged beauty—and very beloved.

After a short stay in the hospital, he was brought home for her to take care of. Gigi thought that he had blamed himself for staying away from home so much. He had given so much of his time, his experience, and his money to the public benefit. He now watched everything he loved being destroyed. The children were the ones who had suffered most.

At first, Gigi hoped that, at last, HJ would retire; but when she heard him talking to his private secretary on the phone, Gigi knew that it would never happen. Gigi listened to the words with a vague trouble darkening over her perturbed spirit. It was the same song he had sung over the years. Gigi had heard it all her married life. Instead of the trim, staid figure Gigi had always known, he looked like a frantic, aging man. She realized that it did not make any difference whether she had things or did not have them. It was inside that one found happiness. Gigi was saddened that they had so much that HJ had to constantly worry over. This final work would steal the last bit of his soul, which Gigi hoped would be hers alone. More than ever, ambition gnawed and chaffed HJ as a new urgency possessed him. Even as HJ was making his final choices, events were moving ahead of him at shocking speed. That year, it seemed to her that both Grace and HJ had been stolen.

Chapter Twenty-seven

All Quiet on the Western Front (1929), *Broadway Melody* (1930), and *Cimarron* (1931) were the lucky winners of the Academy of Merit awards for best picture. Hollywood's films had a sparkling hold on moviegoers' imaginations. The lights, the cameras, the glitter, and the glamour could not be found anywhere else in the world. By 1930, the studios began major construction programs. They needed to turn their studios into sound-film factories. New sound stages were built and new sound departments formed. Gigi believed that motion pictures with sound had established a new and lasting art form. Motion pictures became an intrinsic part of the world's culture.

Amazing advancements in the movies seemed to happen like magic. HJ was fascinated by *Hell's Angels*, an aviation melodrama, which took Howard Hughes over three years to film. *Hell's Angels*, written and directed by Hughes, was the most expensive movie of its time, costing $3.8 million. They saw Jean Harlow, accompanied by Howard, attend the movie's premiere. Gigi found this a little surprising, as she had heard that Howard personally disliked Jean. She guessed that their appearance together was necessary for publicity. HJ enjoyed the extraordinary footage recreating World War I. The authentic dogfights had unmatched realism that truly conveyed the terror of fights to the death. The expressive battle scene between the British Royal Flying Corps and a German zeppelin was especially stunning.

Jean Harlow caught Gigi's eye. She fairly jumped off the screen playing an upper-class floozy. Jean glowed. She was on the fast track to stardom. Jean's appearance solidified her role as America's new sex symbol. Beauty, sex appeal, vulnerability, boldness—whatever the intangible something was, it was clear that Jean Harlow radiated it. She had more glamour than ten women put together. Gigi heard that virtually every man on the set found her endearing and kind and that she was nicknamed Baby. She became so popular with women that they stampeded to their local beauty parlors to become platinum blondes.

Her immortal line, "Would you be shocked if I put on something more comfortable?" made Gigi realize that conventional standards of society were once more changing. There was no attempt made to tone down the fact that she did not want anything to do with marriage. This frankness seemed so shocking to Gigi. It seemed that Hughes wanted to test the limits of public morality. HJ's new town definitely had a never-ending impact on society.

HJ never liked church because people seemed too religious for him. He preferred to just live his own morality. Praying made him feel uneasy because he was afraid that he would not like the answer God gave. Death had occupied too much of his youth. He hoped that there was a heaven but was never really sure. It was late at night, one of those nights when HJ couldn't sleep. He later told Gigi, "I couldn't sleep. I kept hearing music, but I could not tell where it was coming from. So I walked into the garden, and there, under the starlit sky, I saw that the music was coming from above, from where I guess heaven is. And then and there I heard a voice tell me that it was my last chance. I just wanted to tell you that I made peace with God." This surprised Gigi because, in a world of people who walked around talking about God, HJ stood silent on that issue.

When he attended church after that, there was a new calmness about him. He knew that he was saved, just as he knew that the voice from heaven was real. HJ was never the same.

Unfortunately for HJ, the many tragic events in his early life were not fictional stories made up in Hollywood. These events shattered his ability to connect to anyone he deeply loved. He loved his sister, and then she died. He loved his parents; they died. He loved his first wife and daughter; they died. By no longer being able to open up, HJ unconsciously spent many years protecting himself from being hurt. He kept God at a distance. But, nearing the end of his life, he finally felt free to open up. He began feeling the way he had as a small boy, before tragedy struck. He spent more time with his family, loving them the way one should.

It was naïve for HJ to think that Gigi's anger, resentment, and feelings of powerlessness from being neglected her entire married life were going to go away when he began to love her the way she needed. But as Gigi began to understand the bigger picture, that HJ's time on earth would soon end, she softened like a candle sitting in the window on a hot summer's day. HJ was encouraged by the realization that they were fighting less. At last, he was free from the demons that had haunted him most of his life. He let his work slip away. Gigi, at last, was the center of his world. It was a noble deed for HJ to gift her with the chance to cleanse herself of the anger, sadness, and sorrow he had refused to address for so many years.

He spent many hours in the garden with her. It was Gigi's favorite place to relax. In the garden, they could slow down the quickly passing days and feel closer to life. Gigi had designed her garden to delight one's nose and renew a sense of wonder. Complete with a fountain and colorful bougainvillea, the garden was the perfect intimate setting for a quiet time together. Gigi said that her garden was never completely finished but evolved with her over the years. HJ treasured his walks through the garden with her, seeing and smelling the many flowers.

After a morning working in her garden, HJ and Gigi sat in wicker chairs under a canopy of trees, enjoying a simple lunch of cucumber and minted butter sandwiches. Gigi did not even bother to take off the crusts. It was just a simple way to take a break from life. They found themselves so relaxed, enjoying each other's company.

This short period they spent together gave her the needed strength to carry on when HJ was gone. He deprived himself of everything that could have made his life so different, terrified of losing another loved one. Not until the very end did he realize his mistake and the terrible suffering that he caused his family. Remorse overtook him; no one was more penitent than he. He realized that it was more important to live his life with love. He desired to use his remaining time more wisely. He wished his magnificent talents and desire to serve the public had not caused him to sacrifice his family.

HJ told Gigi nothing about his business; when he died, he left her with responsibility she was totally unprepared for. Gigi wished that she would have done without servants the first few years of her married life. Possibly, it would have been easier at a young age to acquire the knowledge and self-confidence her life would now require. People found it so easy to fool her about the business affairs that she now was solely responsible for. As it was, Gigi remained an adult child, letting others take the responsibilities that should have been hers.

Hobart Johnstone Whitley, eighty-three, died peacefully on Wednesday, June 3, 1931, in his sleep at the Whitley Park Country Club at the home of his son, Ross. Although he had become physically frail, he still managed to get around, primarily under his own steam. He died as he lived—on his own terms, in a place that he loved, at home with his much-loved family. He wanted a minimum of fluff and commotion.

It was early morning when Gigi realized he was gone. The sun was almost a semicircle; and the color was strange, a dark shade of orange. It peeped itself over the top of the tall trees in the yard like an anxious child at a window. Sunlight cut through the canopy of leaves; the shadow it cast in the room mirrored the feelings in her heart.

Even as time passed, when Gigi walked past the empty library where she would find him reading, Gigi was assaulted by the silence—the emptiness. Gigi would think, trying hard to listen to echoes and whispers, all those things that remained even though he was gone. One of his most important legacies was what remained in her heart.

HJ told her, "Those that say they can and those that say they cannot are both right. Words are the most powerful things in the universe. The words you speak will either put you over or hold you in bondage. There is creative power within you. Learn to use it wisely."

Life cannot be lived happily without a soul mate, and Gigi wondered where she would be without HJ, standing alone. Gigi missed his kind words that were like dewdrops from a tender plant. His words gave her strength and courage—gifts she would always have.

In his life, he applied the values that sustained his generation. He loved his family, his community, and his nation. HJ never forgot a favor; nor did he fail to note a kindness. His prime directives were to always do what he felt was right and to keep his word. He was willing and able to help others. Gigi remembered his dry wit and keen sense of the humor, noted by the curl of a lip and the twinkle in his eyes.

One fine, warm, summer day, scores of friends of HJ's gathered at the Strother Funeral Chapel. Things would not be the same. They gathered to give tribute to the memory of the pioneer of California real estate, the man who was known as the "Father of Hollywood." A lengthy tribute to him was printed in the *Los Angeles Times*, giving him that much-deserved title. He was the pioneer that named and framed the great city of Hollywood. His friends stood with bowed heads, with hands folded as if in prayer. The afternoon light streamed down, warm, airy, gold; the clouds pressed near in pomp. Peacefully, at last, HJ had arrived in the land of jubilee. Internment was at Hollywood Forever Cemetery. He had come to California almost fifty years earlier.

HJ was a genius a hundred years ahead of the time in which he lived. He knew everyone; but few knew him, for he was mysterious, seeing things so far ahead. No one seemed to comprehend his ideas. HJ was no myth; he was a legend. As said at his funeral, "No one in the whole world has accomplished what he did, putting over a hundred and forty-one towns on the map. He would see other men's dreams, and then he made those dreams come true. HJ Whitley was the great developer, with Hollywood being his finest accomplishment." In fond remembrance of HJ, Gigi wrote:

HJ Whitley, the Father of Hollywood

A game of chance was Hollywood,
Though Nature made it plain
The treasures there were hidden
If you only knew the game.
But not till eighty-six
Did the Wizard come along,
Who understood that game of chance
And played it good and strong.
And he made it mighty easy
To follow in the rear,
Though it took a lot of courage
To be the Pioneer.

For when he got a project
Just strong enough to stand,
Then jealousy came creeping round
And tried to take a hand.
Oh! It took a lot of courage
And perseverance too
To be that faithful Pioneer
Who put that project through.
But he made it mighty easy
To follow in the rear,
Though it took a lot of courage
To be the Pioneer.

Some folks were mighty haughty
When he began the plan,
For lights, for schools, for street-cars,
Said, "They did not give a damn."
They guessed, they knew enough
Without a stranger snooping round

To tell them how and what to do
And spoil their little town.
But he made it mighty easy
To follow in the rear,
Though it took a lot of courage
To be the Pioneer.

For, you know, it's always easy
To blame and criticize
A project in it infancy,
But its work that takes the prize.
Some people never do a thing,
Just follow in the rear
And watch their chance to benefit
From the faithful Pioneer.
Oh! It may be mighty easy
To follow in the rear,
Though it took a lot of courage
To be the Pioneer.

And when he called those meetings
To put his projects through
Most everything that he proposed
They said, "It would not do."
But when he turned the search light on,
Like a magic lantern true,
All eyes were turned toward Hollywood,
And she grew and grew and grew,
For he'd made it mighty easy
To follow in the rear,
Though it took a lot of courage
To be the Pioneer.

So when the task was finished,
The Genius had begun;
And all those songs of praises
To Hollywood were sung.
Then, all the folks were willing
To follow in the rear
And give the name of "Father"
To the faithful Pioneer,
Who made it mighty easy
To follow in the rear,
Though it took a lot of courage
To be the Pioneer

But when I think of all the things
The Pioneer has stood,
Well, then I turn the other page
And think of all the good.
And now I warn you—one and all,
Whatever else you do,
Be grateful to that Pioneer
Who did so much for you.
For he is the "Father of Hollywood"
And he cannot be put in the rear,
For it took a lot of courage
To be the Pioneer.

On a crisp autumn afternoon, nearly a year after HJ's death,
Gigi sat idly under an enormous oak tree, watching as a whirl-
wind whisked across the lawn. As it passed by her, the whirl-
wind scooped up a dormant pile of leaves lying next to the oak
tree. The leaves appeared to come alive, twisting, turning, and
dancing about. They were sporting their new fall colors of red,

orange, brown, and yellow. The brittle autumn leaves seemed to be having a party. As the party moved out of sight, Gigi began to think about the last time she sat under the tree with HJ. The memories of their last visit there were vivid with relaxed and peaceful thoughts motivated by the images, scents, and sounds of him. Her memories contained many images, special places they had been and the adventures they had shared. That was when Gigi decided to write her memoir. It was an essential saga of history.

Gigi wondered whether the public could be beguiled into buying nonfiction of intensity and ideas when it was not rolled in in a truck by a magical marketer. In other words, Gigi questioned whether the public would buy a small, pocket-size book containing writing of merit that cost the same as a large, fat volume copiously padded. Before shouting, "Why, of course they will," Gigi noted that, as far as the general public was concerned (not the discriminating book lover), it was a task she was willing to attempt to conquer. Gigi had to let the world know the true beginning of Hollywood. She was writing the life of a person who accomplished wonderful things now being claimed by other people, who knew that they were not telling the truth; even those who benefited were afraid to speak a word in the defense of the rightful person.

Gigi knew the true story. She had spent her entire married life observing the work of the great developer—one of the greatest in America. Now that he was gone, Gigi was trying to do something in his honor. These facts cover a vast range of our country—the great Northwest, the great Southwest, and his wonderful work in California. Although the memoir was complete before her death in 1951, she never got around to publishing it.

Gifted and noted people of all classes have found their way to Hollywood. All were so charmed by its natural assets that its fame spread around the world. Who was the one that had the vision to see the possibilities the area held? Everyone knew it was the pioneers who paved the way for the artistic things in life, making it possible for others to succeed. Gigi arrived in favored California more than sixty-five years before her death and watched with amazement the rapid changes that took place. Gigi felt honored to have lived with the Father of Hollywood, her beloved HJ.

Epilogue

Whitley Heights was the Beverly Hills of yesteryear, the first royal kingdom for the celebrities. It was there where they went to posh mansions set in the winding hills of Hollywood a few steps from Hollywood Boulevard. The list of its residence could be condensed into a "Who's Who" of rising stars of Hollywood. Its residents included Charlie Chaplin, Rudolph Valentino, Jean Harlow, WC Fields, Cecil B. DeMille, Judy Garland, Gloria Swanson, William Faulkner, Zsa Zsa Gabor, Wallace Beery, Janet Gaynor, Gilbert Adrian, Beulah Bondi, Maurice Chevalier, Harold Lloyd, Marion Davies, Ethel Barrymore, Carole Lombard, Boris Karloff, Francis X. Bushman, Patrick Bauchau, William Bast, Louise Brooks, George Sanders, Bette Davis, Carmen Miranda, Chester Morris, Tyrone Power, Rosalind Russell, Norma Shearer, Francis Coppola's family, and many others.

The Whitley Heights Civic Association was founded in 1923. It was formed to resist efforts of redevelopment and modernization. Unfortunately, in 1948, Whitley Heights was cut in two by the Hollywood freeway. Over protest of residents, the former homes of Valentino and Chaplin were destroyed, along with forty other homes. Threatened with further destruction, the residents mobilized to attract national attention to the landmark.

In 1982, Whitley Heights was placed on the National Register of Historic Places. In 1992, it was designated a historic preservation overlay zone, which means that no exterior alterations can be made without being approved by an architectural review board.

Over the years, numerous publications wrote about HJ Whitley, calling him "The Father of Hollywood." Articles can be found in the *Los Angeles Times, Hollywood Citizens, Architectural Digest, Examiner, San Fernando Valley Today, San Fernando Democrat, Van Nuys News, Little Farms Magazine, The New York Times,* the *American Historical Society,* and many books.

In 1956, the Hollywood Hotel was scheduled to be torn down, losing forever the golden stars that had been painted on the dining room ceiling to commemorate the names of celebrity guests that frequented the hotel. It then became necessary to establish a hall of fame to recognize these historical stars. The tribute needed to be something special, a salute to the celebrities who made Hollywood great—from the silent film stars of yesteryear to the modern action heroes of today's blockbusters. The Hollywood Walk of Fame is Hollywood's tribute to the Hollywood stars for all time. The artistic professionals are immortalized in bronze stars embedded in the sidewalks of Hollywood. Inside each star is engraved with the name of the artist and a distinct emblem identifying his artistic trade—motion picture, television, radio, recording, or live theater. The Hollywood Chamber of Commerce currently oversees the Walk of Fame. Perhaps a new star should be initiated—The Father of Hollywood, located at the corner of Hollywood and Highland Boulevards. Then, at last, HJ Whitley would obtain the star of recognition he rightfully deserves.

Over the years, HJ was instrumental in the development of the following towns: Addington, Agawam, Amorita, Augusta,

Aline, Anadarko, Apache, Avondale, Belleview, Bickford, Billings, Binger, Bison, Bowie, Boyd, Breckenridge, Bridgeport, Canoga Park, Canute, Chattanooga, Chickasha, Chico, Cleo, Clinton, Comanche, Concho, Corcoran, Cropper, Daley, Darlington, Darrow, Doxey, Dover, Driftwood, Duncan, El Reno, Elk City, Enid, Erick, Faxon, Ferguson, Foss, Garber, Geary, Geronimo, Goodwell, Gotebo, Gracemont, Grandfield, Greenfield, Guymon, Guthrie, Harrah, Hastings, Hennessey, Hext Ranch, Hitchcock, Hicks, Hinton, Hobart, Holdenville, Holliday, Hollywood, Homestead, Hooker, Indianapolis, Ingersoll, Isabella, Komalty, Kremlin, Jefferson, Junction, Kidder, Kingfisher, Lahoma, Lambert, Lathram, Lawton, Lone Wolf, Lookeba, Lynn City, Mangum, Marlow, Medford, Meno, Merritt, Minco, Mountain View, Newark, Okarche, Okeene, Olney, Optima, Norden, Paradise, Park Springs, Parkersburg, Pile Spur, Pocasset, Ponca City, Pond Creek, Randlett, Renfrow, Reseda, Richards, Ringgold, Ringwood, Roman Nose, Rush Springs, Rusk, Saginaw, Sayre, Seminole, Stoneburg, Sugen, Temple, Texhoma, Terrill, Tinney, Tyrone, Union, Van Nuys, Walter, Walthall, Watonga, Waukomis, Waurika, Weatherford, Wewoka, Whitley Gardens, and Wilcox.

The Ridge Route is a historic California highway and only one of two California highways on the national register.

About the Author

Gaelyn Whitley Keith is a California native and a graduate of Cal Poly, San Luis Obispo. A writer, she wrote for *South Bay Magazine* and was awarded top honors in a national writing competition. Visit her Web site at

www.TheFatherOfHollywood.com.

My writing gives an honest picture of two people I have greatly learned to love. I am proud to be HJ and Gigi Whitley's great-granddaughter. I would love to have my great-grandfather walk out of history to tell his own story, with Gigi at his side. What I have told about them is true, as conveyed in Gigi Whitley's memoir. I want the world to know and cherish my great-grandparents as I do, for HJ Whitley is the Father of Hollywood.

listen|imagine|view|experience

AUDIO BOOK DOWNLOAD INCLUDED WITH THIS BOOK!

In your hands you hold a complete digital entertainment package. Besides purchasing the paper version of this book, this book includes a free download of the audio version of this book. Simply use the code listed below when visiting our website. Once downloaded to your computer, you can listen to the book through your computer's speakers, burn it to an audio CD or save the file to your portable music device (such as Apple's popular iPod) and listen on the go!

How to get your free audio book digital download:

1. Visit www.tatepublishing.com and click on the e|LIVE logo on the home page.
2. Enter the following coupon code:
   0e46-598a-c633-1f99-9452-b83b-7ae1-028c
3. Download the audio book from your e|LIVE digital locker and begin enjoying your new digital entertainment package today!